LIVE/WORK

Live/Work

Working at Home, Living at Work

Deborah K. Dietsch

Foreword by Sarah Susanka

An Archetype Press Book

ABRAMS · NEW YORK

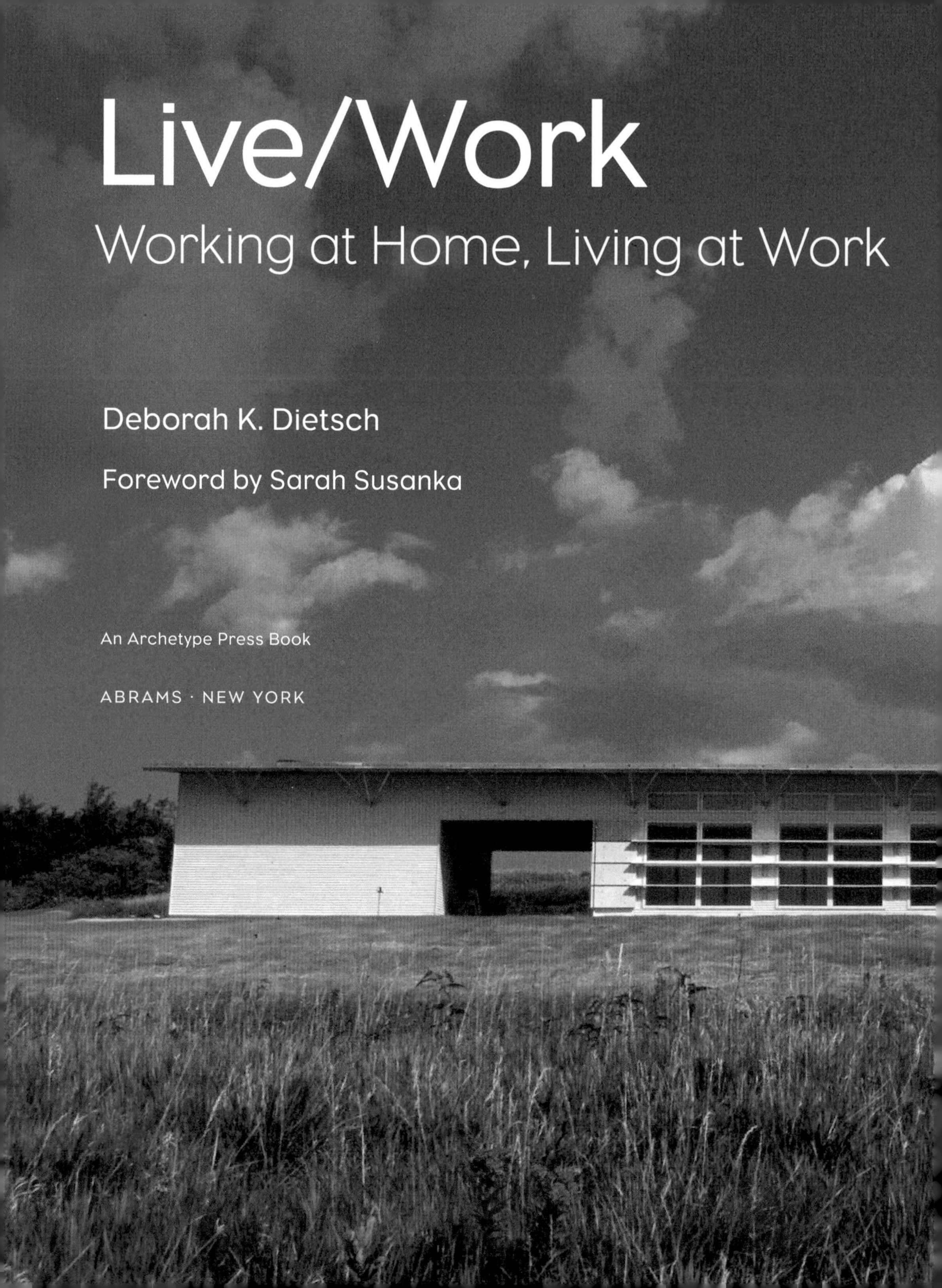

Contents

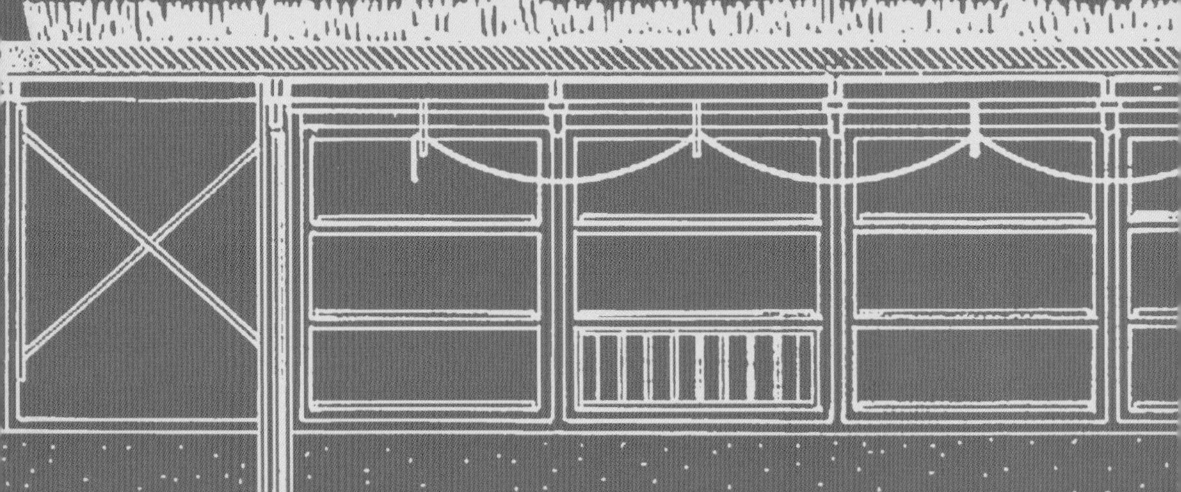

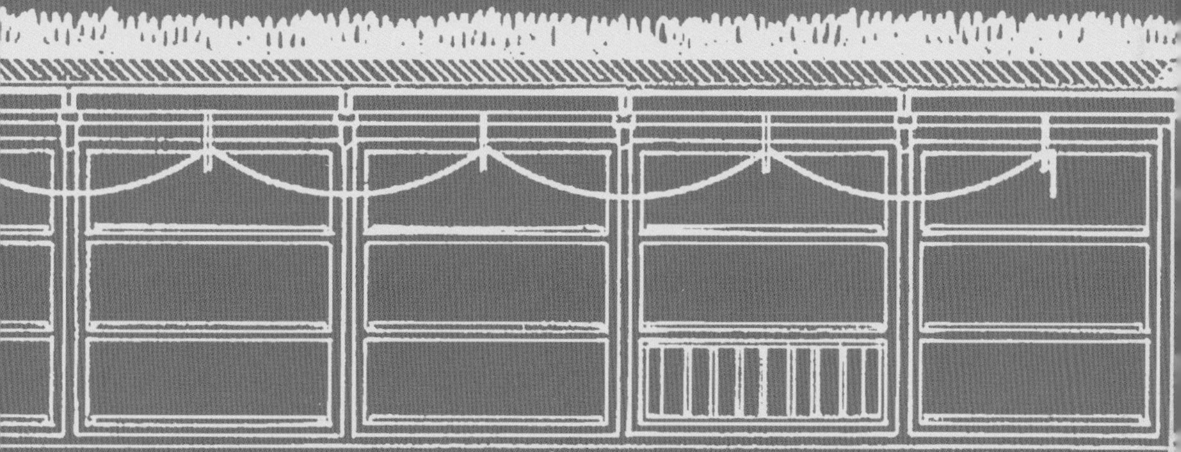

FOREWORD

Sarah Susanka

In the mid-1990s, when I built my first Not So Big House in St. Paul, Minnesota, I planned to leave the walk-out basement unfinished to save money. But then my life as an architect began to change. I started writing about how to make houses warmer, more personal places designed for the way we *really* live, instead of for impressing the neighbors. With this new avocation came a new need: a place to work at home.

Suddenly that unfinished lower level looked awfully attractive. I realized that I could line the walls with countertops, providing many linear feet of layout space for all the graphics I needed to illustrate my ideas. I could build an outside stairway down the side of the house and make the walk-out-level door into the main entry for my new home office. That way, visitors to my workplace could come to my office door without having to traipse through the house to get there. I could even include a small conference table for meetings with my colleagues and clients.

Fitting in
Sarah Susanka (left) has gained wide acclaim for her approach to designing the Not So Big House. For her new home in Raleigh, North Carolina, she added an office over an existing garage, with large windows turned to the back yard. A green spiral staircase leads up to the office, where the architect works with her assistant, Marie St. Hilaire (right).

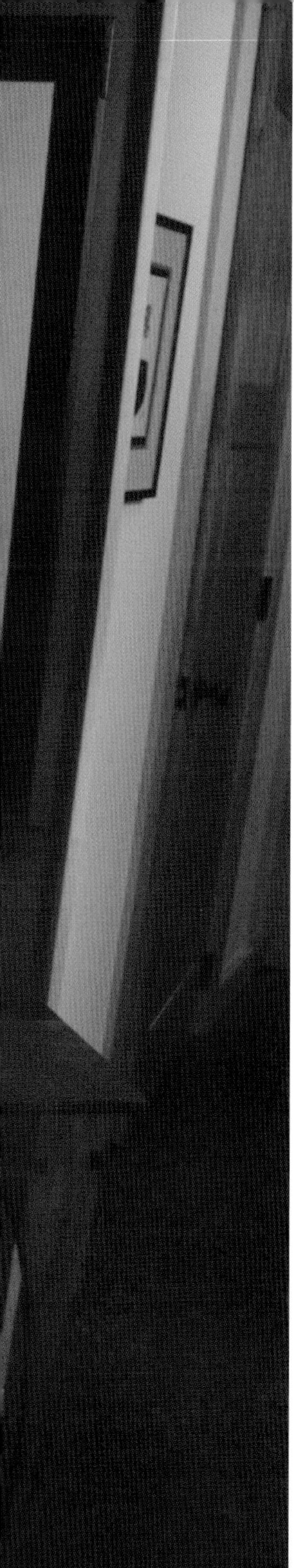

Although at the time it felt like an extravagance, my lower-level office space turned out to be a terrific investment and a really wonderful place to work. I had views out along the Mississippi River valley and a constant flow of wildlife—from deer and fox to wild turkeys and bald eagles—all making my work time a magical delight. I now realize that if I hadn't carved out a place in which to work from home, that first book in my Not So Big House series might never have come into existence. And it wasn't long before I was wondering why I was driving to work every afternoon after I'd finished the writing part of my day.

Fast forward a decade, and once again my life has changed. Now I live in a Cape Cod-style house in Raleigh, North Carolina, that I've remodeled. But instead of being an afterthought, my workplace was the first thing on my list of renovations. I'd discovered the delights of working from home, and nothing would persuade me to go back to the off-site alternative. In fact both my husband and I now work out of our house. We converted the old living room and dining room into his office, while I transformed two bedrooms on the second floor for my own.

Compared to my previous office, these small rooms were pretty tight quarters, and I sorely missed my lovely view of the great outdoors. So I decided to add on—not a lot of space, though, just two hundred square feet, enough room for two desks plus the requisite copy machine, file cabinets, postage machine, and storage. I also converted part of one of the old bedrooms into a lovely entry space to the office that opens from the stairway landing. Having this small separation between the "live" part of the house and the "work" part makes all the difference. I actually feel now that when I step through the door and walk into this daylight-filled "lobby," I'm going to work. It is clearly somewhere different from the place we live, and yet it is only a few feet and one story up from the kitchen where I just ate breakfast.

Another important feature of my new remodeled office is a small, acoustically separate room where I give radio interviews, a common occurrence in my life as an author. At some point in the future, it may become someone's master bedroom closet or perhaps a sauna, but for the time being it provides me with an ideal and relatively soundproof location from which to speak to the world.

Transitioning
A serene Japanese painting announces the office tea room, dividing the main offices on the left from the inner office at right. The latter is reached from a narrow hallway to provide a feeling of transition.

My favorite space of all is one that used to be the ugly duckling of the house: a room atop the garage with steeply sloping sides that reach down to around three feet off the floor. I added a skylight and a dormer to match the others on the front face of the house, lined the two low walls with continuous countertops like my old St. Paul house, and then completely filled the end wall with bookshelves—my favorite type of wallpaper. Not only is this garret a cozy and personal spot to write, but it also doubles as my private sanctuary—a room of my own where I also meditate, listen to music, and read.

Snuggling
Susanka calls this inner office over the garage a "room of my own." Built-in bookshelves line one wall, making use of every inch of space. Both a niche above the window and the windowsill hold objects on display. Magazines are filed under the base of another angled wall.

As someone who has lived the live/work vision of everyday existence for a dozen years now, I can attest to the fact that it can completely change your life once you give yourself permission, even if only on a part-time basis, to try it out for yourself. As you'll see in the pages that follow, there are lots of tricks and design strategies that architects around the country are exploring to help differentiate the "work" part of the house from the "live" part.

Although millions today are working from home, few people realize how limited are our visions for combining living space with work space. For those of us who work at home on a daily basis, the as-is basement and extra bedroom just aren't good enough. They need a makeover in order to provide the proper support for work life. We need more inspiration, more solutions, and a new vision for what is possible when combining living and working environments.

All sorts of live/work spaces are included here, each one designed for an individual with specific needs that are now perfectly accommodated by their new in-home office. The people you'll read about include visual artists, architects, photographers, musicians, filmmakers and screenwriters, chefs, small business owners, graphic and software designers, a psychologist, a dancer and exercise instructor, a color consultant, and jewelry and fashion designers. The new and renovated buildings featured provide all the inspiration we need for this new way of working and reflect many of the lessons that I learned from my first home office. In my experience, the key is this: to be truly successful, the live/work combination must be intentionally designed, preferably from the ground up, but if this is not possible, then with all the care and attention one would give to a living space. Let's face it: we spend a huge segment of our lives in our work space. It is time to make it just as enjoyable a place to be as the space we retire to when our work is done.

This wonderful book is the first step in helping bring these new design notions out into the open so that all of us who choose to work from home can do so in style, in comfort, and in our own uniquely personal way.

Differentiating
Niches within the office are painted different colors to set them apart as separate areas, even some holding light switches. Susanka also chose different shades of wood to impart a sense of depth to the office spaces. Throughout she followed her governing principle of theme and variations to add character while unifying the compact workplace.

INTRODUCTION

Working at home is becoming more commonplace as corporations downsize, employees telecommute, and entrepreneurs start their own businesses. The Census Bureau's Working at Home 2000 report estimated that 4.2 million self-employed Americans worked at home, and five years later the federal government's American Housing Survey revealed that 5.75 million were spending forty hours or more working from home. The numbers, understandably, keep growing. Who doesn't want the freedom to be her own boss, work in his own personal space, and set flexible hours away from the pressures of corporate life?

Yet despite the millions of Americans working at home, most are making do with casual, even uncomfortable environments. They are discovering that the average home's rooms are not easily converted into spaces suitable for full-time work. With this realization has come the need for intentionally configured spaces that mesh the worlds of living and working within a single property. Successfully working from home requires more than a desk shoved into an extra bedroom, a laptop opened on the dining room table, or a basement corner converted into an office. It demands the same attention to design as is paid to "real" offices and work spaces in commercial buildings.

Living and working
Matthew Hood, a Michigan developer, liked the model apartment in one of his projects so much that he moved in himself. Now he works from the mezzanine that opens onto his airy two-story live/work space in the Detroit suburb of Royal Oak.

Converting
When a light industrial area was rezoned, Hood moved quickly to convert an old lumber warehouse into eight apartments. Sleeping bays added to the front and generous walls of glass inserted at the back help create the feeling of urban loft spaces.

The homeowners and residents featured in this book are pioneering new territory in both working at home full-time and inventing the space to do it in. Instead of putting up with makeshift solutions, they have intentionally created spaces that are truly tailored to the particulars of their occupations. The Maryland musicians featured in the last chapter, who added on a chamber to fit their organ, had very different requirements from the Minnesota color consultant in chapter four who needed room for her swatches and computer.

Common to these professionals is the view of working at home as a way of integrating their business and personal lives. "I don't consider work as separate from my life," says a Washington, D.C., photographer. "In fact, I don't like the word *work*. It comes with the negative connotation of someone else's agenda." Work and life may be inseparable for some, but all the people represented in this book insist that some division be drawn between the office or studio and the domestic sphere. As a Los Angeles therapist notes of her back-yard commute, "I wanted to work *at* home but not *in* the home." Several are parents who have decided to work at home in order to balance the demands of raising children while pursuing their careers. "Working at home has allowed me to watch my kids grow up," says a father who is an architect. "I want to be around while they are still young."

Each chapter tells how these individuals have come to make the choice to live and work in the same space and how they created the means to do so. Represented are married couples with and without children, same-sex partners, single professionals, and retirees. Most are creative entrepreneurs—artists, architects, photographers, filmmakers, chefs—whose live/work settings draw the public and often advertise what they do. To show how the designers of live/work spaces themselves live and work, we also include the homes and offices of several architects as well as their clients.

From tree house-inspired pavilions to urban lofts, their designs reveal that there is no single model for working at home. The setting may be a brand-new building, a home addition, or a renovated factory or warehouse. The office may be customized for solo endeavors and occupy its own floor, or it may be divided among separate levels or several freestanding buildings to accommodate employees. The styles are as varied as the owners whose ingenious solutions underscore the spatial richness of this hybrid building type.

All recognize that work—an activity that situates us within the world—deserves a space of its own, just as home—a retreat from the world—also needs its special place. Striking a balance between the two can be difficult, especially when family members, site conditions, zoning codes, and other practicalities are factored into the equation. "We realized that we needed to fight for living and working in the same place," says a Kansas

Hiding out
Working at home allows for family time during office hours—and the White House is no exception. In 1963 President John F. Kennedy was conducting the nation's business in the Oval Office while his three-year-old son, John F. Kennedy Jr., found a good spot to play under the historic *Resolute* desk.

chef featured in this book. He was forced to remodel his home-based restaurant to meet local commercial building codes after city officials shut it down. Such valuable lessons learned are highlighted in every profile to help readers plan their own spaces.

Inventing
At Monticello, his Virginia home, Thomas Jefferson designed a sunny work space next to his built-in bed so he could work round the clock. He fitted the leather chair with a movable table and candlesticks for reading at night; the ottoman allowed him to stretch out his legs. Jefferson invented the double-pen device on the table to make copies of his writings.

Past Is Prologue

Making a living at home is peculiarly American. It reflects our country's values of independence and self-sufficiency. It saves time by eliminating the commute and money paid for office rent. It offers other economic benefits as well, including a single mortgage to finance both a home and a workplace and tax deductions for a home-based business.

Leading the way are our presidents, who conduct the nation's business from home. George Washington presided over the country from his Philadelphia house before John Adams and his successors moved into the White House. Since 1909 our leaders have worked in the Oval Office, which was moved to its current location in 1934 for easier access to the residence.

The comforts of working at home were appreciated in this country even before the American Revolution. In his first design for Monticello, Thomas Jefferson drew a semioctagonal room that would eventually become his "cabinet" for reading, writing, drawing, and scientific observation. Jefferson made sure that the room was light filled by setting windows into the angular walls so that sunshine would come in from different directions. He furnished the space with such user-friendly designs as a movable table, a chair fitted with candlesticks, and a revolving bookstand, which permitted him to consult multiple texts at once. A copying machine allowed Jefferson to write with one pen, while another followed his movements to make an exact replica. Contemporary versions of his conveniences can be found throughout the interiors featured in this book.

Home-based enterprises were common until the late nineteenth century, when stand-alone office buildings began to rise in cities from Chicago to New York to San Francisco. Even as they created similar groundbreaking designs, architects such as Frank Lloyd Wright preferred to work at home. Wright's Oak Park studio is part of a long tradition that includes such distinctive buildings as the paired home and studio shared by Charles and Ray Eames, the Los Angeles designers responsible for much of the midcentury-modern furniture back in vogue today. A handful of examples in this book reveal more recent variations on those architects' live/work spaces, from a compound of cottages in Maryland to a combination field office-vacation retreat in Montana.

While the Industrial Revolution separated the workplace from the home, the information age has reconnected them. Advances in computers and digital equipment have made setting up a home business easier and more

Living above the store
The two-story Field-Pacheco Building in Brownsville, Texas, exemplifies how residential and commercial uses were combined during the early 1900s. A general store occupied the ground floor behind arched doorways, while living quarters were located on the second level. The brick building came to house a variety of businesses, including government offices, a dressmaking factory, and an electrical shop—testifying to the adaptability of its simple design.

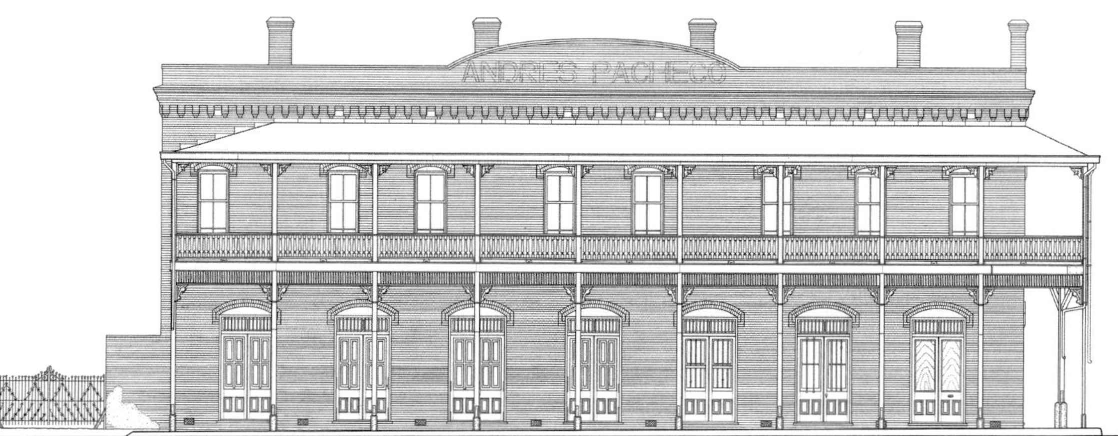

Living
The husband-and-wife design team of Charles and Ray Eames created their joined residence and studio in Pacific Palisades, California, in 1949 as part of the Case Study program, which was sponsored by *Arts & Architecture* magazine to promote modern residential design. Each part was constructed from the same prefabricated steel frames and fitted with glass and colored stucco panels to create checkerboard facades resembling Mondrian paintings. Their architecture of flexible spaces continues to be an influential model in the design of contemporary live/work buildings.

Working
The loftlike studio where the Eameses dreamed up their midcentury-modern furniture, fabrics, and films is a smaller version of the couple's adjoining home. Like several examples in this book, it was designed to function as a guest house as well as a work space. The two-story pavilion incorporates an office mezzanine built over a small kitchen, bathroom, and darkroom. Visible through the doorway is the planted courtyard between the studio and the house.

efficient. The advent of the Internet and e-mail has made communication with far-flung colleagues and clients instantaneous. Rather than spark futuristic environments, however, this digital boom has helped revive the age-old pattern of Main Street America, where shopkeepers lived above their stores. Such traditional arrangements, the focus of this book's second chapter, have become synonymous with a recent movement to curb suburban sprawl. Called New Urbanism or neotraditionalism, this planning method aims to create pedestrian-oriented communities where people live and work together closely—much like the small towns of yesteryear.

However, few of the hundreds of New Urbanist communities now standing incorporate buildings specially designed for living and working. These hybrid structures are typically the last piece of the development to be undertaken because the revived concept is still seen as new and is often met with opposition by builders used to more conventional housing.

Of those built in the early twenty-first century, most follow the Main Street tradition in combining ground-floor retail with upper-level apartments. Usually clustered in the center of the community, these live/work rowhouses offer alternatives to the typical townhouse or single-family home. They mark a radical departure from standard suburban development, where residences and commerce are separated from one another. Owners of the live/work units are permitted to conduct business at home without having to worry about zoning and building codes and other legal ramifications. Ideally they can walk to nearby services—grocery store, post office, and bank, for example—and enjoy a small-town sense of community shared by other people who live and work in the same place. This book features the home and office of an architect who shaped one of New Urbanism's most successful experiments in live/work: Kentlands, Maryland.

Dining out
The Main Street of Kentlands is enlivened by outdoor dining at Vasilis Mediterranean Grill in one of the community's fifty-two live/work townhouses. Owners and chefs Bill and Julie Hristopoulos live above their restaurant.

In older cities, a widely emulated live/work arrangement is the loft. This wide-open space, typically tall enough to insert an extra floor, developed from the conversion of old warehouses and industrial buildings into studios for artists. The Tower Press Building in Cleveland, Ohio, a remodeled clothing factory shown in this book, is one such example where occupants have the benefit of two-story, live/work apartments, plus a cafe, exhibition spaces, and a meeting room. Such renovations have helped rejuvenate blighted urban districts and led cities to pass new zoning ordinances to encourage and codify live/work developments. A 2000 survey revealed that thirteen cities from Providence, Rhode Island, to Portland, Oregon, had enacted such regulations. Some limit building density and occupancy, while others stipulate the amount of retail space and heights of ceilings. Like politics, all live/work laws are local.

Signing
Old-fashioned signage on Main Street adheres to Kentlands's neotraditional design guidelines. Thyme Out, a meal preparation store, reflects the community's support of locally run businesses in preference to national chains.

Loft conversions in turn have spawned new quarters for artists and others seeking high-ceilinged, open spaces with adaptable mezzanines for working, relaxing, or sleeping. Several examples, including a new artists' building in Mount Rainier, Maryland, are included in this book to show variations on the loft model.

The environmental movement has also fostered an increase in the live/work ethic. Advocates of smart growth claim that mixing stores, offices, and housing reduces sprawl and saves natural resources by limiting residential and commercial development to a single location. It also helps improve air quality by reducing the number of commuters and cars on the road. Many of the homeowners represented in this book have taken this mandate to heart in creating work spaces filled with air, sunshine, and outdoor views—the very antithesis of the "sick building syndrome" that still plagues the sealed-up world of corporate offices. Chapter four shows how some people are using passive solar energy, radiant floor heating, green roofs, and other sustainable practices to save energy and reward the planet.

Vasilis Mediterranean Grill

Cooking
Robert and Molly Krause serve more than family and friends at home: a courtyard in their Lawrence, Kansas, residence is furnished with a full-service restaurant housed in a contemporary glass pavilion. Not on the original menu was a zoning problem that required them to reconfigure the space after the addition had been built.

The New Wave

Although more Americans are working at home, live/work architecture is in its infancy. As noted by several owners in this book, some zoning boards and city agencies are still reluctant to approve businesses in residential areas or living spaces in commercial districts. Even when approved, a live/work building often must comply with commercial building codes, resulting in costly construction of fire-rated separations, staircases, ramps, and parking spaces to meet local requirements. Neighbors too can raise objections, fearing the impact of mixed-use buildings on their property values.

But the live/work movement is here to stay. It has already spread from individuals carving out space in single-family homes to mainstream builders creating multifamily housing with room to work. In some cities, live/work has become as much a popular marketing ploy for loft-style living as a reality for those people who really do it.

As more people choose the live/work life, zoning and building codes will no doubt change to allow additional businesses to operate within residential neighborhoods and housing to coexist with stores and offices in commercial districts. Variety in live/work arrangements will also increase to reflect the demands of different demographic groups, including young business owners starting out, midlife career changers, and retiring baby boomers who will never really retire. This book represents just the beginning of that new wave of Americans who are finding more rewarding ways of working in our increasingly stressful and impersonal world.

Dining
Now back in business, the head chef and the pastry chef welcome as many as thirty gourmands for a high level of home cooking five days a week. The two-story glass addition to their historic home houses the kitchen and the guest restroom as well as a mother-in-law suite.

Making music
Accomodating his clients' desire to practice their pipe organ at home proved a challenge for the architect Mark McInturff. His solution was a sculptural addition that encloses the sound while separating Sonja Kahler and Matt Larson's practice room from their living space.

Adding on
The music chamber was inspired by a French chapel designed by the noted architect Le Corbusier in the 1950s. While visually separate from the Bethesda, Maryland, house bought just for it, the seven-sided addition connects easily with the living area through sliding glass doors. Here the owners host parties, welcome guests, and give lively concerts.

Lessons Learned

Learned wisdom from the owners of the homes and work spaces in this book, related within each profile, range from where to put the basement windows (low, it makes the room look taller) to when to install a green roof (make sure that the rafters can support one). These spaces also offer larger live/work lessons, including the following:

Anticipate change. You work at home today, but you might not tomorrow. An enticing job offer or loss of a second income through family changes may mean rejoining the nine-to-five commuter crowd. That leaves your valuable investment of work space empty of purpose. Most of the owners and residents featured here anticipated change by building rooms or entire buildings that can easily accommodate different functions. Some inserted multipurpose mezzanines into tall living spaces to serve as offices, lounges, or extra bedrooms. Others added kitchens and bathrooms so their offices and studios can be turned into guest suites or income-generating apartments. One owner even calls his design the Three-in-One House, citing its unity of living quarters, rental unit, and office. He plans to shift his office into the rental unit and incorporate his work space into the rest of the house.

Clearly distinguish working from living. In *A Room of One's Own,* Virginia Woolf suggests designating a space within the house for solitude. "A lock on the door," she writes, "means the power to think for oneself." But even

when locked, a door is probably not enough separation for those working at home full-time. From whining kids to household chores, interruptions and distractions require that an office or a studio be sequestered from living spaces and designed perhaps in a distinctly different style. Clear separation—visual, acoustical, and spatial—is important for getting the job done in peace and quiet. Entering your work space should mean crossing a threshold from the personal realm to the professional world.

Several owners profiled in this book make a strong distinction by dividing home from work space with a patio, a deck, or a terrace. Others extended a bridge between second-floor living and work spaces, leaving its platform open as an extra outdoor space or enclosing it to create extra room for work or storage or a place to unwind after a hard day's work.

Leave room on top. Open, spacious interiors topped the list of must-haves from the owners in this book. As a Cleveland clothing designer noted about his studio, "The high ceilings and big space allow me to think, to concentrate on my work, which is really consuming." Two-story-high spaces afford the opportunity

Retreating
During a renovation project, an artist in Washington, D.C., extended the back-yard deck off her studio. Such outdoor retreats provide extra room for working, relaxing, and dreaming up the next project.

Growing
Madeleine Keesing paints at a custom-designed easel in the two-story contemporary studio added to the back of her house in the nation's capital. The work space also grew within the home to include an upper-level office next to a remodeled master suite.

to insert multifunctional balconies and mezzanines. They can turn a basement into a light-filled studio, as illustrated by a Chicago architect's rowhouse, or a small back-yard pavilion, built by a Seattle filmmaker, into a loft.

Allow room to grow. Business expansion may mean more space for work surfaces, storage, employees, and clients. A property should be large enough for future additions. An artist in Washington, D.C., built the studio she always wanted off the back of her house and then reconfigured the interior for even more work space. A Maryland architect purchased an adjacent cottage, built over his garage, and extended his house to create a live/work compound separated by a garden.

Plan for the downside. Working from home can be lonely. It sometimes means having your professional life overtake your personal life, and staying connected to the outside world without having people around is difficult. Several

business owners in the book anticipated these negatives by moving to lofts with meeting facilities and cafes already built in or by picking neighborhoods near shops and services. "I wanted to be within a five- or ten-minute walk to stores, parks, and restaurants so I didn't feel isolated," relates a Seattle software developer. Others, among them an architect couple in Culver City, California, built their living quarters right over their office and a restaurant.

Set up for work. Determine what you need and want in your work space. This is where you will be spending most of the day, so it deserves as much attention as your living space. Start with the orientation of the room—there should be daylight, breezes, and views; for an Atlanta artist, more wall space than views fit his needs. Because some homeowners wanted the feeling of working outside, they built terraces and decks and installed rolling garage doors to eliminate the barrier between indoors and out.

Move on to the essentials: a work surface at a height of twenty-eight to thirty-one inches, a comfortable chair, a computer, office supplies, convenient electrical outlets, and phone and fax lines. Layer lighting with ambient fixtures that provide general illumination as well as spotlights that direct light to your work tasks and call attention to artwork or architectural

Driving in

Flexibility is built into the Seattle live/work residence of Rob Ferguson and Heather Johnston. She designed the contemporary home so he could work on both his software development and his Jaguar in the comfort of home. Now they live together in the wide-open, industrial-look residence with their son. The motorcycle is a reminder of their first date.

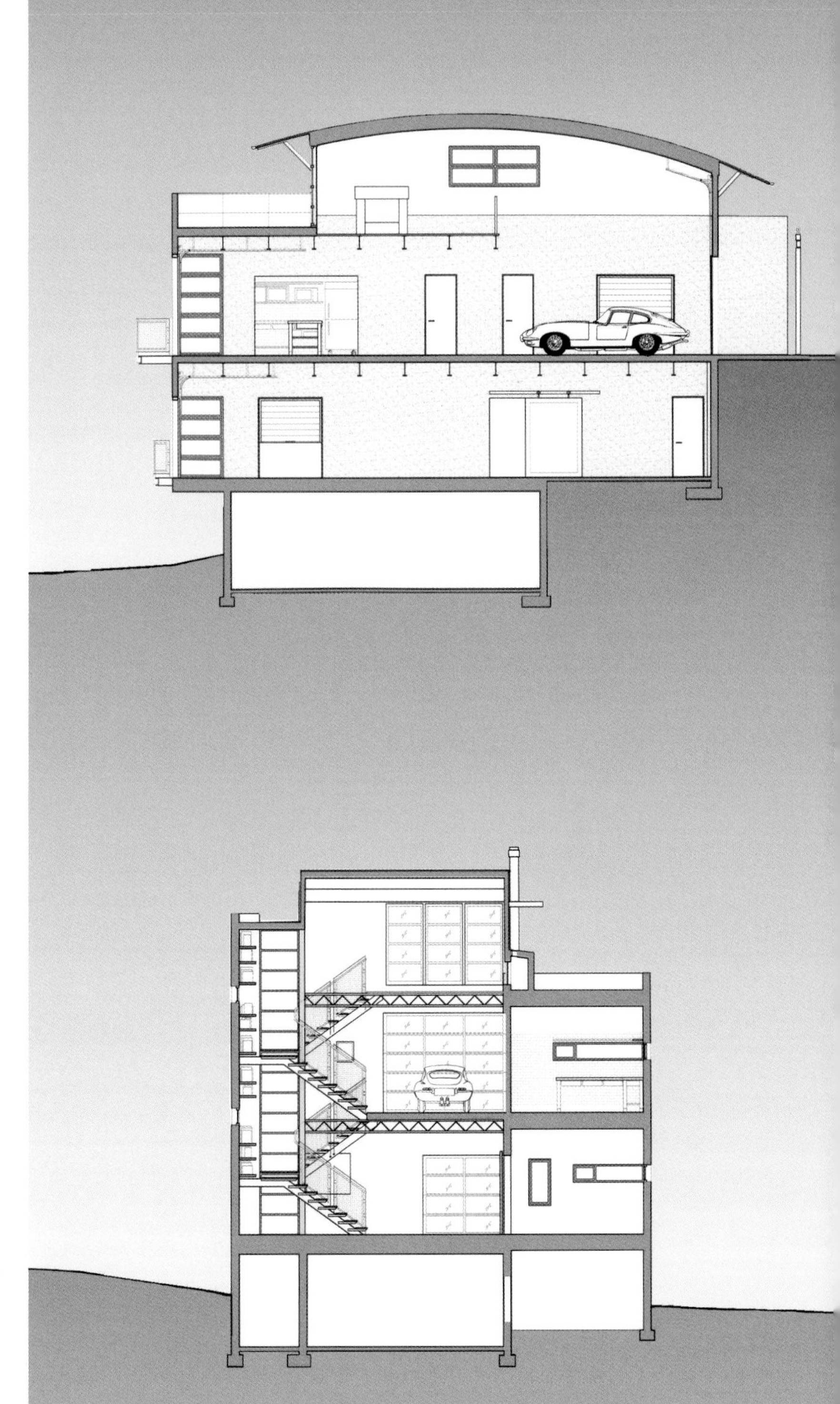

Stacking up

A roll-up garage door allows Ferguson to drive his Jaguar right into the house's main level, where the living spaces are also located, but he goes upstairs, under the vaulted roof, to pursue his software business. Steps lead down the hillside site to the family room and the bedrooms on the lower level.

Celebrating
David Egan, a photographer by trade, lives upstairs in a historic parish house in Baltimore, Maryland. Downstairs his special events company, named Chase Court, hosts weddings and other celebrations in a refined setting suitable for romance, Gothic or modern.

Living
The photographer's unique two-story living space offers a calm respite from the celebrations below. Under a stunning vaulted ceiling, light pours in from arched Gothic windows that were part of the parish house's original chapel. Egan had always hoped to make his home in a loft, but this live/work space, he points out, "goes beyond my expectations."

features in the room. To save space, build in storage cabinets and work surfaces, as many of the owners in this book chose to do. A Los Angeles architect even designed the desks in his office so they can be rolled away when he wants to use the room for parties.

Personalize your space. Business and pleasure do mix. Celebrate your escape from boring office decor by adding touches of your personality to your work space. In addition to colored walls, wood trim, and contemporary furnishings, the owners represented in these pages added everything from movie posters to a sports car to enliven their surroundings. A Seattle filmmaker went so far as to weld the motto "You'll have lots of time to rest when you're six feet under" onto the steel staircase leading to his office. "It reminds me to get to work," he says.

The chapters that follow visit a wide range of live/work experiences exemplifying these ideals. Each chapter highlights a special set of requirements: building from the ground up (Virgin Territory); merging private accommodations with commercial spaces (Living Above the Store); incorporating complexes of buildings and commuting only as far as the back yard (It Takes a Village); using environmentally sustainable designs and materials (Shades of Green); and renovating existing and historic spaces (Built to Last). Modest or grand in scope, traditional or modern in style, urban or rural in location, each project offers tested ideas for maximizing the choice to work at home and live at work.

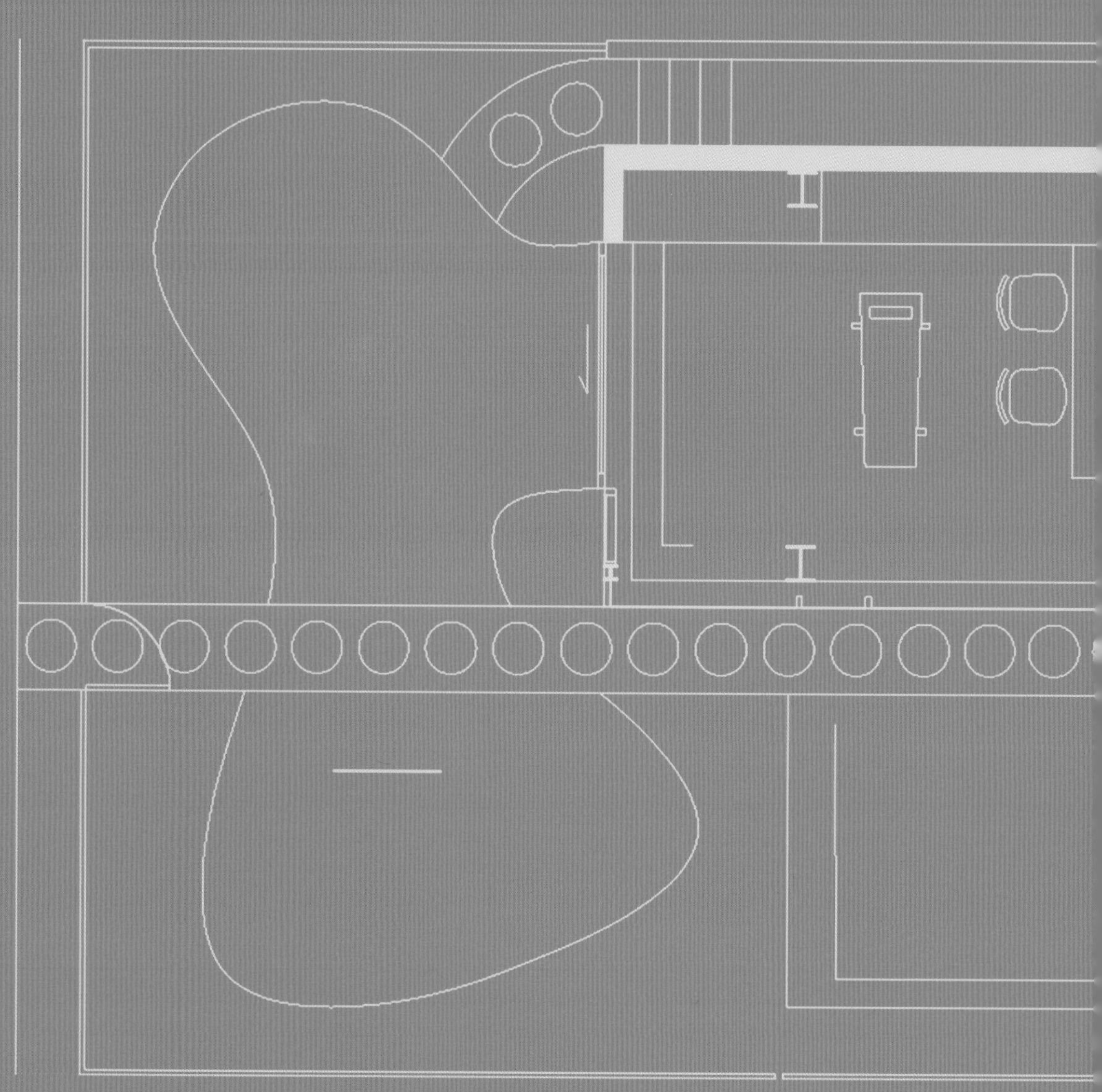

Virgin Territory

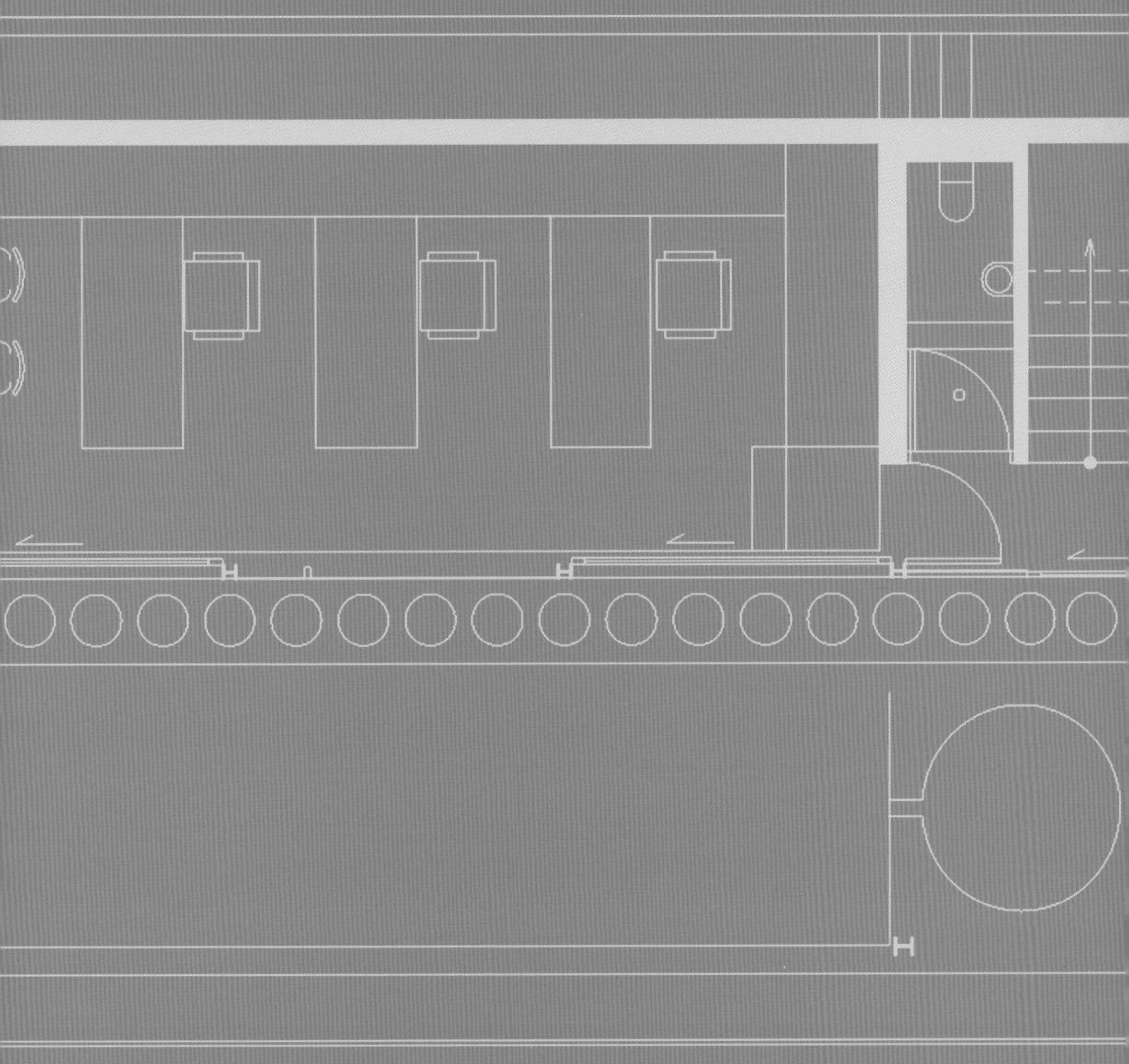

From the Ground Up

THE BEST SEATS IN THE HOUSE

Cheerful color warms the cool modernism of the three-story dwelling where the architect Glen Irani and the artist Edith Beaucage live with their young son, Mario. Painted blue and orange on the outside, the boxy structure of glass, steel, and cement plaster stands out from the older wood-framed houses along a canal in Venice, California. It functions differently too: work spaces for the owners occupy the best rooms in the house.

"Since I spend all day here, I wanted the ground floor next to the pool and garden for my office," remarks Irani, whose design followed two previous canalside buildings in which he also lived and worked. "One of the primary considerations was street access, so people wouldn't walk through the house to get to the office." Where the living room might be is a row of steel-topped desks, which extend from a steel counter along one wall. The arrangement looks rigid but is actually flexible: to free up the room for entertaining, the desks can all be rolled to one end. The glass wall

Greeting
The colorful front facade intentionally stands out from the neighboring canalside houses in Venice, California. Generous glass panes offer views of the adjacent canal from the ground-floor office, upper-story living areas, and top-floor master suite.

Wrapping
Bright stucco panels on the facade repeat the play of colors found throughout the house and the studio.

KATAHDIN
Old Town

opposite slides open to the inviting waters of a lap pool. "Its tranquillity sets the tone for the place," observes Irani. "It dials down the tension when the office gets a little crazy."

On the top floor, Beaucage paints her colorful, biomorphic abstractions in a studio secluded at the rear. "It is a necessity for me to get away to my own space where I can create and think," says the artist, who is from Montreal, Canada. Her small room, furnished with a movable work table on wheels, is framed by south- and north-facing windows to provide plenty of light.

Between the two work zones is an open room on the second floor that is organized into living, dining, and cooking spaces. Walls of cabinets with the rounded edges that reappear in various sections of the house demarcate

Sheltering
The forty-foot-long lap pool next to the glassed-in office—an unexpected bit of tranquility in a work environment—is protected by the overhanging second floor. Rounded shapes on the sandblasted glass wall in front of the upper-story dining area are based on the imagery of Edith Beaucage's paintings.

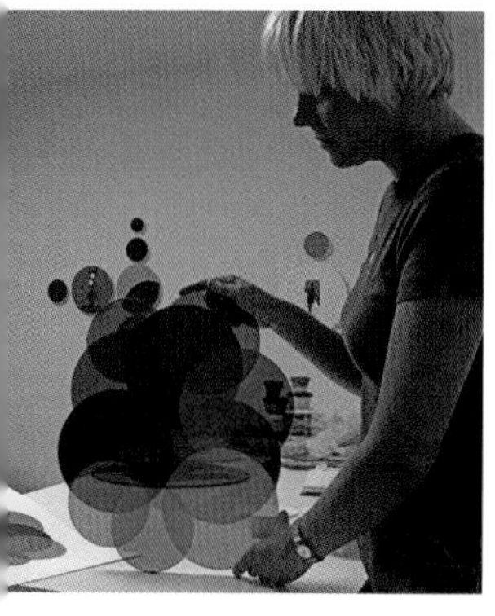

the kitchen and the living room fireplace. The dining table and chairs are pulled up to a window sandblasted with amoebalike shapes reminiscent of Beaucage's paintings. At the back of this level, behind the stairwell, are a bedroom and a playroom for the couple's son.

Irani's deft mix of working, living, and outdoor spaces is all the more remarkable given the constraints of the 30-by-95-foot property, where neighboring houses are only six feet away. This proximity led the architect to hollow out one side of the 3,000-square-foot building to create a terrace off the living-dining area that also acts as a light well, supplying sunshine to the upper-story rooms.

Painting
Edith Beaucage's third-floor studio, the only white room in the house, opens onto a balcony overlooking the second-floor terrace. The bright colors and free-form shapes of her paintings inspired much of the decor found throughout the residence and workplaces.

Where most architects would have insisted on white walls and ceilings, Irani collaborated with his artist wife to turn the modern building into an inhabitable kaleidoscope filled with forty-three colors. "When I met Glen, everything was white in his house," recalls Beaucage. "I exposed him to the beauty and good effects of color over time. He really got into the details of how color absorbs and reflects light." In addition to brightening the rooms, the hues are composed to strike complementary harmonies and contrasts of light and shadow similar to painterly chiaroscuro. Dark flooring, stairs, cabinetry, and window frames juxtaposed against pale walls create depth and lead the eye into the interiors.

"We focused on what occurs when many colors are united in one space," explains Irani. "The shades and tints help develop moods conducive to the different uses of the spaces." In his office, charcoal gray desks under a complementary sky blue ceiling and alongside yellow orange cabinets create an orderly calm, made calmer still by rippling reflections from the lap pool in the adjacent garden. The living space is more energized with nearly all the hues of the spectrum, including scarlet kitchen cabinets, orange-paneled bookcases, and a green wall covered in artificial grass. Arranged around the hearth are purple and blue chairs, each designed by Irani to seat two. Chartreuse, brightened by light streaming in from windows and skylights, practically shouts from the stairway. On the third floor, a Chinese red ceiling saturates the couple's pale blue bedroom and adjacent bathroom; shimmering silver satin curtains at the windows as well as mirrored and shiny acrylic surfaces in the bathroom reflect the ceiling's rosy glow.

"My paintings fit with the house and the house fits with my paintings," muses Beaucage, pleased with the synergy of art and architecture. Her studio, as it turns out, is the only white room in the house. For his part, Irani admits that his first experiments with color in the live/work complex have led him to apply similarly vivid combinations in subsequent projects, including a house with a deep plum facade. "My clients are nowhere as brazen with color as I am in my own house," he acknowledges. "But you don't have to feel threatened by color. In most cases, it's just paint."

Relaxing
Seated on the artificial grass of the second-floor terrace, Edith Beaucage shows her artwork to the noted architectural photographer Julius Shulman. Sliding glass doors open the kitchen and the living area to this outdoor space. By carving such a side courtyard out of the narrow building, Irani was able to bring more light into the interiors.

Living
On the second level, the living area is furnished with chairs designed by Irani to seat two. The kitchen, framed by stained wood cabinets, adjoins the glass-enclosed terrace, with its tent for the couple's son. Reproduction Eames chairs are pulled up to the Irani-designed maple table for dining.

Screening
A biomorphic pattern based on Beaucage's art is sand-blasted on the glass wall of the second-floor dining area to frame the view. It is just one more variation on the house's theme of color and sensuous shape.

Day lighting
Sunshine from a skylight and wall apertures filters into the stairwell, where cantilevered wooden treads are supported by steel rods.

Snuggling
The living area focuses on a fireplace set within steel-faced cabinets, which are curved to match the desks in the office. This consistency of detail helps unify the various spaces and levels throughout the house.

Sharing
Within the open space on the second level, dining and living areas are defined by furniture groupings. Eero Saarinen's Tulip chair is paired with more colorful seating by Charles and Ray Eames around a table designed by Irani. Class doors lead to a terrace overlooking the canal.

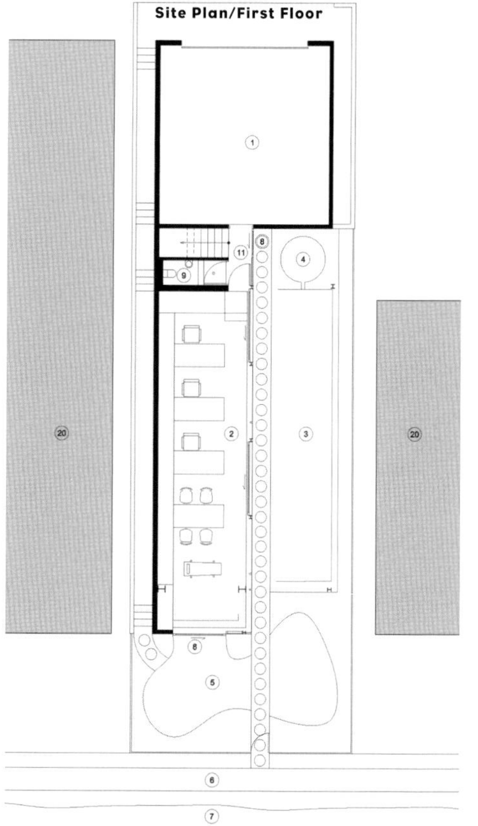

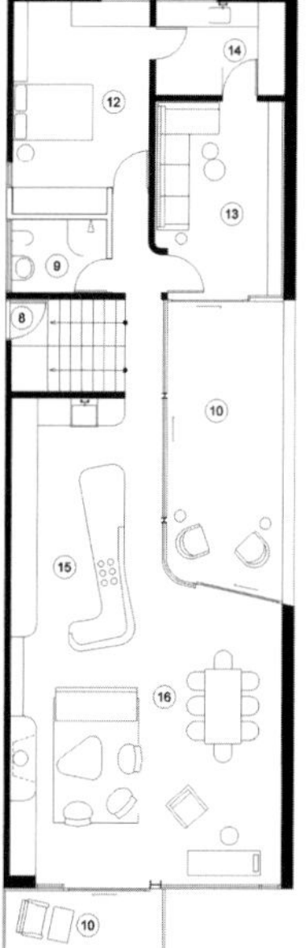

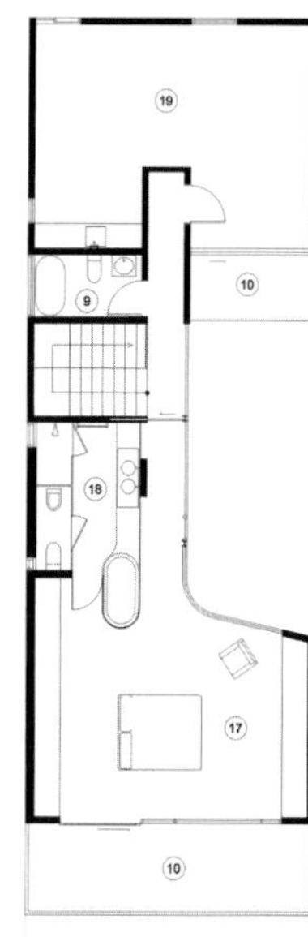

1 Garage/Workshop
2 Studio/Office
3 Lap Pool
4 Spa
5 Garden
6 Sidewalk
7 Canal
8 Entry
9 Bathroom
10 Sun Court
11 Hallway
12 Bedroom
13 Den/Guest Bedroom
14 Laundry Room
15 Kitchen
16 Living/Dining Area
17 Master Bedroom
18 Master Bathroom
19 Painting Studio
20 Adjacent Buildings

LESSONS LEARNED

Design work spaces to do double duty. When Glen Irani took over the ground floor for his office, he also created the perfect setting for parties. During after-hours entertaining, desks can be rolled out of the way, clutter can be hidden in built-in cabinets, and the steel countertop can be transformed into a buffet. Opening the glass wall to the pool provides a seamless indoor-outdoor space for larger gatherings.

Tailor work space to specific tasks. "My office took three months to design because we really thought through every detail, down to the exact places for the electrical outlets," discloses Irani. "The design of your work space should be every bit as functional as your kitchen." Cabinets are configured to conceal office machinery, drawers are sized to hold supplies and material samples, wall shelving is designed to fit product binders and conceal them behind sliding doors of colored acrylic. Lighting is varied to suit the task, including fixtures mounted above the yellow-paneled shelves for general illumination and task lighting under the wall-mounted storage.

Don't be afraid of color. Irani's modern architecture of glass, steel, and cement plaster could have felt cold and austere, but instead it is warmed and brightened by more than three dozen colors. "If you dress your house in beige, it says that you are not living fully," suggests Beaucage, who recommends developing a richer palette, one room at a time. "Start by transferring the colors of your sofa pillows onto the walls. Dive in and enjoy."

Sleeping
The master bedroom occupies two-thirds of the top floor and adjoins a terrace with views of the canal. Irani describes its red ceiling as "like sleeping beneath a Bedouin tent."

Bathing
Curving forms found elsewhere in the house and the office continue in the master bathroom's tub, sinks, and light fixtures. A frosted glass door leads to the bedroom.

CAMERA READY

"I wanted work to have as much weight as living," declares the photographer Rhoda Baer about her dual-purpose contemporary home. Nestled into a hillside within a leafy, suburban neighborhood of Washington, D.C., the concrete-block house balances a photography studio and office on one side with bedroom suites on the other. Bridging the two splayed wings is a glassy living space that angles out from the masonry walls to face the street.

The unconventional dwelling in Bethesda, Maryland, represents decades of dreaming on the part its owner. "I used to design houses in my head while swimming laps," reflects Baer, who formerly worked in the cramped, low-ceilinged basement of a much more typical home. The photographer relates that she always wanted to build her own house, inspired by her mother's example. "She built a house in Stamford, Connecticut, from a kit of plans," Baer recalls. "It was a gutsy thing for an ex-school teacher to do."

Molding
Simple concrete blocks allowed the architect to mold space into angles that contrast nicely with the lush wooded setting of the photographer's live/work space.

Shooting
Inside the nearly eighteen-foot-high studio, white walls and a concrete floor provide a changeable backdrop for Rhoda Baer's photo shoots.

Photographs by Maxwell MacKenzie

After buying the steep, tree-filled lot, Baer went through an intensive interview process to select Ralph Cunningham of Cunningham and Quill Architects. He used the hilly site as a starting point in designing the 3,450-square-foot live/work space. "There was a reason why this lot wasn't developed," he explains. "It is a trapezoid in shape, very steep, and sits on a rock outcropping. We looked at it as an opportunity to break apart the program, to separate the studio and make it independent of the house."

His angular design edged in steel and copper is unabashedly contemporary, but the house is organized according to the classical model of a *piano nobile*. Living spaces, the main bedroom suite, and the office occupy the higher floor, allowing treetop views. The studio and less frequently used spaces—the guest bedroom, laundry, and storage and utility spaces—are arranged on the ground floor. "I wanted to build something that I could navigate as I got older," explains Baer.

Siting

One constraint in designing Baer's house was a local zoning restriction requiring that it maintain a generous distance from adjacent properties. "It made sense to align the volumes to the setbacks. That's why the two wings are skewed to each other," says the architect, Ralph Cunningham. "That made for a lot of interesting geometries inside the house."

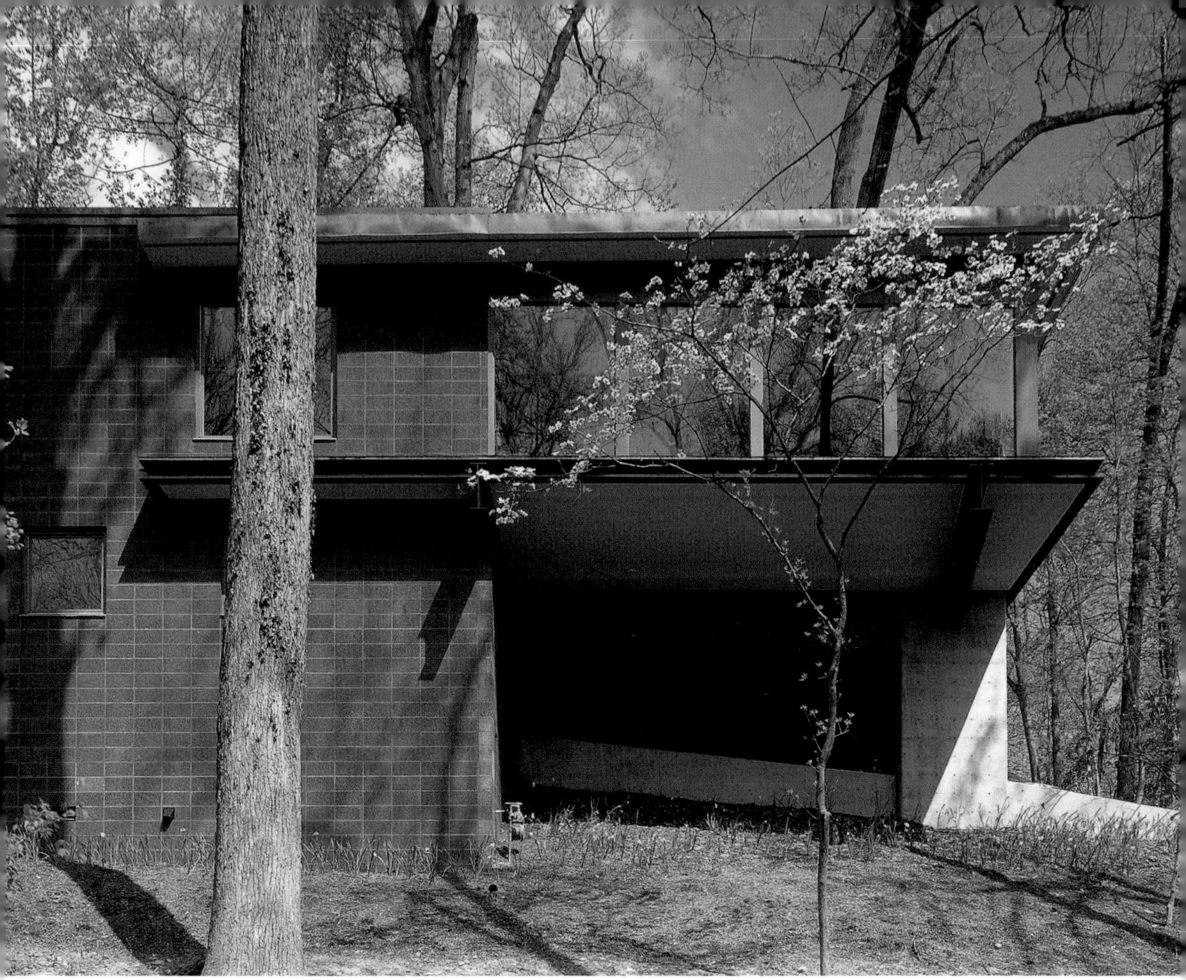

Bridging
The residential section is entered from a sloping driveway and parking area at the rear. From there the role of the bridge in separating working and living spaces becomes clear.

The physical division between living and working is accentuated by the sloping entrance driveway, which rises through the middle of the house. It leads up from the street under the main living space to a parking court at the top of the hill. Separate entrances to the photography studio and the living wings reinforce the functional distinctions. The door to the studio is located off the driveway, close to the front of the house, while the living space is entered at the rear from a gentle ramp sloping up from the parking area. Inside this back-front door, a glassy corridor connects the foyer to the office and the studio, providing internal access to the work spaces.

Mediating the hillside allowed the two-story photography studio to occupy the front of the work wing, where the slope is lower, yet be integrated into the house's mass. The studio entrance leads straight into this boxy space, with a darkroom tucked into the side. "Now that I work with digital cameras, I hardly ever use the darkroom," admits Baer. "But it comes in handy for the other projects I'm working on." The photographer has recently begun making fused art glass in the utility space.

Driving
The entrance driveway separates the concrete-block wing housing the photography studio (right) from the glass-enclosed living quarters (left). Bridging the divide is the kitchen, with its own terrace above the protruding steel beam.

Living
To help with the decor, Baer tapped the noted Washington, D.C., designer Thomas Pheasant, who softened the rooms with understated, comfortable furnishings, including many pieces of his own design. Upholstery and pillows in muted green shades harmonize with the forested landscape visible through the living room windows.

Cunningham explains that he shaped the two-story studio with future owners in mind: "They could put in another floor and convert the studio into bedrooms," he notes. For now, Baer uses it to snap pictures of people for corporate, commercial, and health-care assignments, among them the Heart Truth Campaign to raise awareness of heart disease among women. "It also becomes a great dance floor for parties," she adds. "It's heaven." In one corner of the tall room, a staircase leads up to the second floor, where Baer works in a small office. "I have meetings with clients here and have used it as a changing room for models," she explains.

By sequestering her office and studio in one wing of the house, the photographer can close the door to these spaces and enjoy kicking back in the living and bedroom wings on the opposite side without having to be reminded of work. Most of her down time is spent in the bridge over the driveway, where living, dining, and cooking are combined in one big, loftlike room. "When I was growing up, everyone had a beautiful living room that no one went into," she remembers. "I don't think people should live like that. When I entertain, I want to be in the same room as my guests."

Mark Rothko
Irving Penn PASSAGE

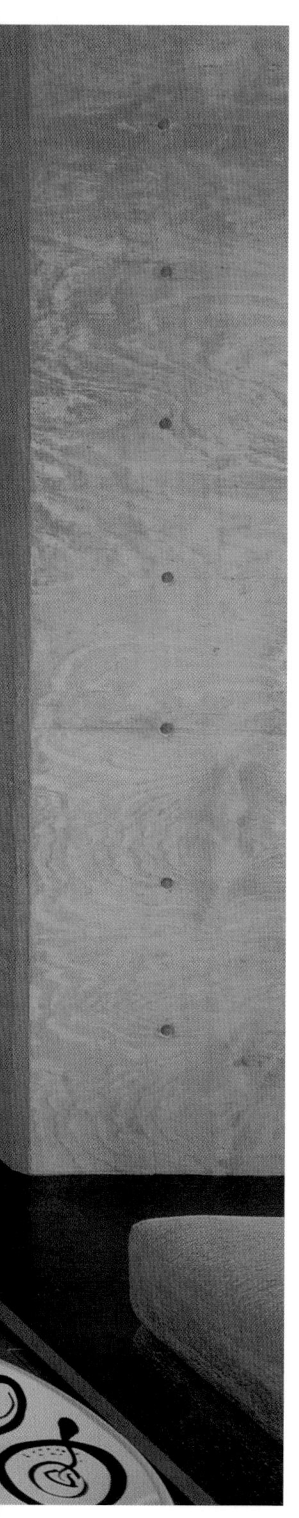

The elevated space, enclosed by glass on two sides, overlooks leaves and branches. Stretching along one side of this tree house, the galley kitchen is framed by a long island, cabinets, and built-in bookshelves, all in white. "If you are going to expose the kitchen to the living space, it should be in the background, as visually quiet as possible," maintains Cunningham. On the other side of the living room, a table and chairs are set up for dining, and a seating area for conversation and television watching overlooks the street.

"Building this house made me think about how I live," observes Baer. "I don't consider work as separate from my life. In fact, I don't like the word *work*. It comes with the negative connotation of someone else's agenda. To me, work and life are inseparable, and this house reflects that."

Cooking
In working with her architect, Baer made sure that kitchen countertops, appliances, and door hardware were positioned low enough for her five-foot-tall frame. All in white, they disappear into the background of the living area.

Matching
"I wanted the same look in the kitchen and the bathroom," says Baer, who installed matching ivory Corian countertops and Navajo white wood cabinets and walls in both spaces.

LESSONS LEARNED

Interview architects to find a good match. After drawing up a list of ten architects, Rhoda Baer decided to hire Ralph Cunningham. "I liked that he had experience designing commercial buildings," she remarks. "I wanted the architect to really understand the studio part of the house and to use nontraditional materials. Ralph was the only one who saw the studio and the living area as two distinct parts of the house."

Use a landscape element to separate living and working spaces. To distinguish the building's living and working portions, Cunningham extended the driveway up through the house instead of placing it to one side (which also limited construction on the site). A pedestrian walkway, an outdoor deck, or a pool could perform the same role.

Build for tomorrow. Keep in mind possible expansion or changes to your own living and working arrangements as well as how the structure could be marketed for sale. Live/work spaces tailored to the needs of the original occupant may not fit potential new owners, limiting the resale value. The two-story studio was designed so it could be divided into bedrooms with the insertion of an additional floor or turned into a rental apartment or a guest suite with the addition of a kitchen and a full bathroom in the darkroom.

DOWN-TO-EARTH DIVA

Rob Ferguson and Heather Johnston spent their first date on a motorcycle, riding around Seattle to survey local real estate. Ferguson, a software designer, had decided that it was time to move from his Craftsman-style bungalow to a setting more accommodating to his home-based business and his hobbies: photography, welding, and car repair. "One day I had my Jaguar's entire engine spread out on newspaper in the living room," he recalls. "I realized then that my life and my house weren't meshing."

His search for an old warehouse to renovate led to the realization that dot-com companies had already snapped up most of the city's few industrial buildings and that other desirable properties were too costly. Ferguson then risked his budding romance with Johnston, an architect, by asking her to design him a building from scratch. "Most of my friends thought that I was out of my mind," he laughs. "But we shared the same modernist aesthetic, and I was struck by her understanding of the beauty and directness of simple materials. So we drew some very clear lines between our personal and professional relationship."

Siting

Diva, the house, is built on a Seattle hillside so that it appears from the street to be just two stories. Rob Ferguson can drive his car or his motorcycle up the driveway and through the garage door—right into the main wing. His office is tucked under the curved metal roof, while his workshop occupies the smaller, stucco-clad building at one end of the house. A bridge on the other side leads to the entrance and the stair tower connecting the three levels.

Ferguson ended up buying a dilapidated house in Seattle's Fremont neighborhood and tearing it down to make way for a three-level structure with enough room for his various pursuits. "Because I work at home," he explains, "I wanted to be within a five- or ten-minute walk to stores, parks, and restaurants so I didn't feel isolated." Another benefit of the hillside site he found is that it is high enough to offer views of Puget Sound and the Olympic Mountains on a clear day.

Multitasking
Reflecting Ferguson's hopes for a multifunctional space, the main level resembles a warehouse with exposed trusses and concrete floors. Here Ferguson can repair his beloved 1969 E-type Jaguar, work on his computer, and entertain. At the rear of the open floor space, the living and dining areas are within reach of the balcony. The loft above this main level provides office space for Ferguson's software business.

Ideas for the design came from one of the couple's favorite films, the 1981 French thriller *Diva*. The movie's quirky lofts and warehouses inspired similarly large, open rooms that can be transformed for ever-changing purposes. "Rob told me that he wanted a space where he could restore a car, run a software company, raise a family, and throw a dinner party without having to renovate the house every time," relates Johnston, who heads Place Architects in Seattle and designed the live/work project in collaboration with the architect Kevin Spence.

Indeed, the airy main floor off the street serves as a showroom for Ferguson's 1969 E-type Jaguar, a living room, an entertaining hub, and an office. The lower-level loft has been turned into a family room, with furniture clustered around a blackboard for creative doodling. On the top floor, under the vaulted roof, is Ferguson's office, a retreat where he works on the computer. It is also a second living room, furnished with a vintage George Nelson desk and 1950s chairs paired in front of a fireplace. The aerie opens to a terrace where the Canadian-born software developer can work on his laptop while enjoying mountain views. Balconies supply similar outdoor spaces on the lower levels.

Given their shared background in the theater, Johnston and Ferguson interpreted the house as a set for the drama of everyday life. "The big, open space with the car on the middle level is the stage where everything happens," Ferguson points out. "Backstage" is a narrower, bar-shaped projection at the side of the house where more practical, private activities take place. The second-floor kitchen, darkroom, and half bath and the lower-level master suite occupy this more confined wing of the house but to feel connected, open to the larger, multipurpose lofts on both floors. An attached garage on the street side provides a workshop for messy automotive repairs. "In a loft, it's often hard to find a cozy corner, while in a house you often feel that there is nowhere to stretch," comments Johnston. "We tried to bring together the two types of spaces."

Entertaining
For parties the owners move the dining table front and center within the main level, turning the Jag into a sculptural conversation piece. The concrete floors are fitted with electrical outlets so furniture and lamps can be easily reconfigured.

Living
Evidencing the architect's blend of the intimate and the open are the sofa, nestled into an alcove, and the dining table at the center of the main level's expanse. Even when closed, the glass-fitted garage door and the corner window allow the family to enjoy views of nature as they dine.

Working
In the top-floor loft, Ferguson works at a George Nelson desk next to a fireplace with a concrete hearth and a steel mantel matching the exterior's Cor-Ten panels. Metal mesh railings recall those used on the staircase and the decks.

Cooking
Heather Johnston, the designer-owner of the house, prepares a meal in the back-corner kitchen. Open shelving provides easy access to tableware and cookbooks. Subway tiles, a stainless steel exhaust hood, and tinted concrete countertops extend the architecture's industrial feeling.

The couple nicknamed the house Diva, but it is far from fussy or high maintenance. "Rob asked for a building that would last a hundred years," reports Johnston, "so we chose materials for their durability and economy." On the exterior, panels of rusty Cor-Ten steel covering the main building and yellow stucco on the side wing and the stair tower clearly differentiate the house's various parts. Aluminum windows and roll-up garage doors draw on the straightforward appeal of warehouses. Steel trusses are left exposed inside, and fir decking serves as both ceiling and floor. Staircases are framed in steel with balustrades made of wire mesh.

Happily, the process of creating Diva brought Johnston and Ferguson closer together. They now share the house with their young son, Ewan, who sleeps in a space partitioned by Ikea office furniture in the lower-level loft next to his parents' bedroom. The house has proven as adaptable as intended, allowing the couple to install a home theater and to turn the darkroom into a storage area for motorcycles and tools, among other changes. When the couple entertains, the car is rolled from the loft into the garage and the computer work station next to the front door is set up as a buffet. "The great thing about Diva is that it can be whatever I need it to be, whenever I need it," asserts Ferguson. "I've held business meetings, done photo shoots, worked on cars and bikes, written software, designed and built electronics, hosted large parties—all in the same set of spaces, easily rearranged to suit the particular task at hand."

Connecting
The steel staircase linking the home's various levels projects from the side of the main wing to leave uninterrupted floor space. Built-in fir bookshelves free up room, underscoring Diva's industrial, multifunctional nature.

Gathering

The lower-level family room opens onto a balcony and includes a space for Johnston to work on her architectural projects. Furnishings include reupholstered 1950s chairs and a blackboard for creative brainstorming. As on the upper levels, the ceiling's metal joists and wood decking are left exposed.

Screening

The family room's back wall doubles as a screen for showing movies. A reading nook is furnished with vintage 1950s chairs and a table for Johnston's architectural drawings.

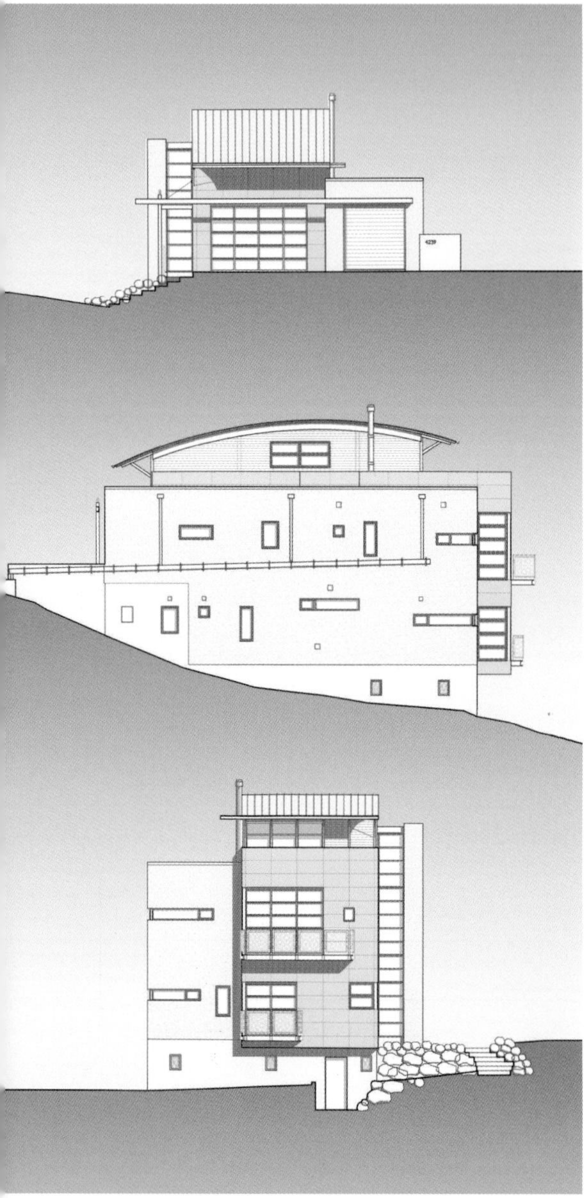

Loft

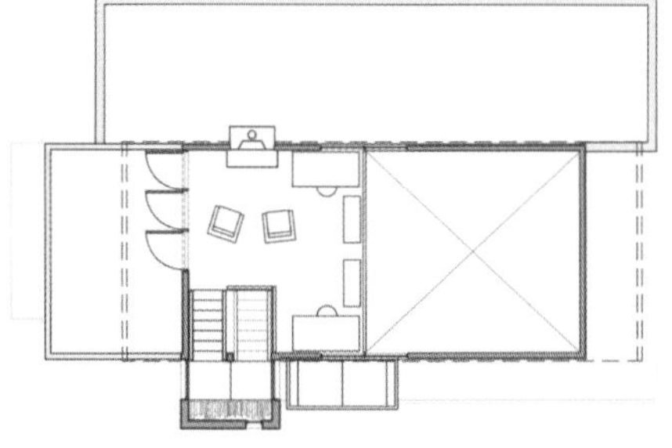

Main Level

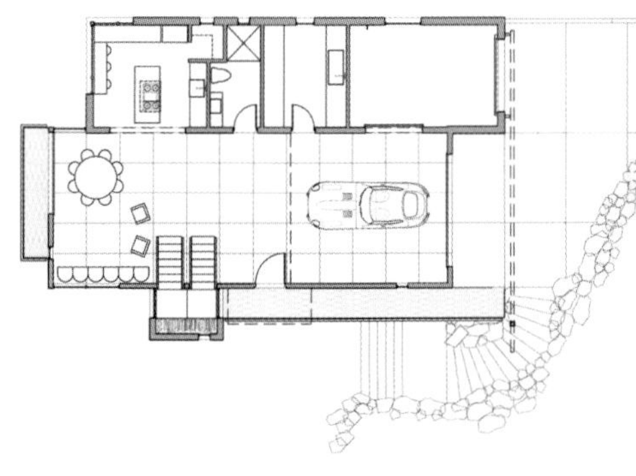

Lower Level

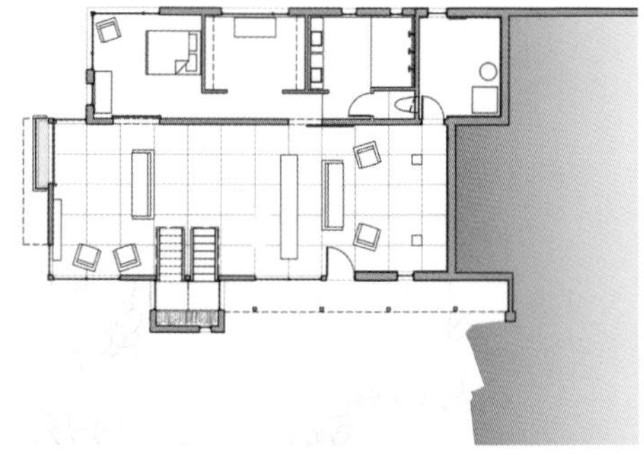

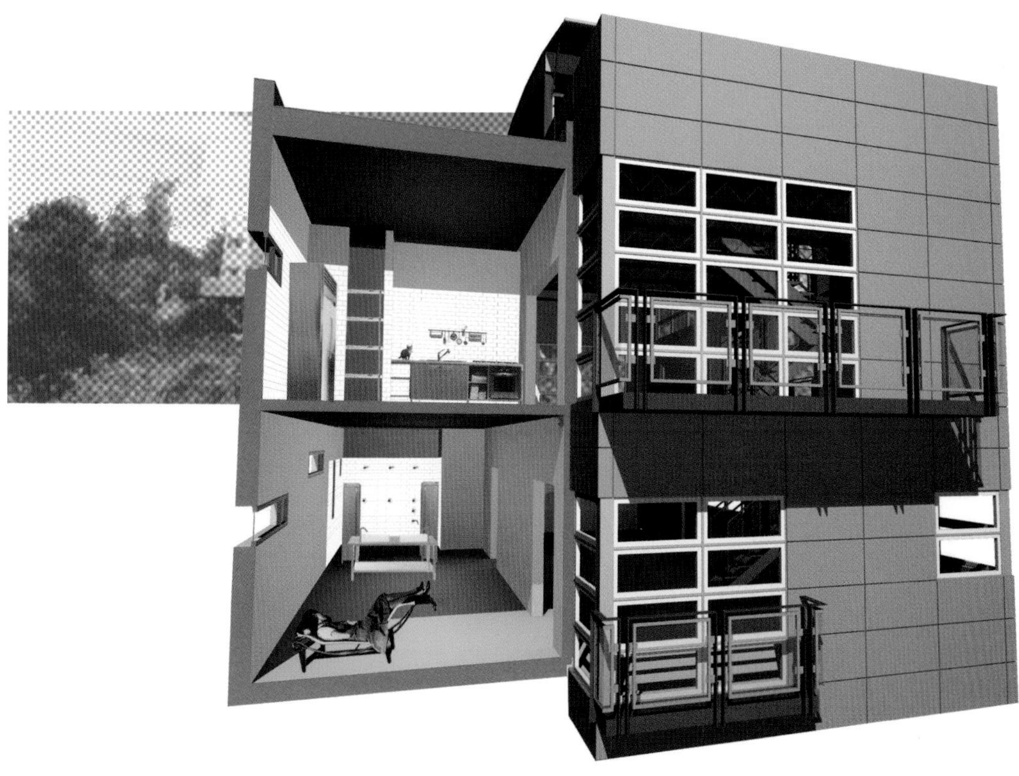

LESSONS LEARNED

Vary the space, vary the function. Instead of shaping each space with a specific purpose in mind, Heather Johnston kept the floor plan flexible so that the bigger rooms can be used for working, entertaining, or displaying Ferguson's prized Jaguar. The house has no formal dining space and only one bedroom, which could be converted into another use. "I wanted malleability," Rob Ferguson observes. "It's hard to move walls around after the fact."

Find beauty in industrial details. Johnston ordered off-the-shelf elements from catalogues to keep costs down and convey an industrial look. "Diva is a warehouse in its soul," she acknowledges. Bathroom vanities are made from restaurant tables, and towel bars are metal railings attached with pipe fittings. Openings are fitted with rolling garage doors. Tool carts supply office storage, and science lab tables provide kitchen counter space. Even the door knobs are a sturdy design intended for schools.

Create more than one work space. Ferguson's main office, a retreat on the top floor with a fireplace, opens onto a terrace where he can work outdoors on his laptop. He also keeps a computer work station on the main floor next to the front door. "The flexibility is important because it means that I can always accomplish what I need to in the most natural way possible," Ferguson remarks. "My business and my life are always changing, but even so, I never feel constrained by my house. I feel liberated."

STOCK OPTIONS

Radcliffe Bailey mixes old family photographs and vignettes of black history into brightly colored abstract paintings as improvisational as jazz. His large artworks are created in a studio connected by an enclosed bridge to the house where Bailey lives in a neighborhood west of downtown Atlanta. The setup is as fluid as the artist's brushwork, allowing for togetherness when the divorced father's young son and daughter visit as well as seclusion for painting alone. "I wanted an open space that I could work in," notes Bailey, "and with a skip and a hop, attend to a child."

Nestled into forested acreage adjoining a nature preserve, the house and studio complex takes advantage of the views while providing enough introspective space to create and contemplate art. "I avoided having windows in the studio because I needed as much wall space as possible to paint," explains Bailey. "And I didn't want to stare out at the woods all day." To design the two-bedroom home and studio, he tapped the noted Atlanta architects Mack Scogin and Merrill Elam, whose freewheeling design sensibilities are in sync with his collaged shapes and colors. "I felt like I was commissioning a sculptor to shape a piece that would sit on my property," adds the artist.

Working outdoors
A covered porch at the end of Radcliffe Bailey's studio provides a sheltered place to create sculpture next to the trees.

Linking
Projecting from the house's second story is a bar-shaped wing linking house and studio. The fiber cement-paneled bridge projects over the entrance to create a sheltering porch and a carport. The projection is a visual play of solid and void—sculpture designed to uplift the property.

Painting
Bailey creates his colorful artworks in a 2,000-square-foot studio. Viewing windows as a distraction, he opted instead for more wall space. Light filters into the space through plastic-covered gaps in the eaves, a low-cost alternative to skylights.

GEORGIA
PALMARES
4
BATOE

Constrained by a tight budget and an easement for a gas line on the property, the architects organized the living spaces into a cube and the work area into a shoebox; each two-story building comprises about 2,000 square feet. On the ground level, the house and studio are separated by a deck and a carport, and on the second story, they are linked by a wide, enclosed bridge, which is used as a library, work area, and guest room.

Although straightforward, the design proved expensive to build. Bailey turned to John Wieland, an arts patron who owns several of his paintings, to provide a more economical solution. As one of the largest homebuilders in the Southeast, Wieland specializes in efficient construction, providing everything from exterior cladding to kitchen equipment from his own building supply companies. He agreed to construct Bailey's house and studio from those stock items, leaving the architects to translate their custom design into standard materials. "That led us to find ways of using the elements in different ways, such as taking windows that are limited in size and grouping them into bigger windows," relates Elam, who managed to preserve the design's modern intent with large expanses of glass and crisp planes.

"Walking up the trunk of a tree" Inside the two-story living room, a sculptural staircase winds around the fireplace chimney to a mezzanine laundry room and the upper-level bedrooms. Here Bailey has found places to stand and enjoy all the architectural angles.

Dining
On one side of the sculptural staircase, a dining table contrasted with Philippe Starck's transparent polycarbonate Louis Ghost chairs is in easy reach of a built-in sideboard and the adjacent kitchen.

On the exterior, unfinished fiber-cement boards and corrugated fiberglass panels are simply bolted onto the walls, with the stainless-steel connections left visible. The translucent fiberglass is placed over silvery, reflective insulation so when hit by sunlight, the facade glows. "The budget didn't get in the way of the architects' creativity," says Bailey.

Inside the house, the ground-floor living area is airy and sunlit from the industrial-sized window assemblies framing views of trees and greenery. Centering the two-story space is a sculptural staircase winding up around the fireplace chimney to a mezzanine laundry room and upper-level bedrooms. "It's like walking up the trunk of a tree," observes Bailey. "There are lots of places to stand on and enjoy the different angles of the house." The top floor, in contrast, is more inwardly focused, with closets and bathrooms placed at the building perimeter. "This makes the bedrooms feel more protected and creates a change of environment within the house from the more transparent level below," explains Elam.

Bailey's studio resembles a big warehouse with wooden ceiling joists and few windows, allowing him to mount canvases on the walls and to paint in the shadow-free, artificial light he prefers. "If he changes his mind and wants to go to daylight, it's a simple procedure to put skylights in between the joists," notes Elam. At one end, a roll-up garage door opens onto a deck where Bailey, who studied to be a sculptor, tinkers with three-dimensional work. "Space away from people and space away from your work are both important," he maintains. "This house gives me those options."

Climbing
The staircase leads from the living room past a built-in bookshelf on the mezzanine. There angular nooks and crannies offer places to take in both outdoor and indoor vistas.

Sleeping
The main bedroom suite on the top floor offers several vantage points to enjoy treetop views, including a deep window seat with storage for books.

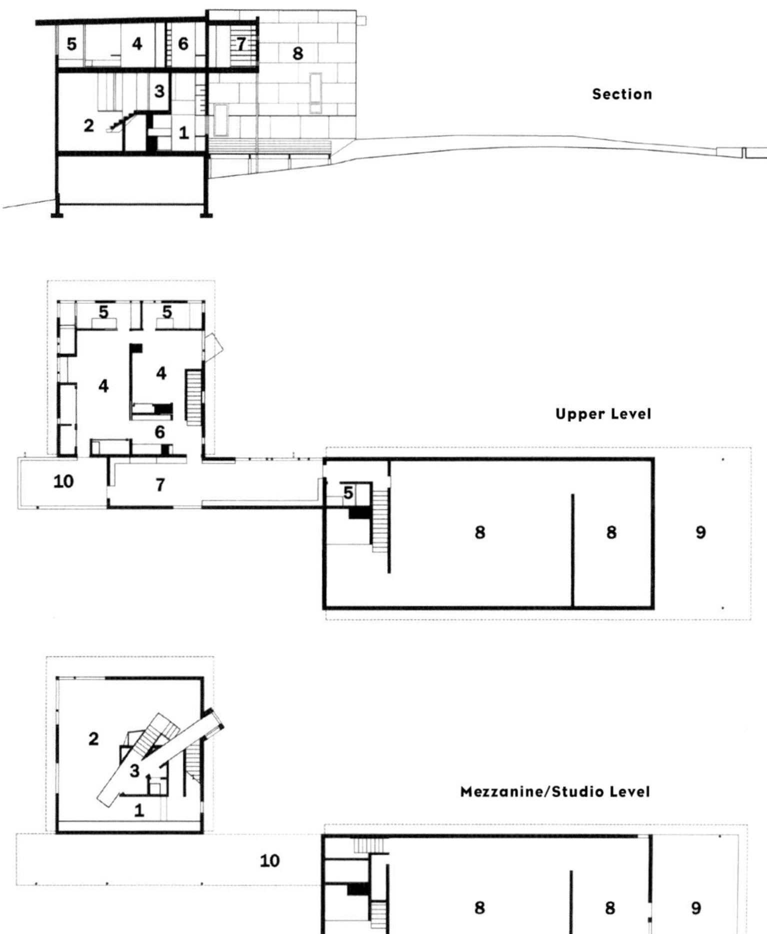

1 Kitchen
2 Living/Dining Area
3 Mezzanine
4 Bedroom
5 Bathroom
6 Office
7 Library
8 Studio
9 Outdoor Studio
10 Deck

LESSONS LEARNED

Get creative with off-the-shelf elements. Here standard building elements were recast into inventive architecture. Stock windows are grouped into larger areas of glass, and inexpensive fiberglass and cement-board are fastened with stainless-steel bolts to create a streamlined look. Over time, the house and the studio can be upgraded with finer finishes.

Build in nooks and crannies. "The house is full of unexpected areas where you can pull up a chair and stare out into the woods," states Radcliffe Bailey, pointing out windows at the ends of hallways and in closets. An alcove off the mezzanine and an angled bay window provide cozy places for thinking about the next creation. A deck off the studio provides an outdoor alternative to the main work space.

Turn a hallway into a room. The bridgelike corridor connecting Bailey's house and studio is wide enough to serve as a second work area, a guest room, and a library. Horizontal windows are spaced to accommodate shelving and still provide views.

THREE-IN-ONE HOUSE

"All over Los Angeles, tons of people work at home," observes the architect Roger Sherman. "The phenomenon is widespread but not acknowledged in terms of new architecture." As one of those people, Sherman worked in his garage until he could afford to buy a lot and build his own live/work abode. His space-efficient dwelling in Santa Monica is as much an experimental prototype as a family home, shared with his wife, Jennifer Schab, an architect, and their two young daughters.

Divided into living quarters, an office for Sherman's practice, and a one-bedroom rental unit to help pay the mortgage, the narrow, hillside structure is aptly named the Three-in-One House by the architect. "With such a mix of spaces, the building couldn't be a simple object on the lot like a conventional house," he notes. "We treated it like urban infill and modeled it on a railroad flat with the rooms arranged so they unfold in a linear way down the hill."

Linking
Set apart with its own entrance, the kitchen occupies the center of the house. Beyond the bookshelves in the dining room at the top of the stairs is Sherman's office.

Siting
The narrow, metal-clad house—modeled on a railroad flat—cascades down the hillside. Windows in the kitchen and the upper-story bedrooms overlook the terraced garden.

Positioned at the street are the office and the rental unit, each with its own entrance. Here the facade's main feature is the angled shape enclosing the interior staircase, which ascends to the second-floor rental apartment bedroom above the office. At ground level, Sherman's one-room studio adjoins the house's dining room, and behind it the kitchen occupies the center of the house with its own entrance. Up a few steps at the rear, the living room juts over the lowest part of the hillside to create a carport underneath the building. "The girls will be in the living room playing with their toys, my wife will be in the kitchen reading, and I'll be in the studio working, yet the sightlines and openness let us feel like we are all together," remarks Sherman.

Although small compared to suburban McMansions built today, the 1,900-square-foot, three-bedroom home feels expansive and bright. Along the house's inner side, Sherman installed glass walls and a balcony to overlook terraced gardens that follow the contours of the site. He alleviated the sense of compartmentalization inside by inserting light wells between the bedrooms and unifying the open ground-floor spaces through continuity of

Planning
From the street, the office is entered from a pathway leading to the door on the left. Clearly discernable on the facade is the angular shape of the staircase, which connects both levels of the rental apartment, built into the hillside; its door is on the right. Roger Sherman designed the building so he could eventually move his office into the apartment.

materials. In the kitchen, a concrete tabletop morphs into the countertop and the dining room floor. Plywood paneling reaches from the stairs to cabinets and columns. A wooden shelf used to display architectural models in the office projects into the dining room to become a bar and extends into a kitchen shelving unit.

Sheltering
The concrete staircase leads from the terraced garden down past the kitchen entrance. At the house's rear, the living room extends over the driveway to create a carport, which also serves as a play area for the architects' daughters. Among the unusual materials selected by Sherman is bonderized sheet metal, a cheaper alternative to lead-coated copper.

"Almost every space was meant to do double duty," relates the architect, who firmly believes in quality over quantity. "Too many houses today are built too big." Like Sarah Susanka, author of the popular Not So Big House books (and the foreword to this book), Sherman believes in replacing big, formal rooms with smaller, multifunctional spaces that are comfortable and frequently used. At the back of his house, the living room serves as family room and play area, focusing on a fireplace fitted with shelves that form both bookcase and entertainment unit. The dining room is more often used as an extension of the office and a conference space than for meals; when the homeowners entertain, they close a curtain lined in nylon and metallic linen to conceal the office. In the entrance foyer, a thick door hidden in the wall can be pulled out to direct visitors into the office and away from the home's front door.

While the architecture is space efficient, it is also enriched by sculptural shapes rendered in a variety of unexpected materials. Metallic floral wallpaper, bonderized sheet metal, birch plywood, and translucent polycarbonate paneling replace conventional finishes such as painted drywall, which is limited to the ceilings on the main living level.

The multifunctional building is still a work in progress, according to Sherman. One day he hopes to convert his 200-square-foot office into a den or a library and move his studio into the 630 square feet now occupied by the rental apartment, which has its own patio. "The design is meant to change over time," he points out. "The different functions are interlocking but not entirely separate. The dining room doesn't always have to be the dining room, for instance; this ability to imagine future scenarios became the principle charging the architecture."

Flowing
To emphasize the union between living and working spaces, a wooden shelf winds from the kitchen (opposite top) through the dining room (opposite bottom left) and to the office (below). The panels of birch-veneered plywood covering the stairs leading from the kitchen to the family room are repeated on the adjacent walls, column, and countertop (opposite bottom right) to erase boundaries between the spaces.

Multitasking
The living room does double duty as a family room with a multipurpose wall unit—part fireplace, bookshelves, and media cabinet—covered in the same bonderized sheet metal as the exterior. Feeling that most new houses today are too big, Sherman chose to fit family life and work into spaces only as large as necessary.

Sleeping
In the master bedroom, a skylight, a window, and walls made of translucent polycarbonate panels filter sunshine into the small space to make it feel brighter and bigger than it is.

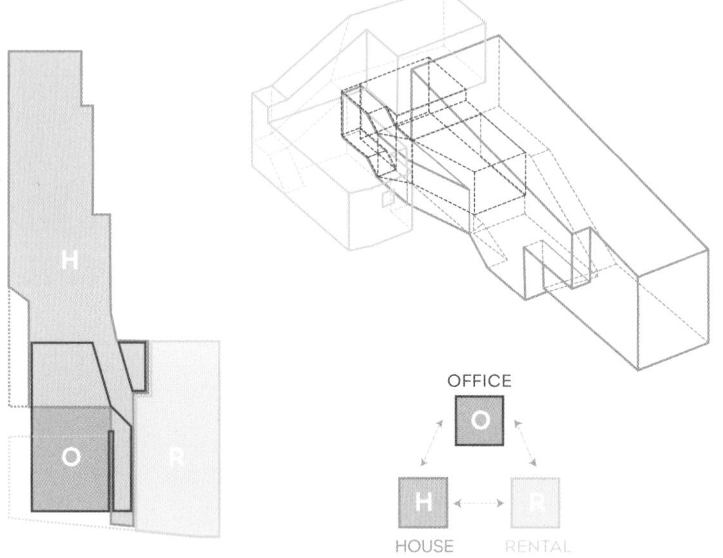

1 Desert Garden
2 Guest/Studio Path
3 Guest/Studio Entry
4 Studio
5 Conference Room
6 Dining Room
7 Powder Room
8 Back Entry Landing
9 Kitchen
10 Stair to Bedrooms
11 Living Room
12 Parking Area
13 Outdoor Terrace
14 Rental Patio
15 Rental Kitchen
16 Rental Living Room
17 Rental Entry/Stair to Second Floor
18 Front Lawn
19 Trash Area
20 Rental Stair
21 Rental Bedroom
22 Rental Bathroom
23 Office Lightwell
24 Children's Bathroom
25 Laundry
26 Corridor Stair to First Floor
27 Child's Room
28 Child's Room
29 Master Bedroom
30 Master Bathroom
31 Outdoor Deck
32 Stair to Lower Terrace
33 Upper Terrace
34 Front Yard Lookout

LESSONS LEARNED

Build for lifestyle, not design style. "Don't get hung up on what things look like but how they function," advises Roger Sherman. "Think about where you spend your time and how your family interacts." He recommends building only those spaces that will really be used. Instead of separate living and family rooms, this house has only one place in which the family can watch television and the children can play. The dining room serves as work space, conference room, and entertaining space. "If you are going to stay for the long term, think about how the architecture will change with you," he suggests.

Invest in unconventional construction. Sherman did not scrimp on adventurous shapes and materials, choosing unusual finishes over boring drywall. A wall of polycarbonate filters light into the master bedroom, bonderized steel (a smoother-looking alternative to the more familiar silvery, flaked finish of galvanized sheet metal) clads the fireplace and facades, and metallic wallpaper and fabric contribute sheen to the kitchen and the dining room. "Many of these materials aren't expensive, but the labor to apply them was more than what it would have cost to paint wallboard," he observes.

Plan to swap a rental unit for office space. Sherman's unusual architecture has attracted tenants involved in design-related professions, and income from the one-bedroom rental property pays a third of the mortgage costs. In the future, the rental apartment, with its own entrance, will be converted into the architect's office when his current studio becomes the family's library or den.

Second Floor

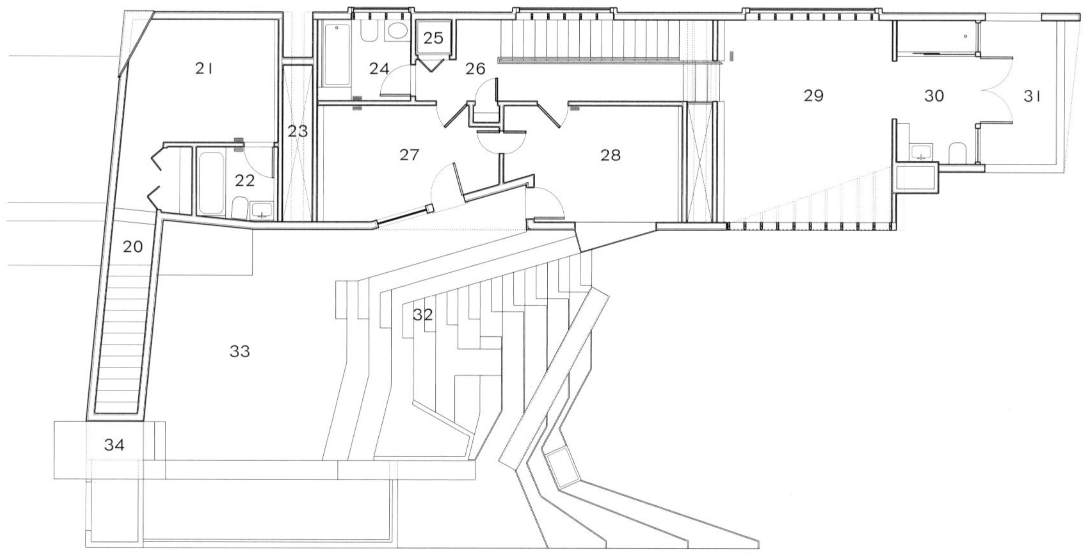

Ground Floor

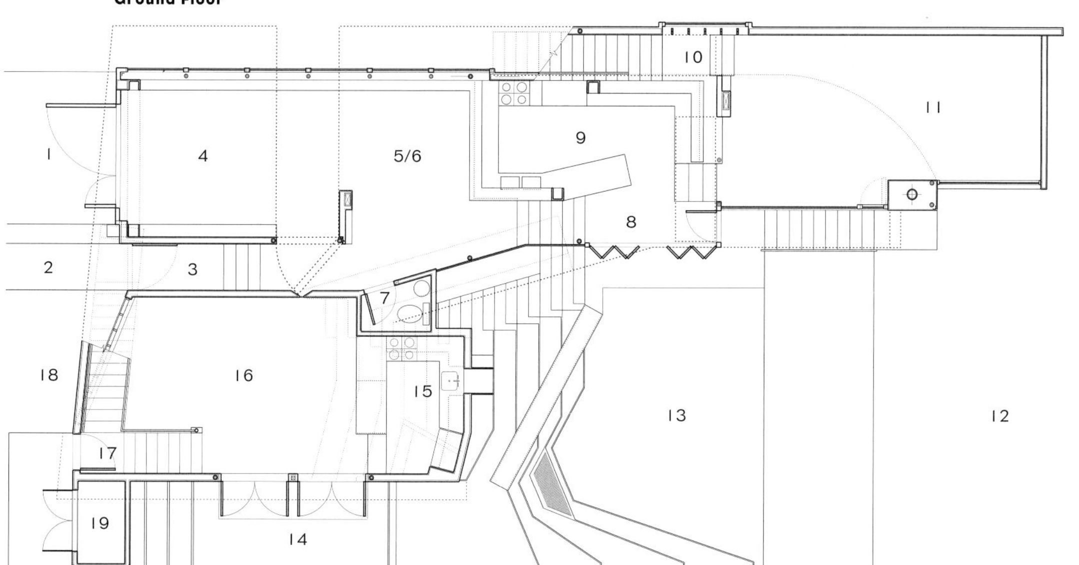

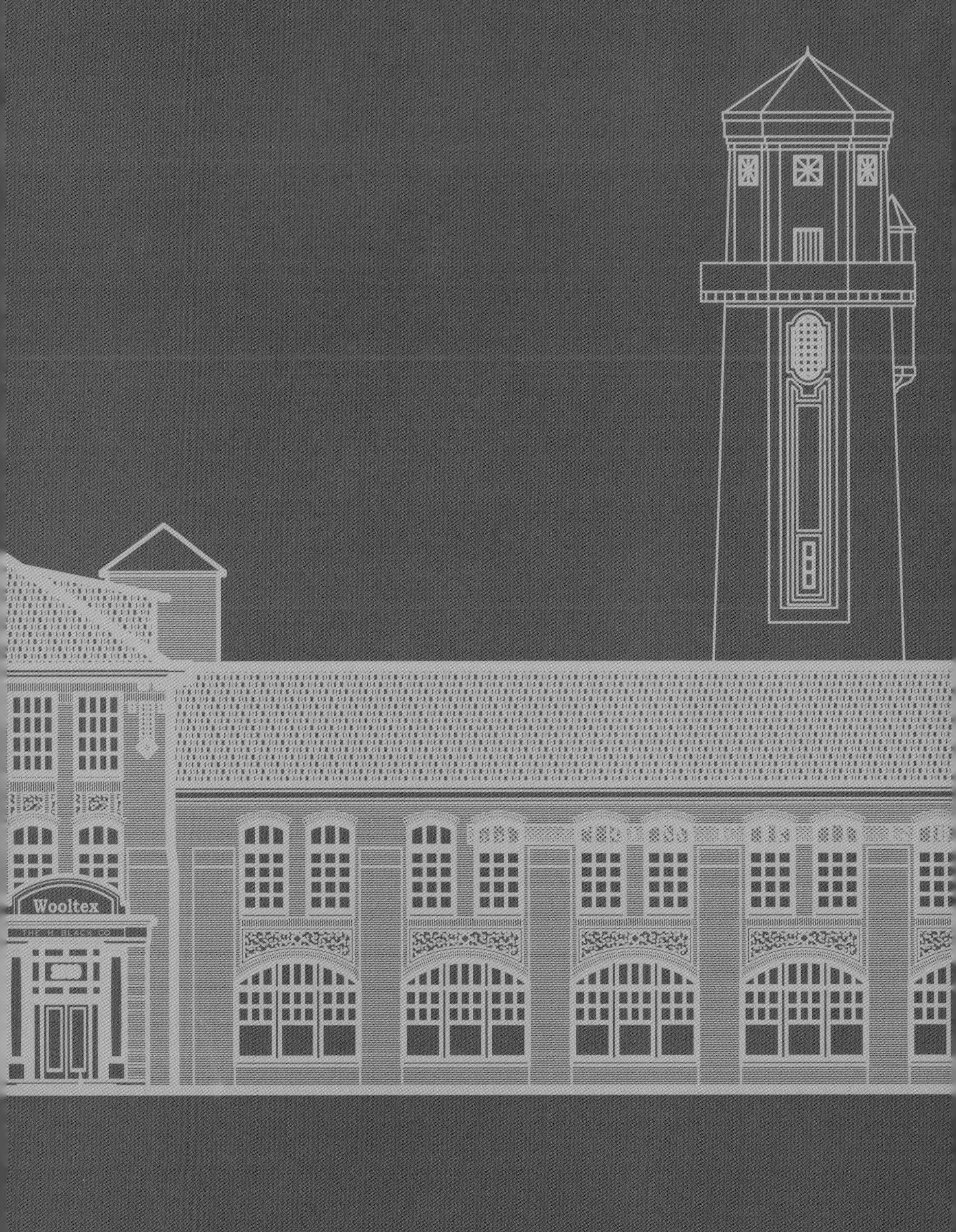
Wooltex
THE H. BLACK CO

Living Above the Store

Shared Spaces

CHANGING FASHIONS

Like many creative urbanites, the Cleveland artist and fashion designer Krisztina Lazar enjoys living and working in a renovated loft. But the place she now calls home—a renovated clothing factory—is particularly suited to the handcrocheted gowns she designs. Known as the Tower Press Building, the eighty-loft enclave is Cleveland's first legally zoned live/work compound.

This block-long, Mission-style structure was designed by the New York architect Robert D. Kohn and built in 1907 on Superior Avenue in what would become Cleveland's garment district. Intended to provide a humane environment for workers, the U-shaped factory was given big windows and skylighted sewing rooms to ensure plenty of light and air. Brick facades with raked purple joints, decorative tilework, tiled roofs, and a 130-foot-tall water tower reflect a high level of artistry and craftsmanship. Kohn went on to serve as president of the American Institute of Architects and as President Franklin Delano Roosevelt's director of housing in 1934.

In 1928 the building was converted into offices and a printing plant for a branch of the Evangelical Press. By the 1980s, however, it stood vacant while artists and designers settled into industrial structures nearby. "The best-kept secret in Cleveland is that hundreds of artists live and work illegally in warehouses," discloses Joe Cimperman, a city councilman. "We created a live/work ordinance

Styling
It takes a month for Krisztina Lazar to crochet each of her unique gowns. Mannequins are kept in her loft to display her work for customers, who can come to regular showings or make an appointment to visit her in her Transcendent Bird Studio and Gallery.

Creating
"The building has made me more focused," says Lazar, who paints in the Renaissance-based *mische* technique that layers oil and tempera. "It's good to be a part of a community here." The artist paints, sews, cooks, eats, and lives on the lower level of her Tower Press Building loft, which includes a sleeping mezzanine.

Artists Work
Tower Press
Wooltex
1900
BUS STOP

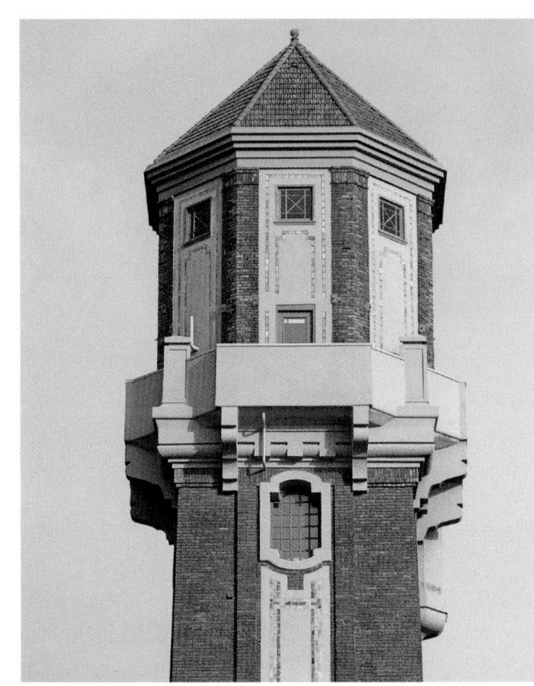

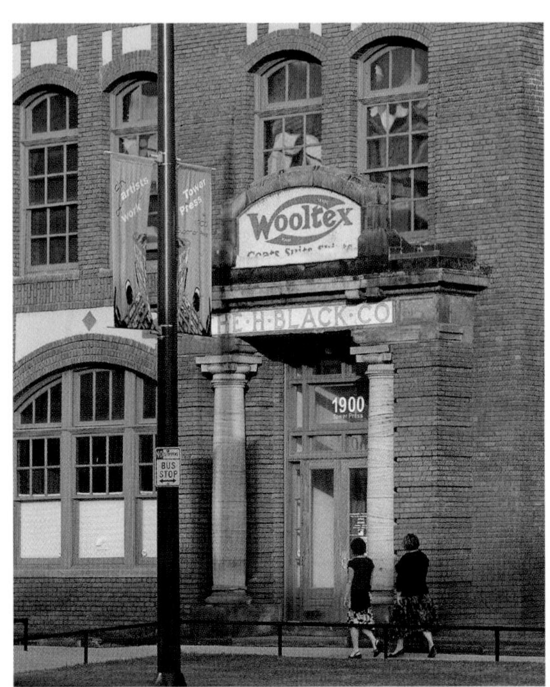

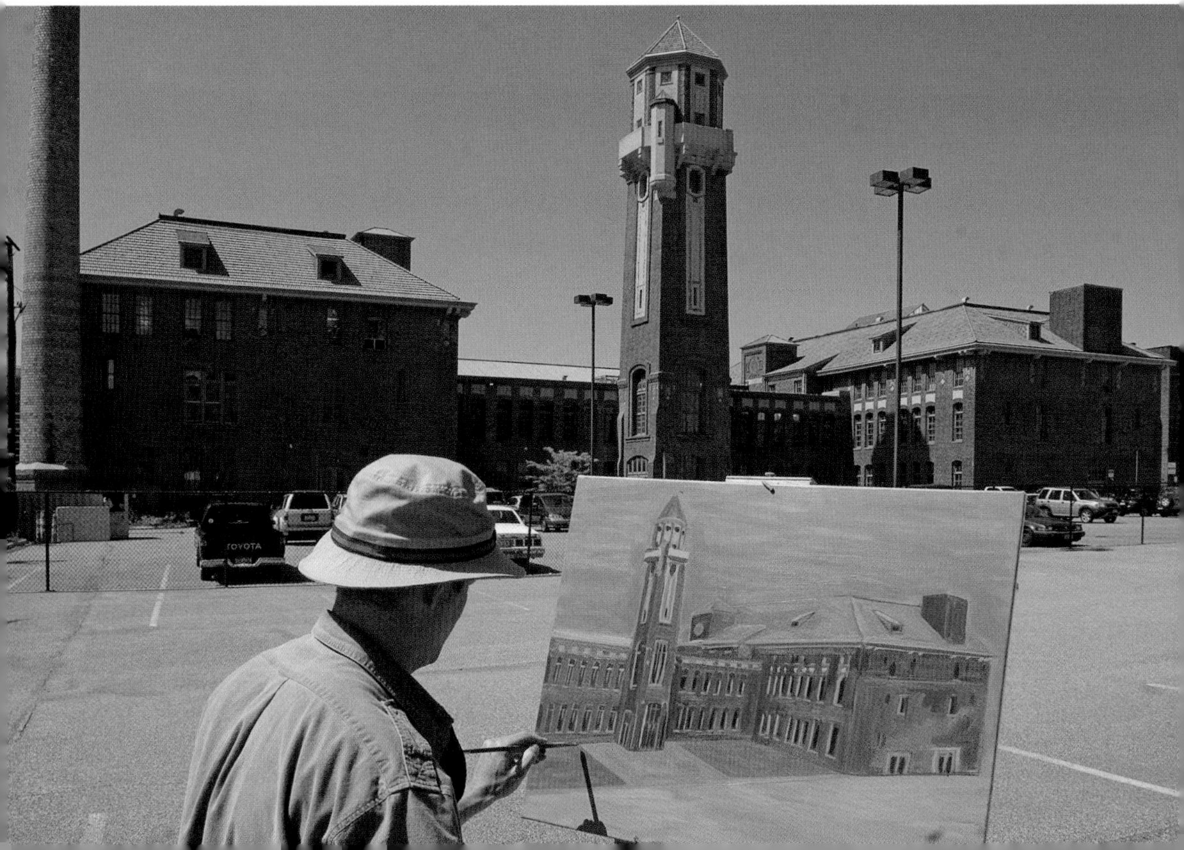
TOYOTA

Thriving
As Cleveland's first reinforced-concrete factory, the Tower Press Building was built to emphasize functionality—but its sturdy red brick is leavened with a multitude of details, colors, tiles, generous windows, and an elegant water tower. Three-story wings are connected by a two-story center section, both featuring segmental-arched windows trimmed in green.

Painting
Patrick Haggerty is a designer who works out of his home in Cleveland Heights, but when he saw the Tower Press Building he was inspired to paint it. His work was later included in one of the building's juried shows featuring Cleveland artists.

Noshing
With the *Cleveland Plain Dealer* headquartered across the street from the Tower Press Building, newspaper employees such as Margaret Bernstein, a features reporter, often find their way to the Artefino Café on the converted factory's ground floor. Started by the artist Hector Vega, the eatery is now owned by Karen Perkowski, the wife of the building's developer.

to address that and revive the city's abandoned industrial structures. Now live/work has become the new buzz in real estate marketing. Even people who aren't artists want to live in live/work buildings."

While the city ordinance was being developed, the derelict Tower Press Building was renovated in 2001 by a local developer, David Perkowski, with the help of public subsidies, including community development funds from the federal government and state historical tax credits. "The biggest challenge was the deterioration of the building," recalls Perkowski. "The roof had collapsed in the central section, exposing the concrete structure. It wouldn't have made it through another winter." To repair and stabilize it, he tapped Sandvick Architects, a Cleveland firm that specializes in historic preservation. The architects meticulously restored the exterior, down to the original shape of the roof tiles, and remodeled the interior into eighty live/work rental units, including sixteen leased to artists at below-market rates.

The ground floor facing the street has been converted into communal spaces for both tenants and the public: a conference room, an exhibition gallery, and a cafe. Also sprinkled into the mix are offices for artist groups, including Cleveland's Partnership for Arts and Culture, which helped develop the city's live/work ordinance. The old water tower is now a five-level apartment with a staircase leading to an octagonal observation room. The trek up some 110 steps—there is no elevator—rewards climbers with panoramic views of the city.

"The building definitely provides great live/work spaces," observes Krisztina Lazar, "but it is also a space for creativity. In fact, it's a hotbed of creativity." The artist's unit is often used as an exemplar for would-be tenants: interested visitors are invited to tour her airy work space with its bedroom mezzanine above. Here she paints, crochets ballgowns, and customizes jeans with personalized scenes or poetry. "The space is very versatile. There is enough room for everything I need," she adds, pointing to her sewing machine in one corner and her easels and paint in another area. To bring her residency full circle, she also works in the street-level Artefino Café—a social center for meeting just about everyone in the building.

Patti Choby had not lived in a multifamily building since college, so the Tower Press Building proved a slight adjustment for this suburbanite. After a residential development she liked was delayed, she happened upon the new live/work space. "Wow! Here's an opportunity that I hadn't thought of," she recalls thinking. "Why not take advantage of it?" Because she was in need of office space too, it was perfect for her consultancy work in change management and economic and community development. Choby and her son became two of the original tenants.

Socializing
Named after the building's original women's garment business, the Wooltex Gallery is a key gathering spot for residents and visitors. Elizabeth Davis, the gallery director and marketing manager for the project, regarded the building so highly that she made it her own home.

Since opening the Tower Press Building, Perkowski has transformed another sturdy brick industrial building into a live/work complex for filmmakers and musicians. This renovated warehouse, now called Hyacinth Lofts, is located in an old working-class neighborhood near a steel mill named Slavic Village. Once used by the city's board of education, it is now home to fifty-one rental

apartments, some with soundproof editing rooms. Residents have free use of shared facilities, including large spaces for filming, casting calls, and set making, as well as a back lot for outdoor shoots.

Pointing to the wide range of residents and lifestyles in the Tower Press Building, Patti Choby notes, "It's a completely different dynamic here than in an apartment building. The whole concept of live/work," she stresses, "needs to be taken more seriously given the way people work today." For Choby, living above the store—twenty-first-century style—is a way to bring people together, to develop a sense of real community.

Upper Level

Lower Level

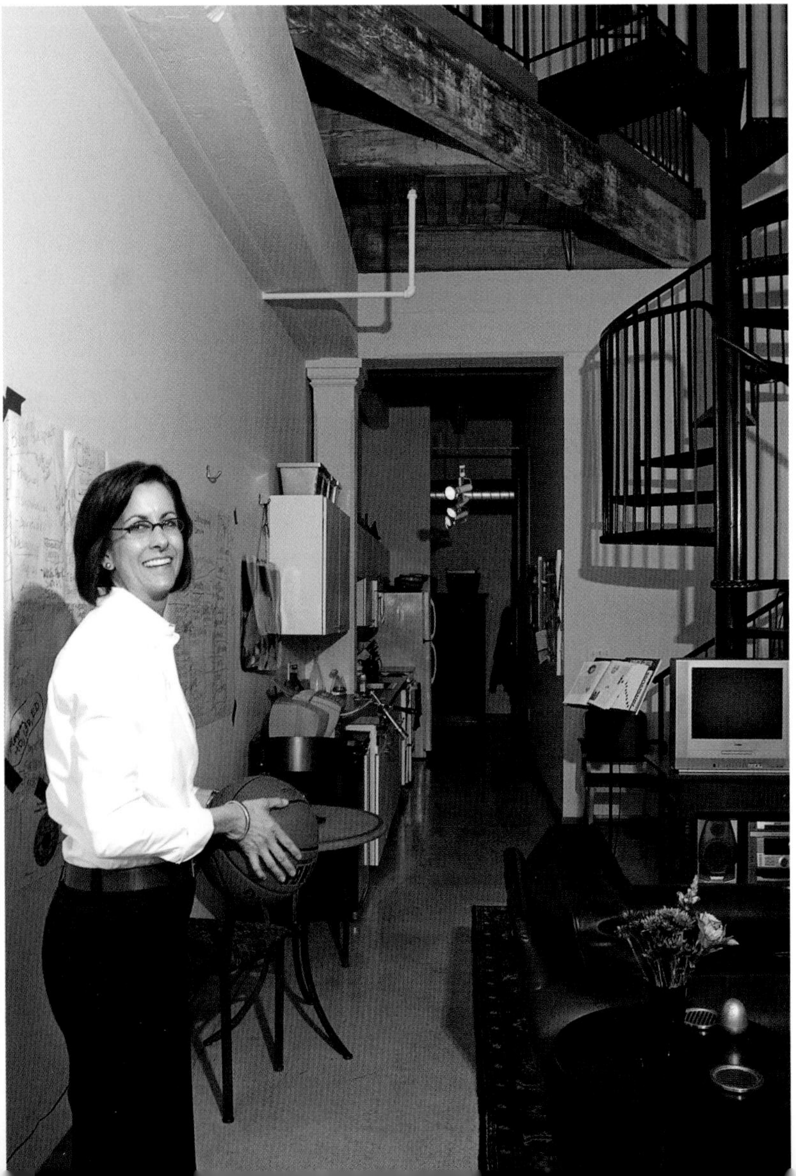

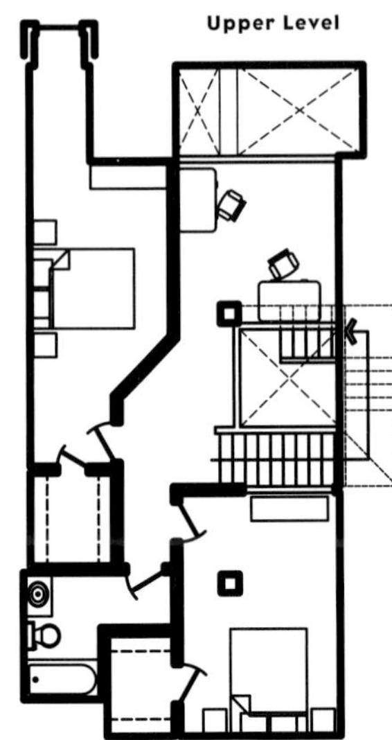

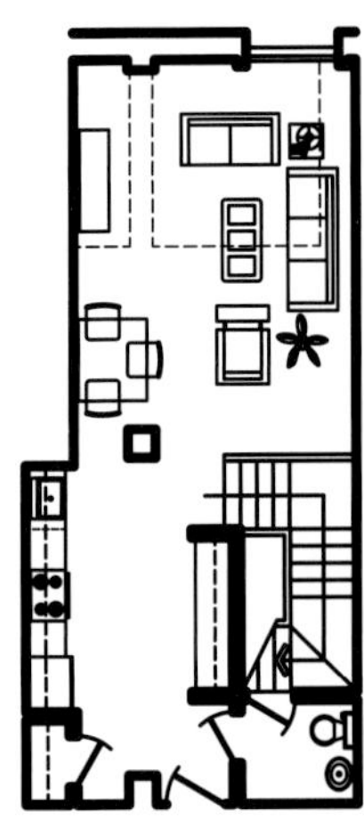

Living and working
Patti Choby's company has a "virtual office" policy, so moving into the Tower Press Building proved an ideal solution for her living and working needs. The two-story loft on the third floor that she shares with her son features high ceilings and a spiral iron staircase. Sometimes her support team meets and works in her space.

Shooting
The photographer Eartha L. Goodwin and her son, Claus, occupy one of the spaces reserved at a special working artist's rate—a right won in a juried competition. She turns her 750-square-foot space into a darkroom by using red vinyl-coated paper to filter incoming light.

Stretching
At the Tower Yoga Studio, Lynn Kennedy teaches classical yoga in the Satyananda tradition. The broad arched windows of the historic building offer plenty of light as well as a contemplative environment for yoga.

LESSONS LEARNED

Make sure your live/work space is legal. Cleveland's zoning code was amended in 2004 to allow live/work projects such as the Tower Press Building and Hyacinth Lofts in former industrial areas. According to the new ordinance, work space must occupy at least 50 percent of a unit's total floor area, and the living spaces must be accompanied by a kitchen and a bathroom. Such laws ensure livability while protecting against potentially unsafe and incompatible uses nearby, such as manufacturing facilities. By encouraging renovation of vacant and neglected buildings with round-the-clock activities, these laws help revitalize blighted urban areas.

Join two units to distinguish living from working. Once his business grew, one Tower Press tenant rented the duplex across the hall to supplement his original live/work unit. His second home, joined to the first by a pair of mezzanines, provided living, dining, and sleeping space and allowed additional space for work-related activities.

Build in communal space. Social isolation is the chief drawback of working at home. The Tower Press Building solves that problem with a conference room, gallery, and cafe on the ground floor where residents can meet each other as well as business associates and friends. The cafe and an adjacent gallery, which can be rented for events, offer amenities to the public and connect the complex to the neighborhood.

OUR TOWN

Kentlands is one of the earliest and most successful experiments in New Urbanism, a planning strategy for replacing suburban sprawl with pedestrian-oriented, mixed-use neighborhoods. Modeled on a small town, this 352-acre community in Gaithersburg, Maryland, outside Washington, D.C., has steadily grown over the past two decades to embrace a variety of houses and apartments, a commercial district, and civic buildings.

The latest additions to Kentlands's new urban mix are fifty-two live/work townhouses built in the early 2000s. These duplex apartments over storefronts, constructed between the community's residential and commercial districts, resemble buildings on a typical American Main Street. Their ground floors are now filled with shops, hair salons, restaurants, and other small businesses, with a few owners living above their stores. The live/work concept at Kentlands has proved to be popular, but builders were slow to climb on board. "It was a new 'product,' and builders and developers had no track record with it," reflects Mike Watkins, who designed the buildings.

Living and working
In the heart of Kentlands are fifty-two live/work townhouses that recreate the time-honored, mom-and-pop tradition of a small-town Main Street when business owners lived above their stores. Storefronts are now filled with small businesses such as restaurants that keep the street life active. Some owners live above their stores, while most rent out their apartments for extra income.

333

"They held out to the absolute last moment to do the live/works. In fact, they tried to get the city to allow them to do townhouses instead. The city agreed, but there was demand for the commercial space, and, interestingly, every single unit wound up with commercial on the ground floor."

As the town architect responsible for overseeing this development, Watkins practices what he preaches. Ever since he helped plan Kentlands with his employer, Duany Plater-Zyberk and Company, Watkins has worked in one of

Evoking the past
Designed to resemble the traditional architecture of an old Main Street, the three-story live/work townhouses incorporate storefronts and signage based on historic shop windows.

the tract's original farm buildings. The one-story shed is still home to a branch office of the Miami architecture and planning firm known as DPZ, but now Watkins's commute is much shorter. In 1999 he moved into his own live/work unit, a three-story "tower" he designed and built from scratch with living quarters on the top two floors and a storefront on the corner. The architect occupied the apartment but leased the ground-floor commercial space to a real estate agent before taking it over as his office in 2006. The work space currently serves as an annex to the main office in the shed, just steps away. "Renting it out was the only way that I could afford to live in Kentlands," Watkins discloses, referring to the continuous rise in the community's property values since the mid-1990s.

From the outside, the live/work building resembles a taller version of the nineteenth-century buildings that still survive from Kentlands's days as a farm. Like those older structures, it is built of load-bearing brick with historically correct windows, pediments, and moldings. "I wanted it to fit in with the neighbors, using the same structural brick details," explains the architect, pointing to the slightly rounded arches over the windows.

The storefront, framed in a wood-composite material, is based on old shops in Baltimore, where Watkins lived before moving to Kentlands. It has its own entrance with no internal connection to the upper-story living quarters, which is reached from a staircase under the side porch.

Serving
Shops and restaurants are mostly one-of-a-kind businesses rather than franchises of national chains. Upper-story windows, shutters, and cornices recall nineteenth-century architecture.

330
KENTLANDS REALTY

Scanning

A two-level wooden porch extends off one side of Mike Watkins's New Urbanist live/work building in Gaithersburg, Maryland. Atop the gabled roof is a belvedere (a lantern cupola shaped like a small Greek temple), providing views in all directions. The brick material as well as details such as pediments and rounded window arches pay homage to the neighborhood's past.

Working

After first leasing his corner storefront to a real estate agent, Watkins claimed the ground-level space (based on an old shopfront in Baltimore) as his own office. He turned it into an annex of the Maryland headquarters of his employer, Duany Plater-Zyberk, located in a converted farm shed just steps away.

"I installed a lintel in the structural brick wall and filled in the framed opening with brick and drywall," notes Watkins. "If I ever want to enclose the stair as part of the storefront, I can knock out those infill materials since the lintel is already in place." Inside the storefront, administrative staff work at desks next to the window, while the architect occupies a separate room at the rear. A kitchenette-file room and a bathroom are tucked into the side farthest away from the street.

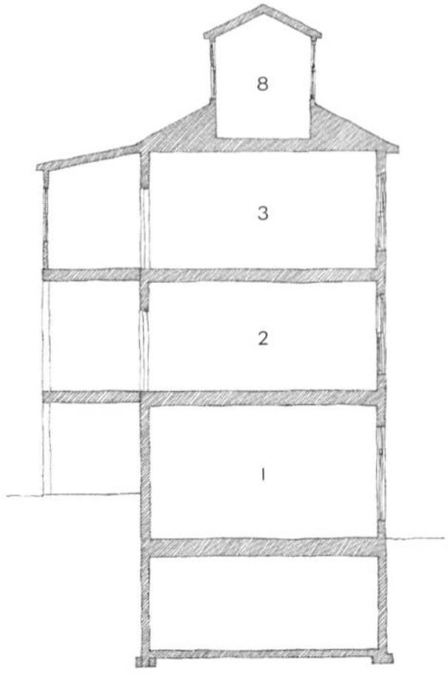

On the private second floor, beadboard wainscoting and Mission-style furniture provide cozy comfort in the big room that combines living and dining spaces. Along the back wall is a galley kitchen. Space-saving designs include bookshelves built into the back of the kitchen island and a wide chair rail for displaying the architect's collection of Russel Wright pottery. Upstairs the small master suite and an adjacent bedroom are furnished with iron beds, and an enclosed side porch doubles as another guest room and office. A narrow staircase pulls down from the hallway ceiling to provide access to the belvedere ("beautiful view"). "I find it a peaceful escape," comments Watkins. "It allows me a certain distance from the neighborhood."

Such retreat is rare for this architect, who welcomes chance meetings with his Kentlands neighbors in shops and restaurants just a short walk away. "It's not the physical place that is the most satisfying accomplishment of working here," the architect says of the pioneering community he has helped design. "It's the opportunity to enjoy other people's company."

1 Office
2 Living/Dining/ Kitchen Area
3 Master Bedroom
4 Bedroom
5 Bathroom
6 Deck
7 Enclosed Porch
8 Belvedere

Second Floor

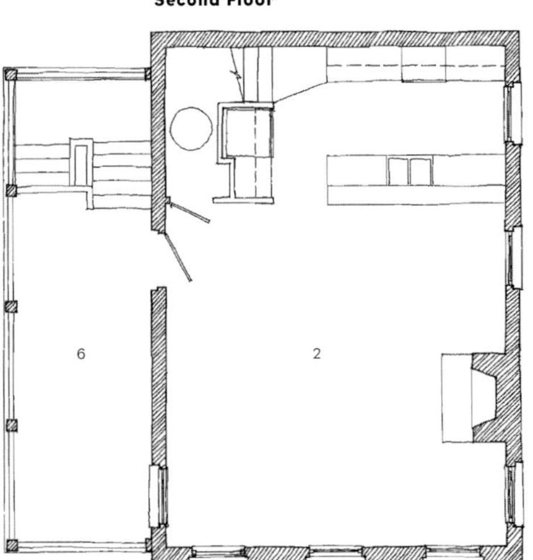

Third Floor

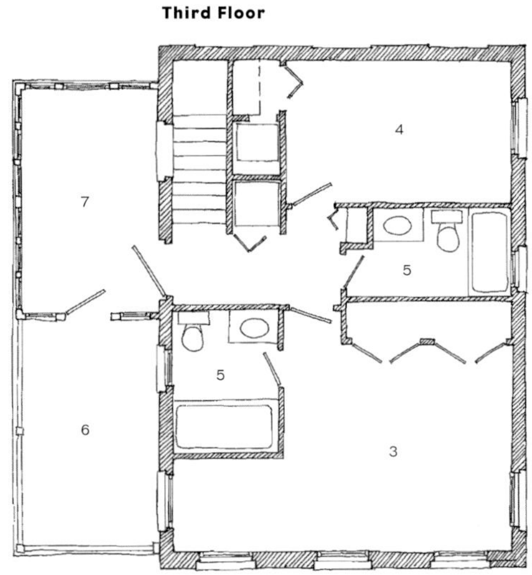

Living
The private second floor of the Watkins building combines living and dining spaces plus a galley kitchen along the back wall. Space-saving designs include bookshelves built into the back of the kitchen island and a wide chair rail above beadboard wainscoting, on which the architect displays his collection of Russel Wright pottery.

LESSONS LEARNED

Rentals help pay the mortgage. Mike Watkins rented out his storefront to a real estate agent until he was ready to turn it into office space. Other live/work owners at Kentlands lease their apartments while maintaining their businesses on the ground floor.

Integrate signage and lighting into the storefront. "Too often signage and lighting are an afterthought," asserts Watkins, who based his corner storefront on historic designs. "Sometimes there isn't room for the lettering, and the lighting highlights the building and not the sign." For shop owners, he recommends hiring a retail designer to configure the storefront as well as the displays of merchandise inside. "And remember to keep the glass clean."

Create an outdoor room. Watkins designed the 9-by-15-foot porch off his living space as a warm-weather alternative to his dining space. "It's big enough so I can have four to six guests to dinner at a table with room for a barbecue grill."

STREET MUSIC

Rhythmic patterns of color and shadow dance across the facades as if to represent the activities pulsing inside the building. It is called the Museum of Design Art and Architecture, but there is nothing precious about this multi-tasking structure on a busy boulevard in Culver City, California. Zoltan Pali and Judit Fekete of Studio Pali Fekete designed its 28,000 square feet to accommodate their life under one roof: offices for their architecture firm, a gallery for their favorite artists, and a restaurant on the ground level, topped by six live/work lofts for like-minded neighbors and a spacious apartment where they reside with their two young sons. "Everything we need is here," declares Fekete. "We don't have to leave the building."

The couple designed as well as developed the roughly $4 million building, which has two twenty-foot-high stories. "We were tired of pouring money into leasing old warehouses," explains Pali. "The project started with the idea of building a space for our offices. That led to creating a building for our lifestyle." And he adds, "I had to think like a developer. By keeping the space flexible, we could rent it out should we need to downsize."

Linking
A timber-framed breezeway at the building's rear, reached by outdoor stairways, runs alongside separate entrances to the architects' loft and six other apartments.

Siting
Catching the attention of motorists on a busy boulevard, the mixed-use building known as MODAA (the Museum of Design Art and Architecture) presents a checkerboard facade of fiber-cement boxes above a glass storefront.

Mezzanine Level

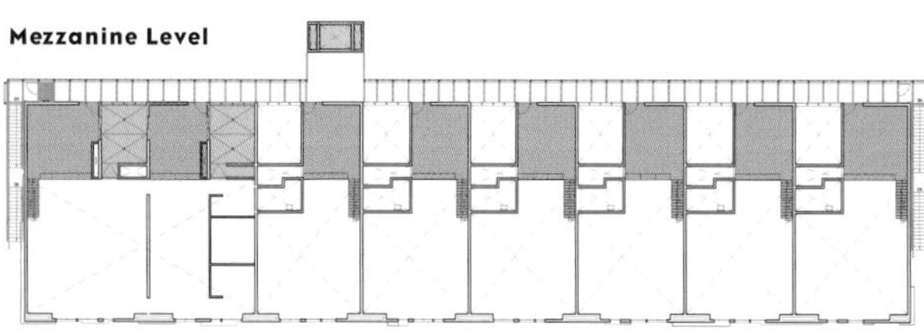

Apartment Level

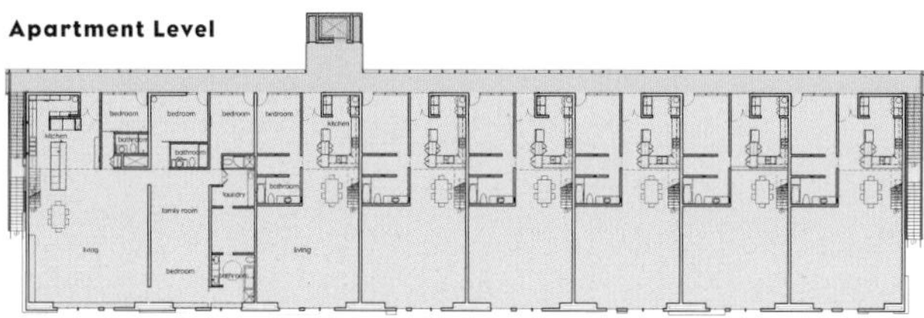

Ground Level

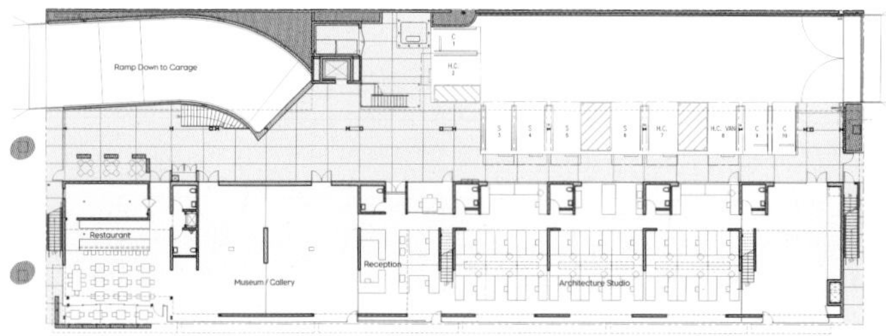

Climbing

A steel staircase leads up the building's side to the living units on the upper stories so that residents do not have to enter the main level. The facade's three-dimensional pattern was designed to create a transitional visual rhythm between the city's gentrified and industrial areas.

Arranged behind the glass walls along the sidewalk is a suite of commercial spaces that bring in the public. Most of this ground level is occupied by the Studio Pali Fekete offices, with a model shop at one end that is visible to passersby. Next to the firm's open workroom is the "museum," a 2,000-square-foot gallery for temporary exhibits that also serves as a conference space; it has become a civic amenity, used for town meetings, high school art shows, and other community events. In the adjacent space, a small restaurant run by the chef Michael Wilson (son of the late Beach Boy Dennis

Browsing
Next to the architects' office is the "museum," a 2,000-square-foot rotating exhibition gallery that also serves as a conference space. Displayed here are works by the painter Chuck Arnoldi and the sculptor Cheryl Ekstrom.

Wilson) also serves the neighborhood. All of the tall storefronts are unified by raw concrete floors, white walls, and few boundaries, so they flow into one another like the spaces within the lofts upstairs.

From their offices, Pali and Fekete take the stairs or the elevator up to their four-bedroom duplex, which combines two of the 1,800-square-foot live/work units. Reflective of the loft vernacular, the main space incorporates a kitchen open to the double-height living area overlooking the street. Ceiling joists, steel beams, and ductwork are left exposed, and flooring is the same unpolished concrete found on the ground level. Softening touches are provided by modern furnishings, a fluffy rug, and white oak cabinets and woodwork. From the main level, a stair leads to a mezzanine. Bedrooms are tucked under this upper level at the back of the building.

The six other units are smaller versions of this residence, including a mezzanine and an enclosed room that can be used for sleeping or work. So far the building has attracted creative types who work at home, including a commercial designer, a movie producer, and a painter. To qualify for residency, occupants must obtain a business license from the city.

Dining
One side of the storefront is occupied by a restaurant run by the chef Michael Wilson. Decorated with a mural of chefs, the eatery attracts a neighborhood crowd and visitors to the building's galleries.

Working

Arranged behind the twenty-foot-high glass storefront is the open workroom of Studio Pali Fekete and its corner model shop. The architects purposely kept the space flexible in case they might want to lease the space in the future.

Living
Zoltan Pali and Judit Fekete combined two apartments into a duplex for themselves and their two sons. The main space incorporates a kitchen with an oak-finished island open to the double-height living area. The stair leads to a mezzanine used as a playroom and an exercise area. Bedrooms are located at the back of the main floor under this upper level.

The lofts can be reached without having to enter the lobby. On both ends of the building, steel staircases lead up to an outdoor breezeway at the back. Climbing the stairs provides a close-up view of the white, gray, and yellow cement-board panels that wrap the facades on three sides. "We wanted to create a vibrant architectural texture, but not with phony historical elements," acknowledges Pali, who compares the patterned relief to a musical score. Its syncopated visual rhythm, he explains, is meant as a symbolic transition between the gentrified area of Culver City to the west and its shabbier industrial district to the east. "We are right in the middle," he notes. On the building's back wall, a cedar screen is more in keeping with the wood-framed houses on the adjacent lots to the north.

The success of their pioneering live/work building has led Pali and Fekete to undertake similar developments in Culver City. "It's a different sensibility for Los Angeles, where [single-purpose] zoning has really messed up the city," asserts Fekete, who describes the difficulty of persuading investors to buy into the still-experimental mixed-use concept. "Though the idea of live/work is new," she continues, "it is important as a way of fostering higher-density urban living and reducing traffic by eliminating commuting. We believe that this is the way the city should go."

The couple also cite the personal benefits of living above the store, such as having places in the office for their kids to do homework or play games after school. "It's a wonderful way to live and be creative," remarks Pali. "Some people say that you need to get away from work, but I'm thinking about work all the time anyway. So it's great to have the office just downstairs."

LESSONS LEARNED

Create a grand entrance as well as a private one. Different circulation routes allow employees, visitors, and residents to easily enter and leave the building yet allow living and working spaces to remain independent. A public entrance leads to the ground-floor offices and commercial spaces and also to an elevator for the lofts. Outdoor staircases along the building's sides connect to the upper-story breezeway at the back, providing direct access to the lofts from the sidewalk.

Consider parking requirements. Pali and Fekete incorporated a seventy-three-space underground parking garage and a surface lot at the back of their building, with room for eleven more vehicles. The numbers reflect local requirements for commercial structures; a strictly residential building would call for fewer spaces.

Make room for a mezzanine. The super-tall ceilings of this live/work development allowed for broad balconies that provide extra room while the main level below rises the full twenty feet. Within the architecture firm's offices, the mezzanine houses a library, a graphics department, and administrative staff. In the owners' loft upstairs, the mezzanine is used as a play area for their kids, an exercise room, and a storage space.

LOFTY ANCHOR

Every morning Dyrell Madison walks from his apartment to the corner coffee house without ever leaving the building. Soon after moving into a new artists' loft compound in Mount Rainier, Maryland, Madison opened the Artmosphere Cafe, where residents and neighbors can enjoy refreshments, listen to live music, and plug into the Internet. "When you are creative, you want to be around creative people," comments the part-time musician and graphic designer. "It feels good to be among people with a common passion."

As a renter and business owner in the new loft building, Madison is optimistic that Mount Rainier, just outside Northeast Washington, D.C., will become the artists' mecca hoped for by local planners and politicians. "It used to be filled with liquor stores and drug trafficking," he recalls. "Now it's changing, with younger people and new businesses like mine moving in. You're seeing more people walking on the streets."

Revitalization has come as a result of the state- and county-supported Gateway Arts District, a once-derelict, two-mile stretch of Route One that is being slowly transformed into an arts and entertainment haven. Near the new lofts are twelve more artists' live/work units in a 1930s-era apartment building recently renovated with green design features. Under development on sites just up the road are an African American museum and cultural center, a performing arts and educational venue, and more affordable places for artists to live and work.

The most distinctive piece of the arts district to be completed so far is Madison's home base, the Mount Rainier Artist Lofts. The colorful, forty-four-unit live/work building, completed in 2005, replaced an abandoned grocery

Living
Thanks to the building's triangular shape, eighteen unit types are available in the artists' building, including this airy apartment occupied by the artist Karen Brown. The range of units, from two-story lofts to walk-out flats, offers the spatial eccentricities found in many remodeled historic structures.

Quilting
Tim Carl underscored the triangular building's prominent location with a bold contemporary design that stands out in the neighborhood. He sectioned the 200-foot-long main facade into a bright patchwork of brick and corrugated steel panels inspired by slave quilts. While clearly contemporary, the building has a base, a middle, and a top, the same organization used for neoclassical buildings.

store next to a traffic circle in the town's center. It was developed by Artspace Projects, Inc., a Minneapolis nonprofit dedicated to creating affordable housing for artists around the country, mostly by renovating older structures. Subsidized by state tax credits and government funds, the $12 million loft project marks Artspace's first building from the ground up to be completed.

Tim Carl of the Minneapolis-based architecture firm Hammel, Green and Abrahamson worked with local artists and community activists to create a bold profile for the triangular building. While injecting a much-needed dose of contemporary design, its bright patchwork of brick and corrugated steel panels is based on building materials and quilts once stitched by slaves in the region. These blocks of color and texture, extending between the concrete block-framed storefronts and silvery metal top story, serve to break up the length of the building, which stretches nearly two hundred feet along Route One.

Living high
This two-story loft is one of the forty-four apartments in the Mount Rainier building: six efficiencies, thirty one-bedrooms, and seven two-bedrooms. Common to all is an adaptable, open layout that allows residents to change living and working needs.

Inside, the lofts, each with its own work space, are arranged on four levels to offer the type of spatial eccentricities found in remodeled historic structures. "We initially had the lofty goal of creating perfect spaces for the different types of artists in the building—wood-sprung floors for dancers and acoustically attenuated walls for musicians—but we couldn't take it that far because of costs," Carl discloses. Still he managed to avoid the dreary cookie-cutter style of most affordable housing, devising eighteen unit types for the wide spectrum of artists who now rent in the building.

These variously shaped efficiency, one-bedroom, and two-bedroom apartments range in size from 700 to 1,700 square feet. Among them are single-level flats and walk-out basement units with access to an outdoor courtyard, as well as two-story lofts with a mezzanine, including a dramatic space in the building's pointed prow. The open living spaces, with galley kitchens extending along one side, have allowed the tenants to customize their spaces for different types of creative work. The painter and jewelry designer Katurah Thomas, for example, divided her kitchen from the living area and studio with a plywood storage partition fitted with shelves and counters for extra work space. Daryl Hunt, a pianist and composer, turned the mezzanine within his sixteen-foot-high loft into a recording studio.

In photographer Valerie Phillips's loft, the mezzanine had been closed off and there was no way of reaching it. So Phillips built a staircase up to the second-floor space, which she turned into a television lounge and retreat instead of a more typical bedroom or office. Stair risers are now decorated

Working
Dancers Laura Schandelmeier and Stephen Clapp and their daughter, Holly, shown here with a friend, enjoy one of the building's two-bedroom apartments. Each unit incorporates a galley kitchen along one side, designed to free up the interior for creative activities. Concrete floors and exposed metal ductwork maintain the industrial loft feeling.

with her photographic portraits, and storage cabinets are tucked into the space underneath. She uses the area next to the kitchen as a studio. "Being one of the first tenants in the building allows you to set the tone and add on to the architecture to make it your own," Phillips notes.

Like other artist lofts, the building incorporates communal gallery, conference, and work space. In the basement, a large room with a slop sink provides more studio space for the visual artists, including a stained-glass artisan and a purse designer. Lobbies and hallways, plus a basement community room, provide places where residents can exhibit their work and share ideas. Commercial space on the ground floor is slowly being filled with arts-related businesses to support the tenants. On the other side of the lobby from Madison's Artmosphere Cafe, a gallery and framing shop recently moved into one of the storefronts along Route One. "Our building has ended up changing the community for the better," reflects Madison. "It's become the anchor for the entire arts district."

Changing
The once-derelict neighborhood, observes the cafe owner Dyrell Madison, now welcomes a more vibrant street scene.

Gathering
Two-story common areas, such as this staircase off the entrance lobby, provide space for exhibits and social gatherings. A courtyard at the center of the apartment block offers an additional place for the tenants to congregate.

One-Bedroom Loft:
a, b, d

Two-Bedroom Loft:
c, e, f

One-Bedroom Flat:
h, i, m, n, o, p

Two-Bedroom Flat:
g, j, k, l

Third Level

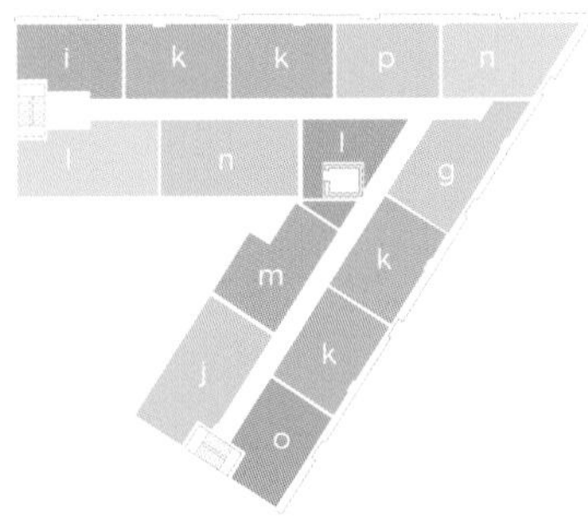

Second Level | **Second-Level Mezzanine**

Ground Level | **Ground-Level Mezzanine**

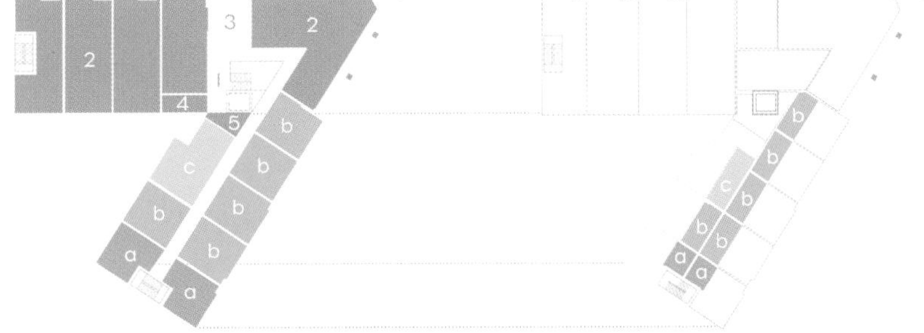

1 Commons
2 Retail
3 Entry
4 Office
5 Mail Room
6 Laundry

LESSONS LEARNED

Reinterpret local history through design. "The artists wanted the building to look like the Guggenheim in Bilbao, but the community wanted a more traditional, neo-Georgian design," recalls the architect, Tim Carl. He satisfied both groups by drawing inspiration from the surrounding area's architecture and culture.

Minimize the number of walls. "If you can have fewer enclosed rooms and more contiguous space," observes the architect of this building, "it allows your living space and business to grow over time. Technical flexibility is also important so you have convenient access to power and data ports." Artists have responded by customizing the open spaces of their units to suit a variety of creative endeavors.

PAS DE DEUX

It took a tornado for Bill Brimm, an artist, and Andrew Krichels, a dancer and exercise instructor, to realize their live/work dream. For years they had coveted a corner property in historic East Nashville that had been home to a grocery store and a photo shop. "We knew that the neighborhood was about to blossom, so we wanted to get in at the front end," explains Brimm. "But it would have taken endless renovations to get the existing building the way we wanted it," adds Krichels.

When severe winds destroyed the old masonry structure in 1998, the couple bought the lot to construct a live/work complex from scratch, with the help of the Mauritius-born architect Patrick Avice du Buisson. "The vision was for me to have a workshop and for Andrew to have space for his Pilates clients," relates Brimm, who co-owns a stained-glass emporium in Nashville where he spends most days. "We also wanted a lot of wall space for art, mine as well as pieces by other artists."

Avice du Buisson, of the Nashville firm Polifilo, divided the property, located next door to a post office, into a two-bedroom house at the corner and a smaller pavilion at the back. Most of the work spaces occupy the ground floor

Separating
The gallery end of the house is set apart with two walls of brick. It has its own entrance on the side to manage the flow of visitors to the live/work compound. A compact balcony off the second-floor living room is framed by two tantalizing cedar walls that stop just shy of meeting at the corner.

Bridging
A metallic bridge links the property's main live/work building with Bill Brimm's office, located on the second floor above his otherwise freestanding workshop.

1113

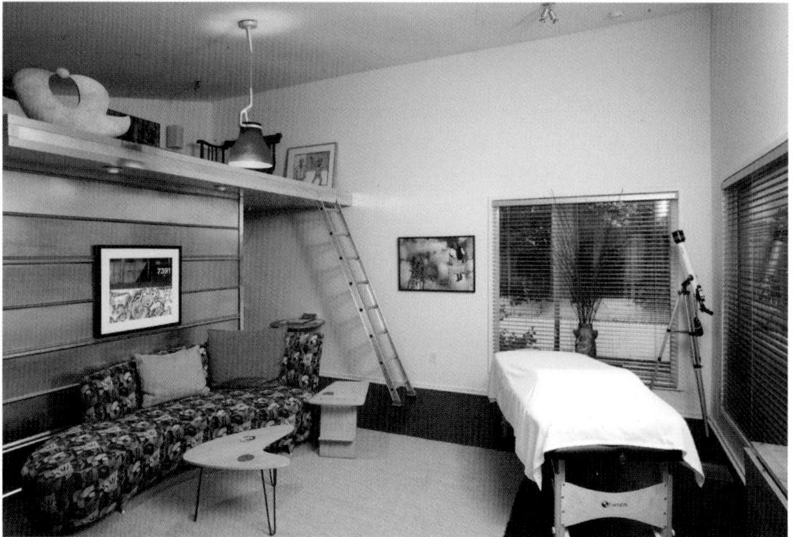

Stretching
Space for Andrew Krichels's exercise business was part of the original design mandate. An oriental carpet makes this room seem more residential.

Visiting
In the guest suite, a metallic ladder beckons up to a cozy mezzanine. Sinuous contrasts come from the amoebalike shapes of the sofa and the table.

Hiding out
A museum-quality velvet rope at the foot of the stairs keeps clients from venturing beyond the designated downstairs areas.

Welding
The steel that Bill Brimm uses for furniture and lamps can be welded in the separate work pavilion without impinging on any of the other living or working activities in the house. He can unload his industrial materials directly from the street.

of the larger structure: a gallery off the street for Brimm and an office and exercise and massage rooms for Krichels. "We wanted to emulate old cities where the family lives upstairs and they have the store downstairs," says Krichels. The couple's private quarters on the second floor are arranged so that the living room, with its built-in seating nook, and the dining room are closest to the front of the house. A galley kitchen and a small office occupy the center, and a guest room and a master suite are placed at the rear.

Behind the house is a ground-floor workroom where Brimm fabricates furniture and lamps of steel, glass, concrete, and found objects. Accessible from the street, it allows the artist to drive up to the door and unload his materials. "I have to pick spots of time when I can create my own stuff," he notes, "so it's nice to walk across the back yard to my work space and spend a half hour there if that's all the time I have, instead of having to drive to a studio." Above his workroom is a guest suite with a kitchenette that could be rented out as an apartment. Altogether the complex occupies 3,370 square feet, 2,400 in the house and 970 in the small building out back.

Although the complex mirrors the old-fashioned idea of living above the store, there is nothing quaint about the architecture. Aluminum-edged planes of wood siding extend from behind lower walls of red-painted brick. Corners are cut away to reveal metal-framed windows and chainlink balconies. All the projections, angles, and notches convey the impression that the house is in the process of being assembled—or dismantled. "The layers give the building more depth and make people wonder what the spaces look like inside," remarks Avice du Buisson. His bold, cubistic design also signals the building's dual purpose and pivotal location between a commercial district and a residential neighborhood. "It's a gateway on a corner site," the architect observes.

Roll-up glass doors open the exercise studio, workroom, and master bedroom to the bamboo-planted garden between the two buildings, where a fountain quietly gurgles. "The whole courtyard has become a second living room," says Krichels. Another bonus space is the chainlink-fenced bridge that spans the courtyard to connect the master bedroom and the guest suite. "It's a great place to have coffee and look over the neighborhood," declares Brimm. "We'll sit out there and watch the fireworks on the Fourth of July."

Flexibility is an important part of the live/work concept, says Avice du Buisson, so that spaces can be changed over time to serve different uses. Krichels's business, Creative Action, quickly grew after he moved in. "We ended up relocating the Pilates machines to the gallery and using the Pilates space for a yoga and mat room," reports the dancer, who now manages five part-time employees. The changes have been easily accommodated in the ground-floor rooms because each has a separate entrance off the street.

Boundaries between home and work, however, are not always easy to maintain, especially when strangers are stretching and straining in the rooms below the couple's private quarters. "Even though it's separate," says Brimm of the exercise room, "you can hear the activity." To make sure that his clients do not venture upstairs, Krichels adds, "We put a velvet rope across the stairs like Studio 54. People respect that, and it's very rare that they come up the stairs."

Since completing their live/work complex, Brimm and Krichels have seen the Five Points neighborhood improve with new art galleries, music clubs, and bars. They too are planning changes to add working and living spaces, possibly turning more of their property into a center for the healing arts. "Our house is more like an organic plant than a piece of architecture," muses Krichels. "It keeps growing and evolving."

Living

Like a *piano nobile*, the living area occupies the second floor to gain the best views. A turn at the top of the steps leads to the dining area and then to the living room, centered around a built-in seating nook. Beyond is a galley kitchen and a small office, followed by the guest and master bedrooms. A colored wall dramatically frames a sculpture of Brimm by Adrienne Outlaw, a Nashville artist.

Sleeping
The choice of roll-up doors for the master bedroom may have been unusual, but it carries through the house's industrial design. An exceptional amount of light filters into the room, which features a headboard wall of reflective metal panels.

Bathing
Over the tub a porthole-shaped window breaks up the lines of the tile and injects a note of humor into the thoroughly modern household. The window looks out onto the second-story bridge connecting the main building and the workshop.

Second Floor

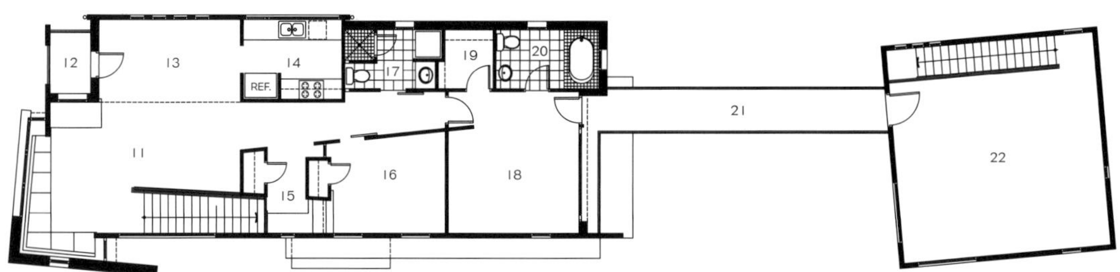

First Floor

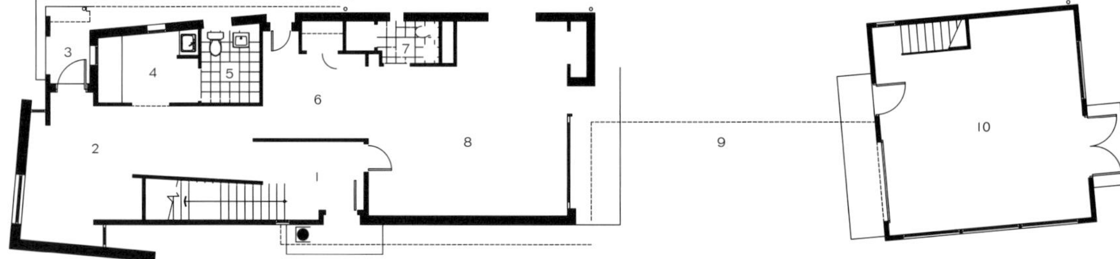

Hanging out
Bill Brimm (left) and Andrew Krichels (right) knew from the outset that they wanted a live/work complex to accommodate their artistic lifestyle. Here they relax in their "second living room," the courtyard between their residence and Brimm's workshop.

Blending in
The exterior of the Brimm-Krichels residence was to be more industrial in appearance—clad in corrugated metal to reflect the spirit of Bill Brimm's art—but the materials were changed to brick and cedar siding so the house could better blend into the surrounding historic district.

1 Entry
2 Gallery/Exercise Space
3 Side Entry
4 Office
5 Bathroom
6 Massage Room
7 Bathroom
8 Pilates Studio
9 Courtyard
10 Workshop
11 Dining Room
12 Balcony
13 Living Room
14 Kitchen
15 Study
16 Guest Bedroom
17 Guest Bathroom
18 Master Bedroom
19 Closet
20 Master Bathroom
21 Bridge
22 Guest Suite

LESSONS LEARNED

A custom home does not have to cost top dollar. To keep costs down (to about $275,000 for construction), Patrick Avice du Buisson eliminated the basement, configured the framing so the joists would not have to be cut, installed inexpensive garage doors and storefront windows, and used single-pitch roofs. Interior plywood-sheathed walls, concrete floors, and sliding doors on tracks also helped economize. "There's nothing out of the ordinary here," maintains the architect. "Saving money is a matter of getting the right builders to understand the design."

Be prepared for design review of changes to historic properties. Building or renovating a property within a historic district designated by a state or a locality typically requires the blessing of a preservation or design review board. Hiring an architect experienced in preservation and having officials review a design before the official hearing can ease the process.

Take advantage of in-between space. Bill Brimm and Andrew Krichels use the courtyard and bridge between their house and studio-guest house as places to socialize and unwind. Garage doors in the master bedroom, dance-exercise studio, and rear workshop roll up to erase the boundary between inside and out, creating the feeling of more room. "When the studio door is open," observes Krichels, "it's like teaching class in the garden even when we're inside."

Both residents and work-space users should respect one another's privacy. At times Krichels has inadvertently become a space invader. "I've found myself running in my undies down to the office, and, oops, I've forgotten there's a class in there," he reports.

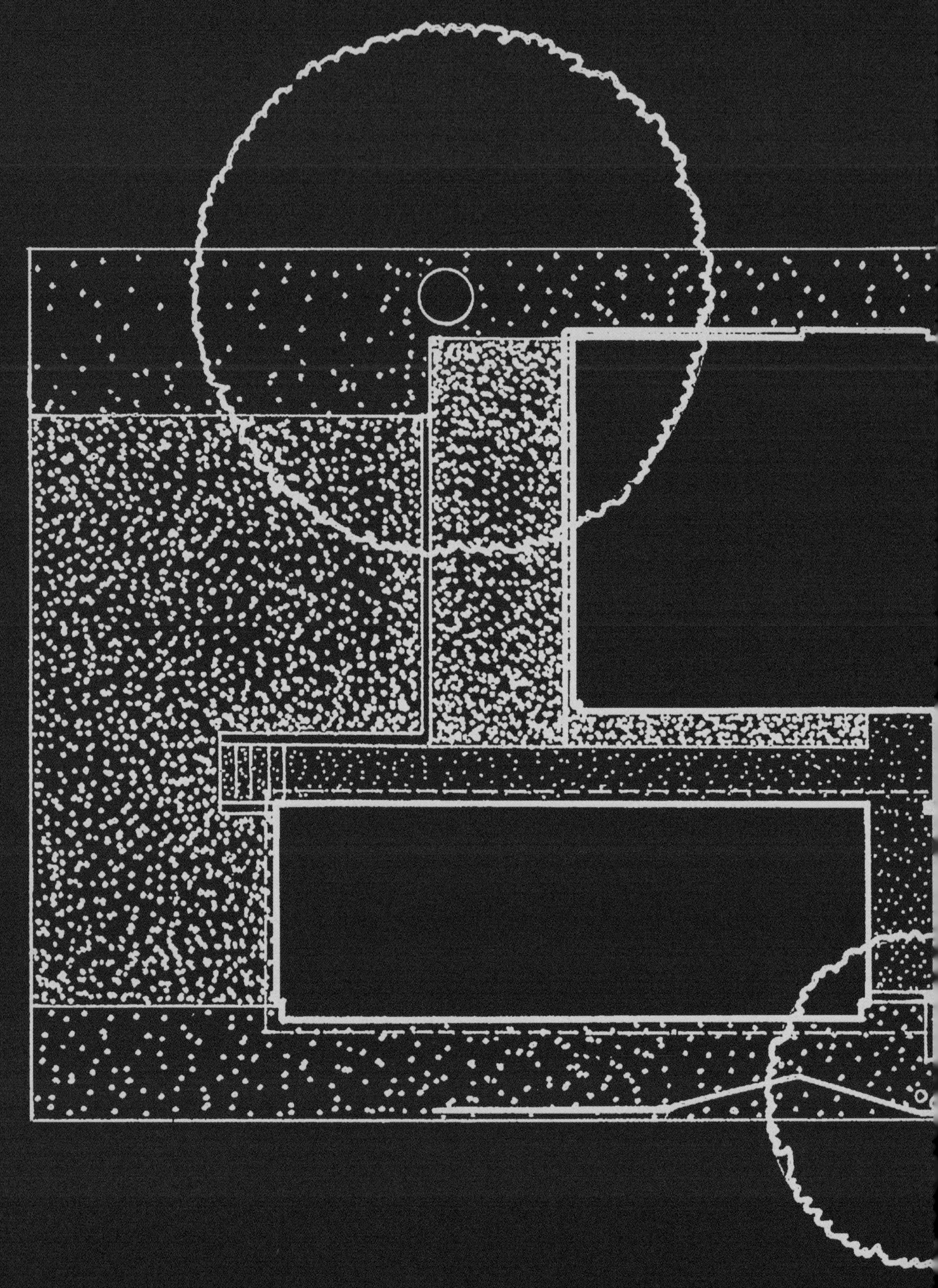

It Takes a Village

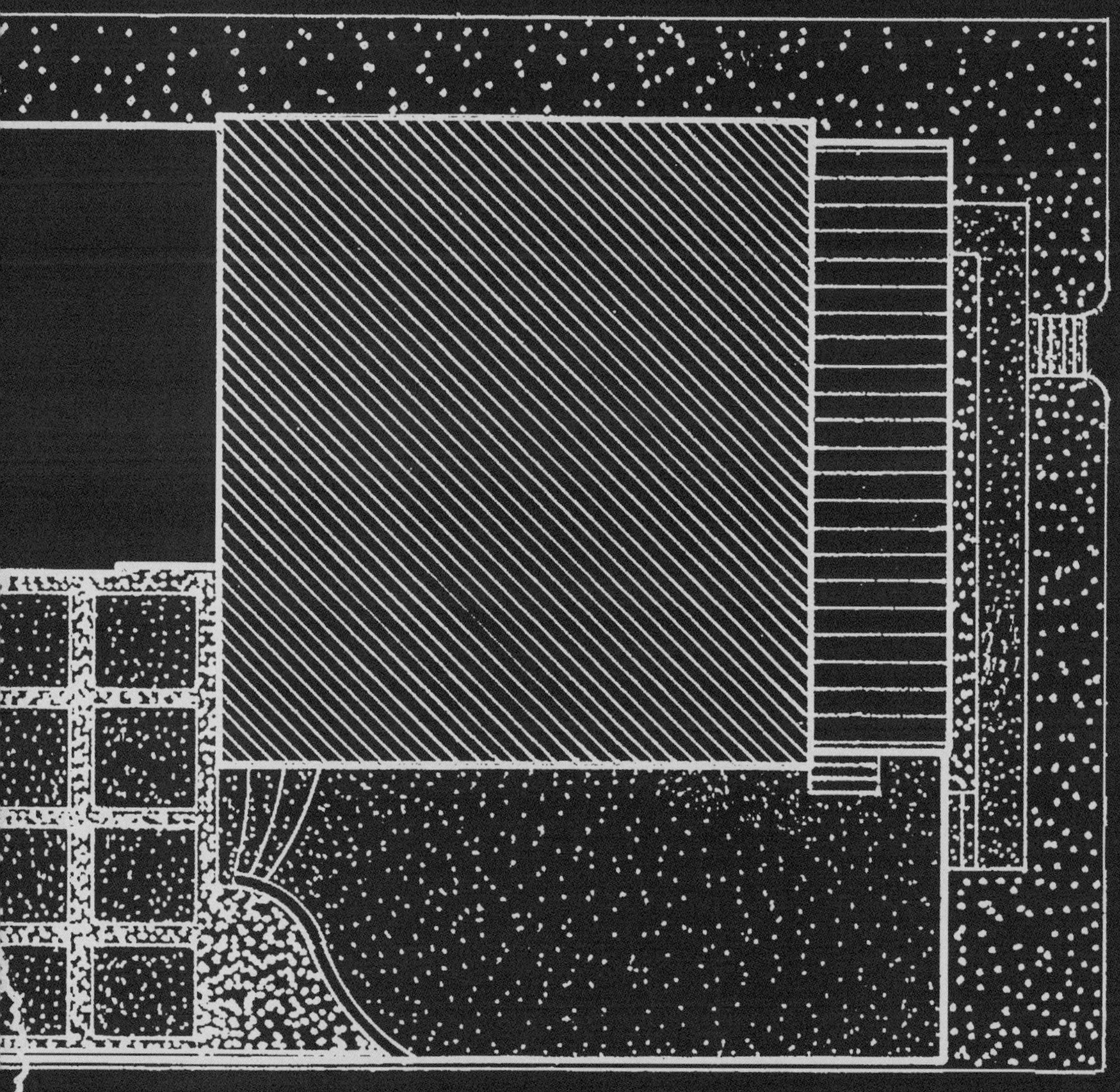

Back-Yard Commutes

FAMILY FARM

"It's like an autobiography," muses the architect Mark McInturff of the hillside compound in suburban Washington, D.C., where he lives and works. The renovated houses and garages evidence not only changes in McInturff's architecture, from historicist to modernist, but also in his life. A divorced father of two children, now grown and gone, the architect still makes his daily sixty-foot trek in the early morning hours, closing his front door to cross a stone patio and descend a flight of steps to his studio. "I used to refer to it as the family farm," he laughs. "We live here, we work here, we just don't have cows."

It's a routine that began three decades ago, years after the young architect and his wife, Cathy, purchased a cluster of ramshackle cottages behind an old gas station in Bethesda, Maryland, near the Potomac River and the

Entering
From the driveway, Mark McInturff's own live/work village is entered along a flagstone path that leads to a courtyard separating the house and the office. A wooden arch adds breathing space, and a teak table and chairs provide a place for the architect and his staff to eat lunch or relax.

Crossing
After closing the front door of his house, the architect makes his daily sixty-foot-long commute by crossing the patio, with its white wooden archway, and descending a flight of steps to his office.

Chesapeake and Ohio Canal. "In 1978, I was driving around looking for a lot near the river and turned down this little street, where I saw four abandoned houses and two garages," recalls McInturff. "I told my wife, 'This would be perfect.' So I renovated one house, sold it, and kept all the rest."

Since then, McInturff has slowly but surely modernized and expanded the 1920s-era structures to create a live/work compound with Shingle Style charm. "It's not a collection of unrelated buildings. There is a strong visual connection between them, even though they aren't quite all the same," he notes, pointing out features representing the different phases of his career as an award-winning architect who specializes in custom houses.

Old wooden porch columns define an octagonal living space in the main house, which the architect has enlarged and refined over the years. The largest structure on the property, it was first remodeled in 1982 and two years later joined to a smaller dwelling next door to create bedrooms for daughter Marissa and son Jeffrey. A decade later, McInturff pushed out the kitchen wall to meet the rest of the front facade, using a window-within-a-window aimed at an outdoor fountain.

All the expanding could have resulted in a hodgepodge of additions, but McInturff unified the pieces of the home within a shingled facade. This is punctuated by a white-painted bay that rises like a Greek temple to a shallow gable. Inside are such quirky features as a dining table made from the floorboards of an old bowling alley and an open bathtub and shower tucked into one side of the master bedroom.

Living
The front door is shielded by a porch under the upper-story balcony, a bay inserted by the architect to knit together his additions. McInturff later pushed out the kitchen wall (right) to meet the rest of the shingled front facade.

Relaxing
Domestic privacy was enhanced by terraces behind the house for barbecuing and relaxing. This side of the "family farm" is strictly private, a place for getting away from the office.

Swimming
Extending across the rear garden terraces is the elevated lap pool, where the architect often sneaks off for a dip during summer workdays. The octagonal bay projecting from the shingled house encloses the living room, with a dormer window lighting its top.

Working
The work building, a smaller cottage down the hill from his house, is reached from the driveway through a gate next to the converted garage (right). McInturff's series of additions are unified with pitched roofs, painted timbers, and shingled walls.

Commuting
A wooden deck joins the work cottage (left) and the meeting-library pavilion (right), with its shingled bay and staircase enclosed by red panels. "Having that sixty-foot commute across the courtyard is important," observes Mark McInturff. "It allows a separation, time to decompress."

Playing
Like the other buildings on the property, the expanded garage (used as a library and meeting space) is shingled and topped by a pitched roof. A basketball hoop allows for office pickup games.

Meanwhile, after starting his own architecture practice, McInturff Architects, in 1986, the owner turned still another cottage on the property into his office. "When we first opened, we didn't even have a bathroom," he recalls. "Everyone had to go to the main house." Nestled into the slope of the hill, the studio opens into a two-story workroom with windows and balconies overlooking the woods surrounding the property.

The architect says that when he first started working at home, the chief benefit was spending time with his family. "In spite of the long hours, I could see my kids every day and my commute time was zero," he relates. Cathy worked as his office manager and bookkeeper. Most of his residential projects were located within a twenty-minute radius of his office, also reducing time spent in the car.

As his firm grew more successful, McInturff expanded the studio in 1997 with a book-lined conference room that feels like a tree house. He then made that space his own office and in 2001 built a one-room library and meeting space over an existing garage next to the studio. Black board-and-batten siding accented by brightly colored paneling on the upper story of the converted structure reflects McInturff's recent embrace of a more modernist spirit in his architecture.

Although a stylistic departure, the converted garage harmonizes with the previously renovated buildings. While he spent years tinkering with his house and office spaces, the architect has consistently applied the same palette of architectural elements—painted timbers, shingled walls, low-pitched roofs—rather than treat each structure as a distinctly different

design. His goal, he explains, has been to respect the cottage character of the original buildings and preserve their orientation within the half-acre hilltop site. "They are not where I would have preferred them to be," admits McInturff. "Sometimes I think I should sell the place and build a cool, new modernist house. But I could never replicate this. I could never have the gardens or the hillside site."

Part of McInturff's mission has been to connect—and to divide—the living and working sides of the property with landscaped outdoor rooms such as a courtyard between the house and the studio. Working so close to home, he notes, has its drawbacks: lack of privacy with employees, clients, and visitors streaming past the kitchen window. "You can't get away from work. There's always the excuse of running back over there to do a little bit more. It's not always best for your personal life to have your office right there." When the architect decided to extend his studio building in the early 1990s, Cathy insisted that he move the addition two feet back, farther away from the house.

After decades of remodeling, trying out design ideas that he has also implemented for others, the architect finally considers his ever-evolving compound to be complete. "For the first time, I'm thinking of it as finished," he remarks. "I really don't need any more space. I don't want the office to be bigger. I don't need a bigger house." But McInturff isn't quite done designing for himself. Currently in the works is a vacation house on Maryland's Eastern Shore that will allow him true escape from long hours in the studio.

Climbing
In contrast to the complex's cottage look, the studio staircase communicates a modernist aesthetic. Stylized, modernistic columns march upward in similar stair steps.

Meeting
Broad wall areas, perfect for display of the architect's work, contrast with the open window areas of the conference room—a rooftop addition to the garage that serves as one of the property's tree houses.

Thinking
An enormous picture window brings the trees right into the architect's office. High above, small squares of glass direct more light into the airy tree house.

POZZI
PROGRESS
neo-ray
COLUMBIA
LUTRON
ICF ICF ICF ICF
LUMA
forms surfaces

Dining
In the dining area next to the living room, Shaker chairs are pulled up to a table made from the floorboards of an old bowling alley. The print is by John Chamberlain.

Living
McInturff added the octagonal living room. Under new pine beams and an upper-story dormer window, a wood stove keeps the space toasty in winter. The coffee table was designed by the architect. Tall windows overlook the rear of the wooded property.

Connecting
At the back of the house, a pine staircase extends from the upper-story bedrooms to the living level and down to the lower-level family room and the back terraces. The blue paint color was selected, McInturff says, "to pull your eye in the direction of the stairs. It works well with the white trim." The abstract paintings are by Marissa McInturff, the architect's daughter.

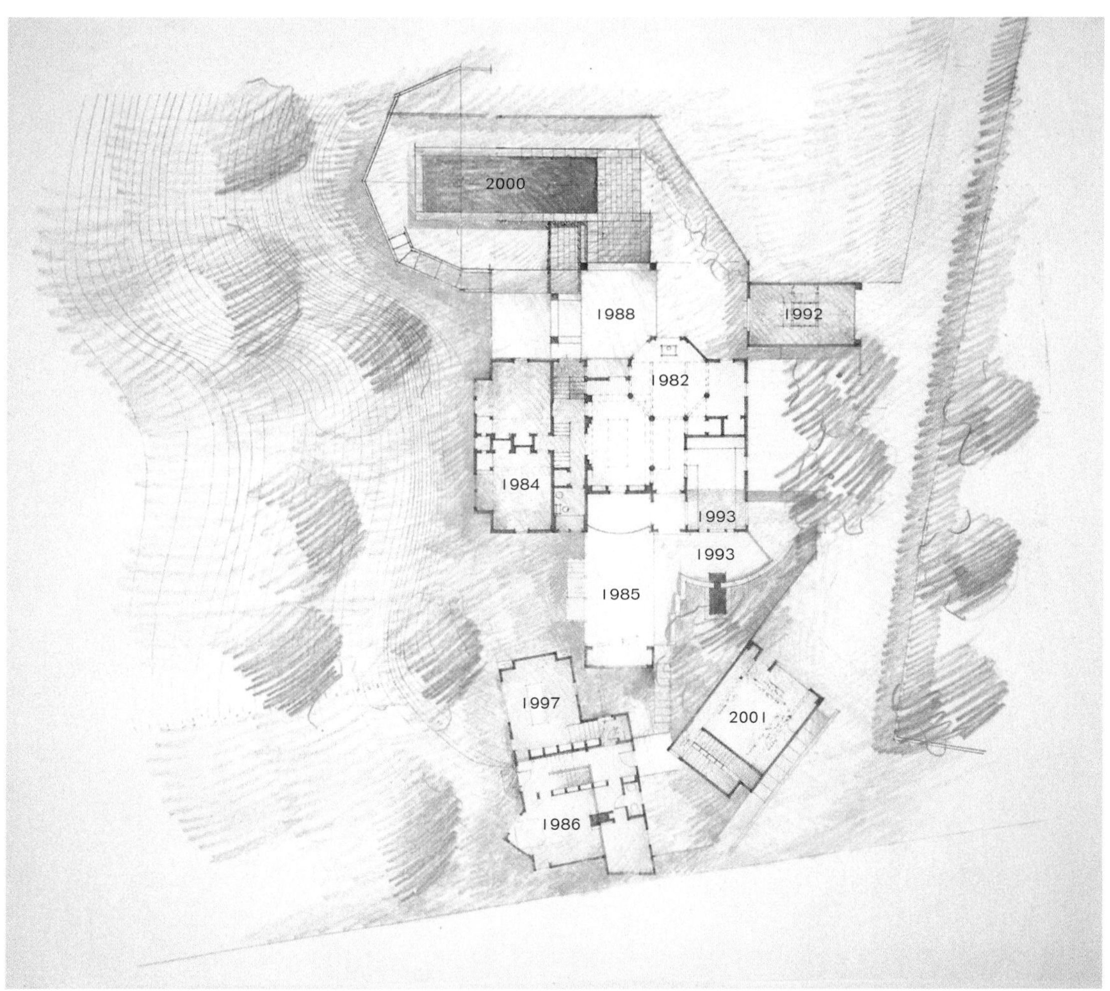

Siting
A model of the McInturff property shows the house at the top of the hill and the courtyard and stairs between the office building (left) and the conference room over the garage (right).

LESSONS LEARNED

Create a back-yard office for the clearest break between living and working. Mark McInturff started his architecture business by turning one of several cottages on his property into his firm's headquarters. "I didn't want to work down the hall or in the basement of my house," he explains. "Having the separation is important to maintaining your personal life away from the office and your professional life away from home."

Relate a group of structures to one another, even if they do not look exactly the same. Consistent building heights, repeated architectural elements, and similar materials help unify buildings in different styles. McInturff, for example, topped the different structures on his property with low-pitched roofs and covered the exteriors with wood shingles.

Maintain a professional atmosphere. When you work alone at home, it is tempting to stay in your pjs or sweats all day. But instituting protocols in your work space, such as a dress code, reflects your seriousness of purpose to employees and customers. "I wanted a professional situation," McInturff underscores. "For years, we all wore ties and shirts to work."

HOME COOKING

Home cooking has special meaning for the chefs Robert and Molly Krause: they run a restaurant in their back yard. Diners cluster in the couple's living room or patio before sitting down to enjoy a six-course dinner in a glass pavilion next to their old stone house in East Lawrence, Kansas. Trained in San Francisco's top restaurants, the Krauses pride themselves on creating a memorable sensory experience, from the sleek modern decor to the colorful sauces on the plates.

Their restaurant grew from a catering business in their late-nineteenth-century home, which the couple purchased in 2000. "A lot of people wanted our food, so we started bringing people to our house in small groups and serving them a nice meal," recounts Robert Krause. Demand for their cuisine led to the addition of the glassed-in dining room and a new kitchen, plus a two-level apartment for Molly's mother, Katie Krider, who takes care of the couple's two young daughters while they work.

The new structures were designed by the local architect Dan Rockhill. He is familiar with every square inch of the house, because in the 1990s he purchased and renovated the historic property, one of the oldest in town. "Before we bought it, the house had been abandoned for nearly forty years," notes Rockhill. "It's in the seediest part of town, next to a bus barn." Located in an industrial area adjacent to a residential neighborhood, the home was once used as a hotel for railroad workers, a boarding house, and a brothel.

Growing
Grass on the roof, which is reached by a custom-made ladder, softens the dining pavilion's modern lines. "I water it, fertilize it, and mow it as if it were a yard," relates Robert Krause, the chef-owner.

Surviving
Once used as a hotel for railroad workers, a boarding house, and a brothel, this old stone house in East Lawrence, Kansas, was remodeled by the architect Dan Rockhill. The dignified late Victorian house, now lovingly landscaped, is in an industrial area of town.

Sitting
The architect added the front porch to an existing concrete deck, recycling light poles from the Kansas Turnpike for columns and freight elevator surrounds for the metal mesh railings. Now furnished with vintage 1950s Russell Woodard chairs, this space is used by the family as a retreat from the bustle of the kitchen.

To create the Krauses' culinary operation, the architect tore down an addition that he had designed and replaced it with a larger wing and a detached metal-and-glass dining pavilion. "We made a concerted effort to have it look different and to use materials that were clearly more contemporary," explains Rockhill, who both designed and built the minimalist new structures. "The contrast strengthens the presence of the older house."

Extending from the limestone home, the two-story, glass-clad wing houses the new commercial-grade kitchen, a restroom for diners, and the mother-in-law suite. The kitchen and the apartment are separated by a two-story foyer used by guests to reach the restroom. Within the apartment, a narrow staircase leads up from the living area to a bedroom, a bathroom, and a reading nook on the second floor. Sandblasted glass panels bolted to vertical steel channels screen the living quarters from view.

Behind this addition, the detached garden room provides dining space for thirty within a glass pavilion framed in steel tubes. Stainless-steel mesh hangs from the ceiling to filter light from the fixtures concealed above it. On the wall nearest the neighbors, glass shelves backed by glowing sheets of polycarbonate hold glasses, wine bottles, and tableware.

Climbing
On one side of the living room, a walnut staircase leads up to the bedrooms. Plaster torn away on the wall of the landing creates an artistic ruin while providing a glimpse of the historic home's thick masonry walls.

Living
Before building their back-yard dining room, the Krauses welcomed guests into their living room for gourmet dinners. Furnishings include ample seating and a modern coffee table, a reproduction of a mid-century design by the sculptor Isamu Noguchi.

A classically trained chef, Robert does most of the cooking while Molly, a social worker turned pastry chef, makes the desserts and serves as hostess. Instead of ordering off a menu, diners are treated to a prix-fixe meal made from fresh ingredients, including tuna and marlin flown in from Hawaii and scallops and sea bass from Maine. The Krauses do not advertise but rely on word of mouth to supply them with customers. Their "modern speakeasy," as Rockhill calls the low-profile restaurant, earned them a glowing review in 2005 from Lauren Chapin, the food writer for the *Kansas City Star*. "Everything is about quality and details," Chapin wrote, "every course is theater, every dinner a carefully orchestrated occasion."

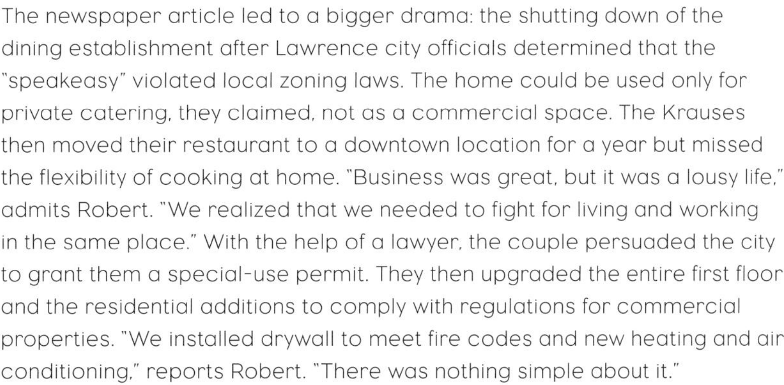

The newspaper article led to a bigger drama: the shutting down of the dining establishment after Lawrence city officials determined that the "speakeasy" violated local zoning laws. The home could be used only for private catering, they claimed, not as a commercial space. The Krauses then moved their restaurant to a downtown location for a year but missed the flexibility of cooking at home. "Business was great, but it was a lousy life," admits Robert. "We realized that we needed to fight for living and working in the same place." With the help of a lawyer, the couple persuaded the city to grant them a special-use permit. They then upgraded the entire first floor and the residential additions to comply with regulations for commercial properties. "We installed drywall to meet fire codes and new heating and air conditioning," reports Robert. "There was nothing simple about it."

The garden dining room, spruced up with a walnut floor and other upgrades, reopened in 2007. The chefs once again serve delicious dinners five nights a week in their home. "We're fortunate to have a great customer base that supported us," asserts Robert Krause.

Traversing
Slate covers the floors of the foyer to the public dining area in the back of the Krauses' stone house. The steel tube-framed dining pavilion abuts a two-story, glass-clad addition housing a new commercial-grade kitchen, a restroom for diners, and a mother-in-law suite.

Dining alfresco
In warmer weather, restaurant patrons sit outdoors on cafe chairs by the Italian designer Aldo Ciabatti that are clustered on the terrace behind the stone house. Their rounded, tubular steel frames filled in with metal mesh harmonize with Dan Rockhill's metal-and-glass additions.

Dining under glass
Designed by Dan Rockhill to be a modernist oasis, the freestanding dining pavilion is situated next to the two-story glass addition housing the kitchen and the patrons' restroom. As part of the recent changes made to meet city requirements, the pavilion was later connected to the two-story addition.

Dining
Separated from the distractions of the house, the restaurant pavilion offers a serene dining experience. Metal mesh baffles hanging from the ceiling, as originally designed by Rockhill, have been replaced by a more sound-absorptive material.

Cooking
Robert Krause prepares gourmet meals in a surprisingly small kitchen within the new addition at the back of the family's stone house. His wife, Molly, a social worker turned pastry chef, likes cooking at home so she can spend time with their two young daughters.

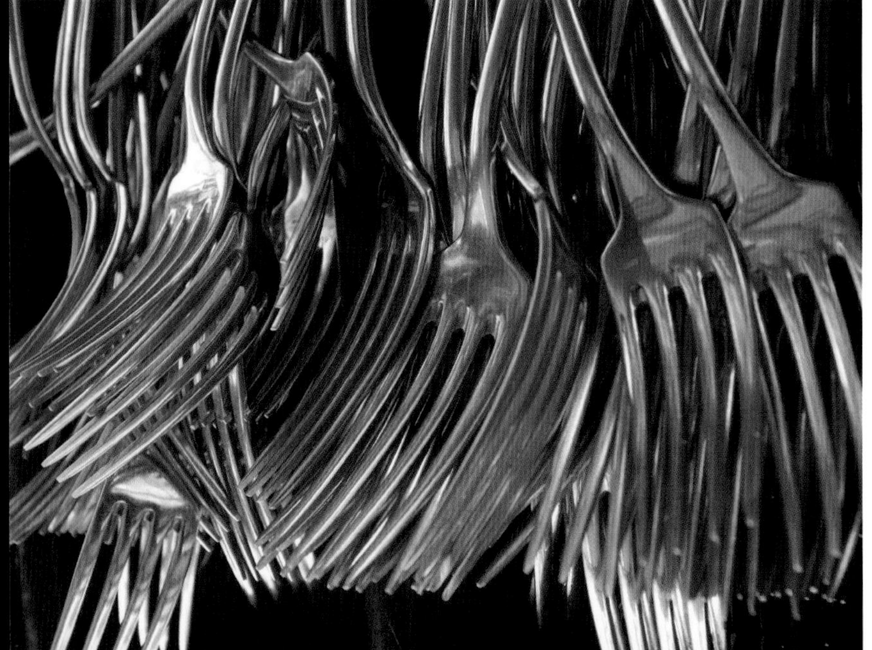

Clinking
On the back wall of the restaurant, glass shelves backed by glowing sheets of polycarbonate hold glasses, cups, wine bottles, and tableware.

Washing up
The modern metal minimalism of Rockhill's addition extends to the stainless-steel basin and towel dispenser in the powder room used by restaurant patrons.

Inspiring
Inspiration for the minimalist additions of metal and glass came from restaurant staples: table utensils, such as these forks, and stemware.

Second Floor

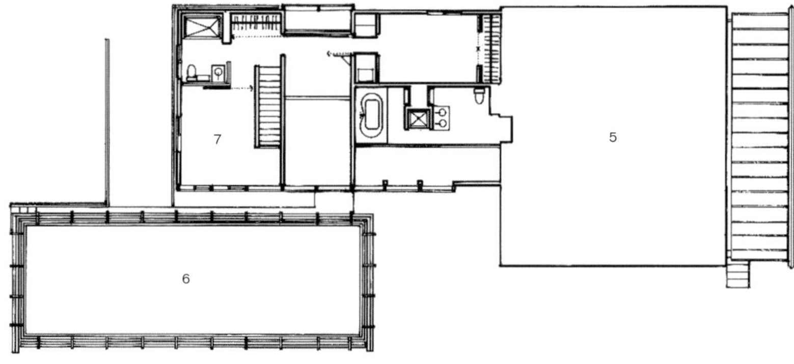

First Floor

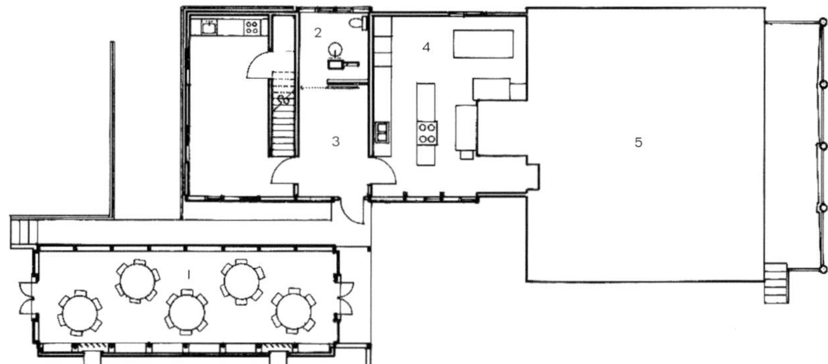

1 Dining Pavilion
2 Restroom
3 Foyer
4 Kitchen
5 House
6 Grass Roof
7 Mother-in-law Suite

LESSONS LEARNED

Look into a zoning variance if necessary. Even if local zoning regulations appear to prevent a home-based business, you might be able to secure a variance or a special-use permit. Upgrades to meet laws governing commercial property can be expensive. The Krauses had to install everything from a new mechanical room in the basement to an entrance ramp to comply with the Americans with Disabilities Act.

Draw design inspiration from your business. In creating the Krauses' dining room and kitchen, the architect Dan Rockhill looked to the table utensils and the stemware on restaurant tabletops to develop minimalist structures of metal and glass. The contemporary architecture complements the Krauses' high-style, sophisticated cuisine, which is served on European dinnerware. "I want my food to look beautiful," Robert Krause declares. "We try to make the highest quality dining experience that we can."

THERAPEUTIC TREE HOUSE

In traffic-choked Los Angeles, being on time for an appointment is a constant challenge. Decades of stressful commuting finally led Joan Willens, a clinical psychologist, to relocate her office from Beverly Hills to a much more convenient location—the back yard of her Brentwood home. "One day I looked up at the top of the hill where we had a gazebo and wondered why I was racing to my office," Willens recalls. "I could see building a space up there in the trees."

Although she wanted to work at home, the therapist insisted that her practice be physically separate from the house she shares with her husband, Leonard Beerman, a retired rabbi, to ensure privacy and avoid distractions. "If you've got one ear cocked for the phone or the doorbell, it interferes with your concentration," she points out. Another requirement was a design that was contemporary but would blend in with the wooded property.

Angling
Joan Willens's corner office rises like a ship's prow from the cedar-clad angular pavilion. Stone steps lead from her house to a private door so the psychologist can enter or leave unnoticed.

Entering
The patients' entrance on the other side is tucked between the prow of the waiting room and a wall adjacent to the hillside with a horizontal opening for looking at nature.

Waiting
Visible through the corner window in the waiting room is a children's tree house on the neighboring property that inspired Kanner's design. A pair of Philippe Starck-designed Eros chairs offer patients a place to sit before appointments. Inspired by the abstractions of Jackson Pollock, Kanner spatter-painted the canvas on the wall as a present to his client.

The Los Angeles architect Stephen Kanner, whose versatile designs range from burger joints to multifamily housing, responded with a contemporary tree house. "It is designed to rise up and aim the views laterally," Kanner observes of his angular pavilion, noting its large windows set into corners shaped like ship's prows. "We didn't want patients to look straight at the main house." The cedar-sided structure occupies a steep hillside behind the house with steps leading up to the clients' entrance on the northern side of the building. Just inside this door, a foyer opens to a waiting room with a view of a kids' playhouse on the neighboring property. At the opposite end of the building, Willens has a separate entrance into her office that is reached from a pathway extending from her residence. "I can run down to the house for a break without anyone knowing it," she discloses.

Looking
Like the office, the waiting room occupies an angular bay that comes to a point above the concrete base. The building sits on what was once a rarely used patio on a steep hillside. Large windows provide views across the property and away from the house.

Office and waiting room are linked by a hallway with a kitchenette and a small bathroom. "It could be turned into a guest house," comments Willens of the 650-square-foot structure. "The waiting room could fit a bed, and the bathroom is large enough so a shower could be added." As part of this multi-purpose strategy, the spacious office could be converted into a living room.

Throughout the interiors, ample daylight and views of greenery through clerestories and big corner windows provide the serene feeling of a retreat removed from the city. Tilted ceilings, white walls, and maple flooring reinforce the uplifting mood. "Patients tell me the space is so peaceful, like a sanctuary," the therapist notes. "It sets a tone that is so different from a typical office building."

The uncluttered, clean-lined spaces, furnished with classic modern pieces, are warmed by Douglas fir beams in the ceiling. The same wood is applied to windows and door frames, cabinetry, and work surfaces to unify the rooms and save the white-walled spaces from appearing cold and austere. During therapy sessions, Willens sits in an Eames chair facing her patients, with a view of the treetops visible just outside the corner window. "Psychologically, it has been transformative," she asserts. "I never realized how tense I was from being stuck in traffic. Now I can set my hours as precisely as I want to."

Screening
Joan Willens's private entrance opens directly into her office. Her Eames chair is pulled up to the space-efficient desk built into the angular corner. Translucent glass on either side of the door screens views into the room.

Working
The office has a residential feeling, reflecting its potential use as a living room should Willens want to turn the pavilion into a guest house or a rental apartment. The sofa is tucked between low, built-in cabinets across from a Mies van der Rohe Barcelona chair. Warm wood tones and views of trees lend the air of a modern Shangri-la.

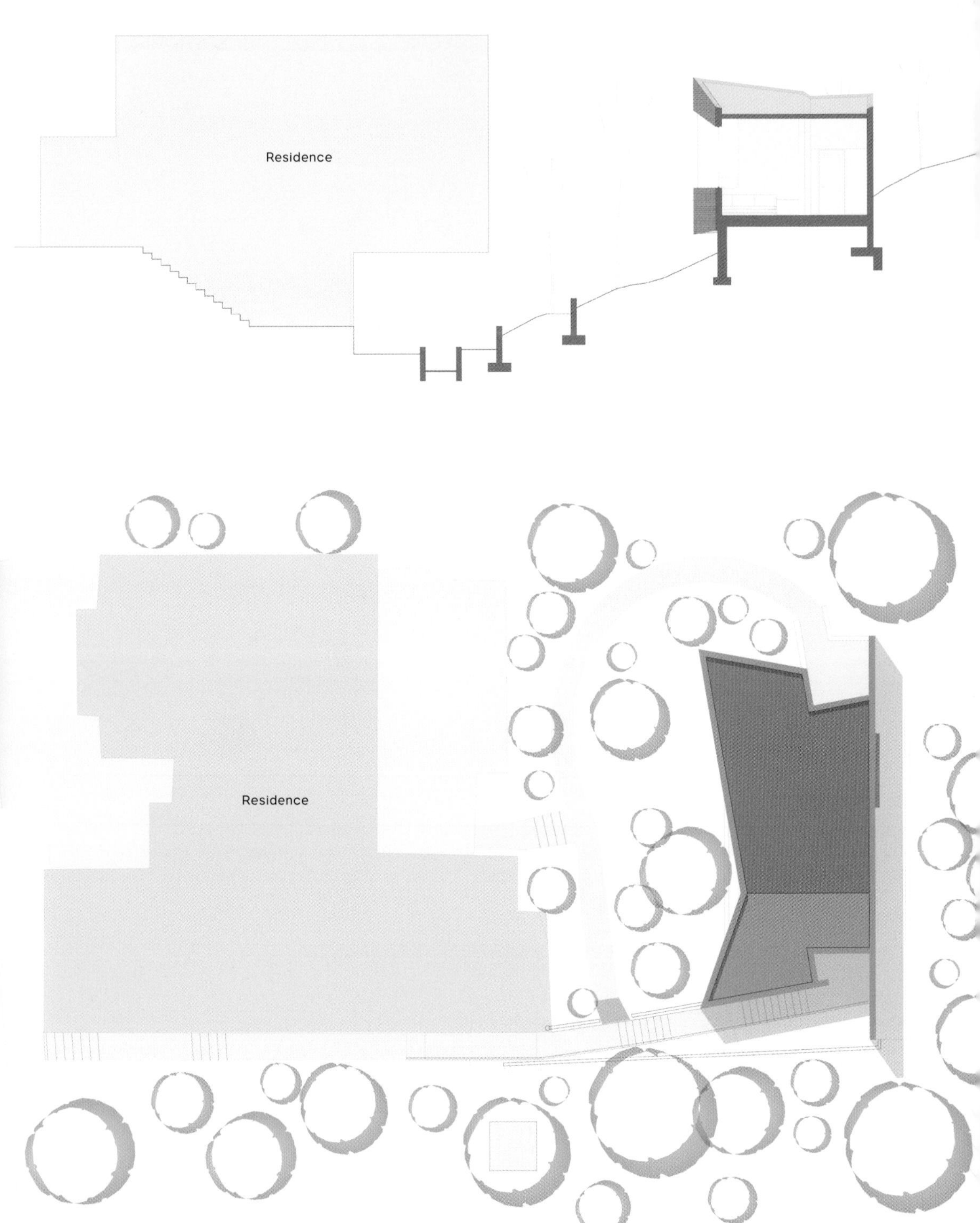
Residence
Residence

North Elevation

East Elevation

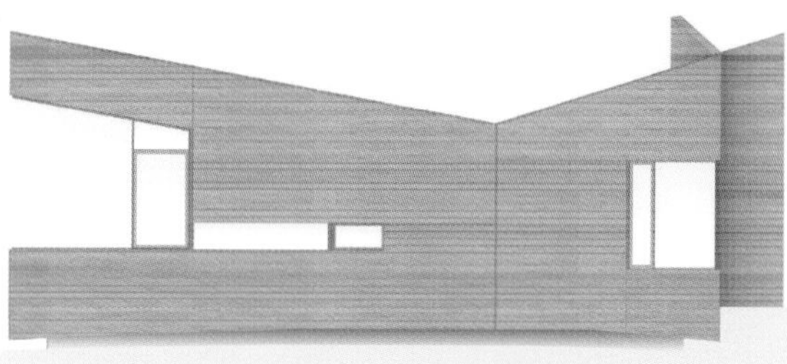

West Elevation

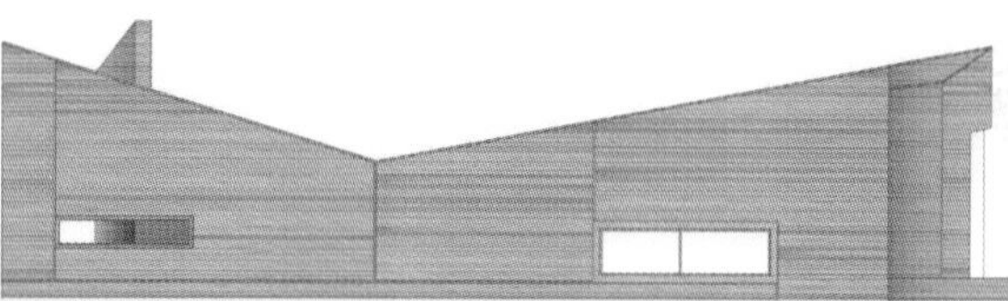

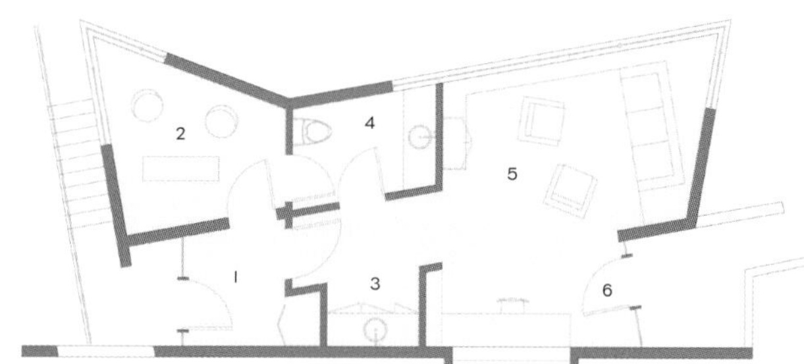

1 Entry
2 Waiting Room
3 Kitchenette
4 Bathroom
5 Office
6 Exit

LESSONS LEARNED

Give visitors a separate entrance. Doors at either end of the office pavilion allow Joan Willens and her patients to enter and exit separately. Inside the patients' entrance, a front hall leads to a waiting room, allowing for privacy before and after an appointment. The same design can be used for other home-based businesses that require frequent visits from clients and vendors.

Treat storage like furniture. The architect Stephen Kanner describes the low cabinets, countertops, and shelving around the perimeter of the rooms as "a protruding ribbon" that leaves space for furnishings. "Raising the cabinets above the floor makes the room feel bigger," he notes. "Detailing them with cutouts in the doors rather than hardware creates depth and a more sculptural feeling."

FORCING A BALANCE

Adele Naude Santos, an architect and educator, has continually renovated old buildings into live/work spaces in the various cities where her dual career has taken her. "Having a busy life in academia and practice, live/work has given me the chance to manage my hours," reflects the South African-born Santos, dean of the Massachusetts Institute of Technology's architecture school. "People always joke with me that everywhere I go, I build myself a place." Her live/work dwellings have included a recycled paint-supply warehouse in Philadelphia and a remodeled printing plant in San Francisco.

After joining MIT in 2004, Santos began looking for an opportunity to create a unique home in the Boston area so she could maintain an offshoot of her San Francisco-based architecture practice, plus entertain, garden, and relax. "Like my other live/work places," she explains, "it would allow me to start in the studio early, go to the university, and work late again in the studio." Her search led to a dilapidated warehouse next to a railroad freight line in Somerville, Massachusetts, near the Harvard and MIT campuses in Cambridge. The old brick building had been built in 1860 as the McCann

Warming
On the north wall of the living space, between the steel beams of the old foundry, an existing niche below the window is fitted with a gas stove. It creates a hearth within a sitting area used for watching television.

Preserving
To honor the past, Adele Santos, dean of the Massachusetts Institute of Technology's architecture school, preserved both the original painted sign on the building's brick parapet and the existing chimneys.

Sunning
The solarium is filled with tropical plants to create a winter garden. The sky-lighted space insulates the old structure's exposed brick walls, reducing heating bills.

Dining and cooking
Just inside the solarium, the dining area is nestled next to the private work area on the foundry's west side. Santos positioned the kitchen under the upper-story guest suites,where plumbing already existed. The kitchen is open to the central living area.

Living
The living area in the center of the converted foundry is furnished with pony skin chairs by Le Corbusier and bentwood Pernilla arm-chairs by the Swedish designer Bruno Mathsson. Collections of artifacts underscore the strong sense of history that pervades the renovated foundry.

Bronze Foundry and expanded with additions over time. In the 1960s a fire destroyed two-thirds of the structure, leaving a portion of the foundry at the north end and a building fragment at the south. Still standing between the two survivors were sections of brick walls and a grape arbor built by an artist who had previously used the property as a studio.

"It was such a ruin, I wasn't going to stop and go in," recalls Santos. "But after being in it for just five minutes, I put in a bid. It felt like being in Mexico or Tuscany." Her impulse buy led to the long, complicated process of stabilizing the crumbling structure, removing insensitive alterations, and renovating it to create habitable space. "The challenge was to modernize without losing the traces of history," comments the architect. "My idea was to make a compound out of it in the same spirit as the foundry."

Her first job was transforming the larger surviving structure at the north end into 3,500 square feet of living quarters and creative space. Santos worked with the historic architectural features to organize the two-story warehouse around a central living area. She left two old gantry cranes in place on the sides and used one to create a second-floor office. This new mezzanine is suspended from the steel beams of the gantry, and the space underneath is also reserved for work.

On the opposite side of the living area, the kitchen and the owner's bedroom suite are arranged under a two-bedroom guest quarters. "This side was mostly windowless and already had plumbing," the architect relates. "I chose to make this a building-within-a-building in contrast to the hanging mezzanine on the other side."

Next, on the property's south end, Santos constructed a 1,500-square-foot studio and conference area with access from the street. It too is glazed along the courtyard side with glass fitted into steel channels. This architecture, consistently applied throughout the complex, is clearly modern yet supportive of the foundry's industrial vernacular.

From the twenty-foot-high existing brick wall along the street, a new roof curves down to the lower courtyard facade, allowing enough height inside for a second-level office and guest suite. The floor of this balcony bends inward to provide views of the studio and the courtyard garden, which can be seen from just inside the front door. Although designed for work, the pavilion incorporates a kitchen on the ground level and bathrooms so it can also serve as a guest house and be rented or sold in the future.

Curving
From the upper level of the work pavilion, sometimes used as a guest bedroom, the vaulted ceiling and its supporting beams were left visible. Santos curved the balcony and the metal railing to maximize the amount of daylight and the sense of space in the ground-level studio, where drafting tables are set up for staff in a corner of the studio.

Converting
Santos rescued this abandoned foundry and converted it into two live/work spaces that face off across a beautifully landscaped courtyard. The solid brick walls seen from the street hide a paradise of glass and greenery within. This south entrance leads into the studio and the conference area.

Working
Just inside the office pavilion entrance are an oval table and Eames chairs for meetings. Santos designed the small building so it could be converted into a guest house or a rental apartment should she decide to move her office to another location.

Looking out
Like the solarium at the opposite end of the courtyard, the 1,500-square-foot studio building is glazed along the courtyard side.

Relaxing
Santos often entertains in the courtyard at a dining table shaded by a grape arbor built by an artist who previously owned the property. She planted flowering trees and shrubs to frame the sides of the outdoor space.

Between the studio and the solarium, the arbor has been preserved as part of the courtyard. This area is now paved in brick and crushed granite and framed at the sides with shrubs and flowering trees. Cherry, crab apple, dogwood, weeping redbud, and other species are planted so that they bloom sequentially from one end of the courtyard to the other. "In summer, I can barely see from one side of the space to the other," Santos observes. "It really becomes like a miniature forest."

The garden comes in handy for the frequent parties and events she hosts as dean of MIT's architecture school. It is also a breather between home and office. "It allows me to make a mental transition between the two," Santos says. "Over the years, I've learned to become very specific about my work space and reduce its intrusion on my living space. You really need the distance between living and working to fully enjoy both."

West Elevation

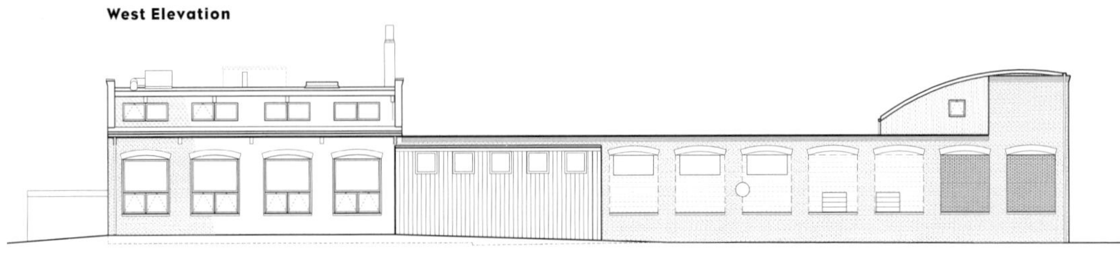

Ground Floor

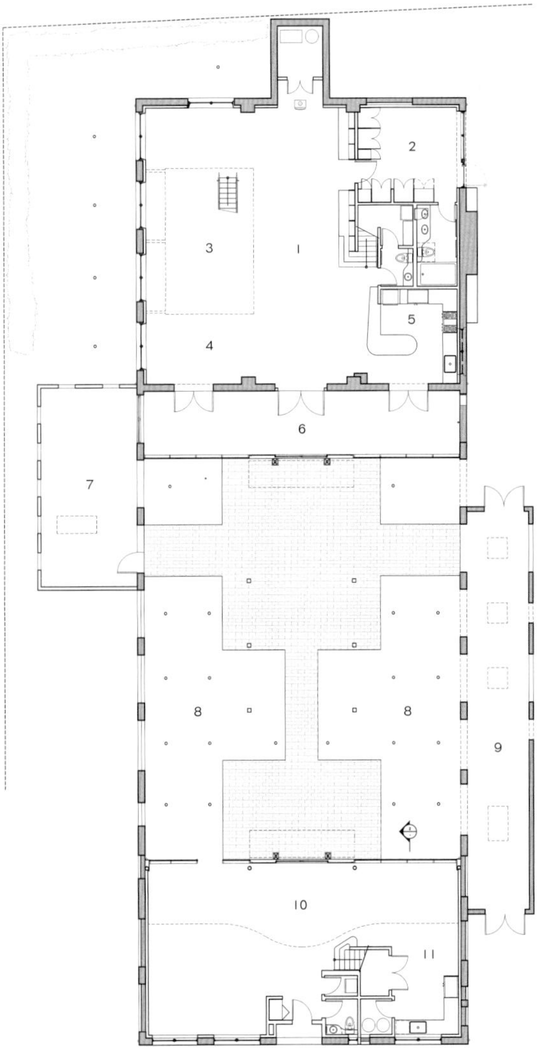

2 3 1 4 5 6 7 8 8 9 10 11

Mezzanine

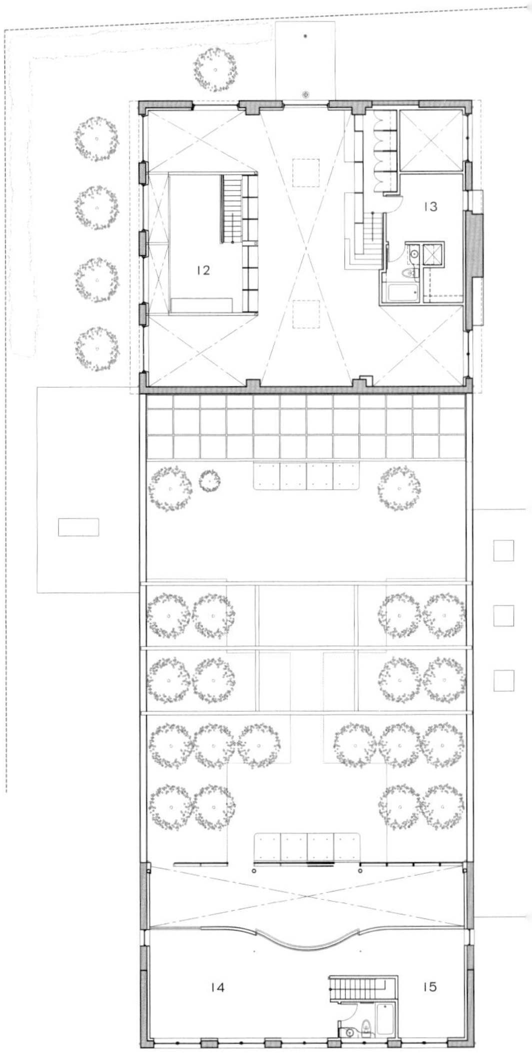

12 13 14 15

LESSONS LEARNED

Respect architectural history. Adele Santos capitalized on steel gantry beams, existing plumbing, and load-bearing masonry to organize and support new live/work spaces. The gantries' wheels and chains were sandblasted and left in place as historical reminders. Old brick walls, industrial chimneys, and worn painted signs also supply architectural character—testifying to the building's former use as a foundry.

Treat the space between living and working as a retreat. "The live/work spaces I have created for myself and others have tended to include a restful garden that implied a creative atmosphere," says Santos. By preserving a grape arbor and planting a grove of flowering trees, Santos turned her once-shabby courtyard into a charming garden and entertaining space. She created a winter counterpart to this outdoor oasis with a passive-solar solarium.

Build in work options. The architect prefers the separation between living area and office provided by the independent studio across the courtyard, but she can still work in her home should the pavilion be occupied by guests or sold in the future.

Suspending
The South African–born Adele Santos suspended a mezzanine from the steel beams of an existing industrial gantry to create an office. Then she turned the space underneath the elevated room into a private studio.

1 Living Area
2 Private Studio
3 Master Suite
4 Dining Area
5 Kitchen
6 Solarium
7 Shed
8 Garden
9 Arcade
10 Studio
11 Kitchen
12 Private Office
13 Suite 2
14 Office
15 Study

ACROPOLIS FOR ART

Retirement offers the opportunity to work at home and turn a hobby into a full-time job. For Kitty Mann, a former media director of a New York advertising firm, it has allowed her time to pursue painting, sculpture, and digital photography right in the heart of wine country. Her studio is just a few steps away from the hilltop home in Sonoma County, California, shared with her husband, Fred, a retired ad executive and architecture buff. "It gave me a way to separate myself from the domestic aspects of the house," says Kitty of the L-shaped work building. "If my studio was part of the house, it would be harder to focus. I would end up doing laundry or cooking."

Or looking out the windows. Fernau and Hartman Architects designed the house and the studio to take advantage of sun-drenched views of ridges, foothills, and vineyards. The Berkeley firm specializes in organizing houses

Siting
To take advantage of the views, the house is perched on top of a flattened hill above a lush landscape of oak trees. Angled roofs and color contrasts inject dynamism into the design and create the impression of a building added onto over time. The architects Fernau and Hartman based their color palette on hues from the surrounding landscape of oaks and grassess.

Painting

A sliding door opens into Kitty Mann's work space in the studio building next to the house. A porch built into the bend of the L-shaped building provides a place to dine or relax with vistas of distant mountains over the treetops.

Gathering

Next to the studio building, a built-in bench and a fountain frame the portion of the courtyard used for barbecues and outdoor parties. A redwood pergola unites the green-stained studio and the ocher stucco house. In contrast to the sloping angles of the house, the studio is topped with a flat roof.

around topographical elements to shape unexpected spatial experiences, but the Manns were restricted to a featureless plateau. "The hilltop had already been flattened by the developer, and we were required to build there," relates Richard Fernau. "So we thought of the site as an acropolis."

Like a smaller version of that ancient precinct, the two-story house and the one-level studio are pushed to the promontory's periphery to command the landscape and enclose a zigzagging courtyard. Each of the two buildings is bent in the middle to cup the stone-paved piazza, and their angular and blocky wings are topped by metal shed roofs sloping in different directions to create the impression of clustered buildings assembled over time. "We wanted the feeling of a little hilltop village," explains Kitty Mann. "Each section of the house is almost a separate building."

Further differentiation comes from the ocher stucco and red-painted clapboard used on the home and the green-stained cedar siding on the garage and the studio. "The intent was to use colors from the surrounding

Climbing
A staircase on one side of the double-height entrance hall leads to the son's bedroom. On the ground level, the kitchen is tucked into a corner of the house facing the courtyard and the pergola.

Living
Beamed ceilings add a rustic touch in the living room. The contemporary furnishings were newly purchased for the home. "With every house, we leave the furniture behind and start from scratch," says Fred Mann. "We travel only with our books and piano."

Working
The red clapboard applied to the home's exterior reappears on the walls enclosing Fred Mann's second-floor office over the front door. A window in the office allows him to look down into the two-story entrance hall. "It's the worm that snakes through the apple, the basic form of the house," the architect Richard Fernau points out. It typifies the unexpected, improvisational quality of the design inside and out.

landscape: dark green live oaks and grasses that change from green in winter to golden yellow in late summer," notes Laura Hartman. "We wanted the house to recede into that landscape."

Rooms are oriented to the light and views so that no two spaces feel alike. The master bedroom at one end of the house, reached from its own staircase, opens up to a panorama of Dry Creek Valley. At the opposite end of the house, the son's hideout has a porch where he can roll out his bed on hot summer evenings. Windows wrap the corners of several rooms to capture multidirectional vistas and break up any lingering boxy feeling.

The Manns commissioned Fernau and Hartman after admiring a home the architects had designed in the Sonoma region. "Fred is an architectural junkie," says Kitty. "He loves architecturally interesting homes." Before moving to Northern California, the Manns lived in the "Pink House," one of Miami's most notable homes on Biscayne Bay, designed in the 1970s by the noted firm Arquitectonica. "It was organized around a long hallway, and the rooms didn't connect with each other," recalls Fred of the linear pink stucco composition. "Our son used to bowl down the hall."

For their California house, the couple sought more casual, collective spaces. "We talked a lot about using every room for more than one activity," recalls Hartman. The idea of a freestanding structure, with two rooms, a bathroom, and a utility sink that could serve as work space, extra bedrooms, or lounges, she discloses, "grew out of the 'Pink House,' where guest rooms and other spaces sat empty much of the time."

Now the Manns enjoy a variety of adaptable rooms and outdoor spaces for pursuing creative work or sipping the local Zinfandel. Barbecues are staged next to the studio, where a long bench and a fountain are built into the side of the courtyard. Kitty Mann uses the second of its two workrooms as a media lounge and a getaway for meditating and practicing yoga, and it is often turned into a guest room for visiting family and friends. "The design works nicely because it gives me space to paint, private areas for my son and our guests, and rooms where we can all come together."

Sleeping
The son's bedroom opens onto a sleeping porch with hillside views. Like health-conscious Californians at the turn of the twentieth century, he can move the bed out into the open air on summer evenings.

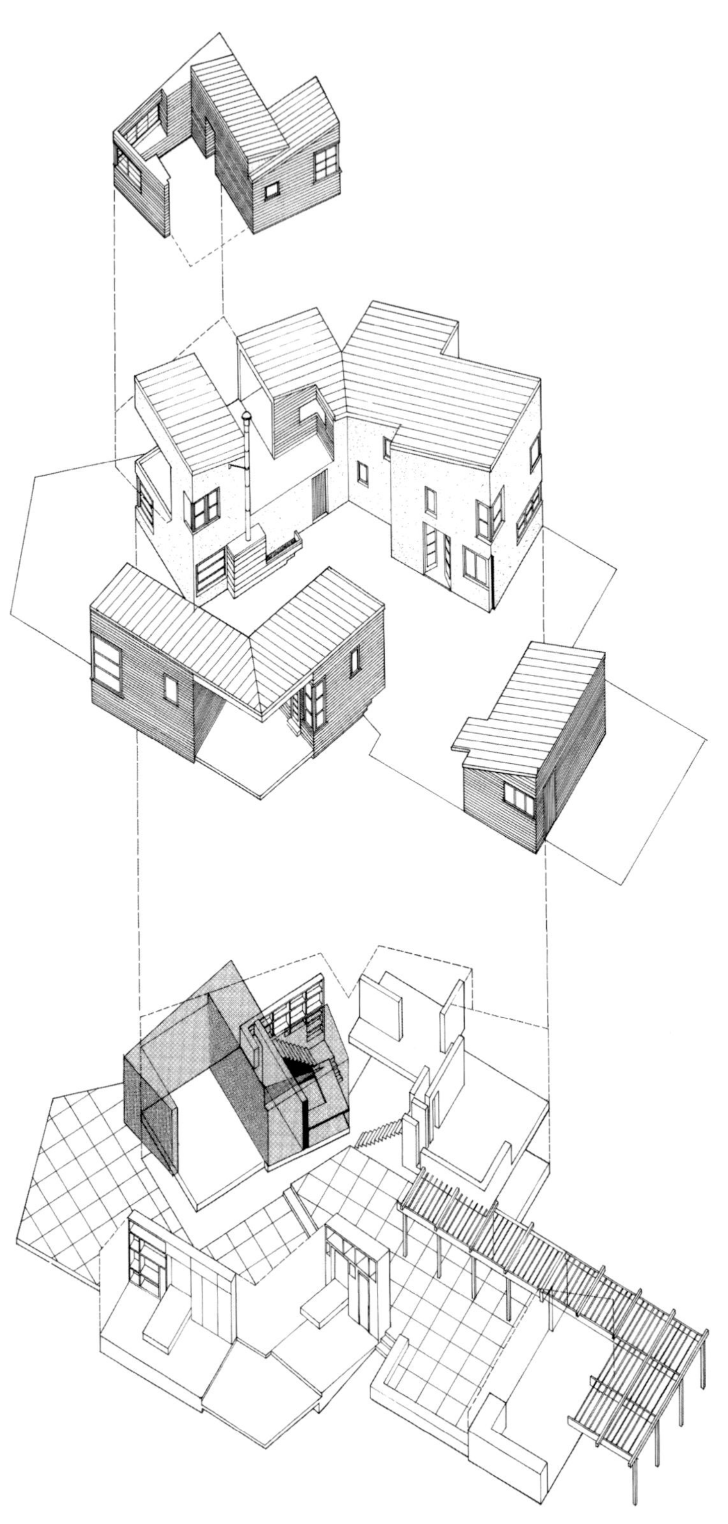

1 Entry
2 Living Area
3 Dining Area
4 Kitchen
5 Media/Guest Room
6 Dog Trot
7 Studio/Guest House
8 Courtyard
9 Garage/Laundry
10 Carport
11 Master Bedroom
12 Study
13 Open to Below
14 Study
15 Sleeping Porch
16 Son's Bedroom

LESSONS LEARNED

Create outdoor spaces for different times of day. Instead of surrounding the house and studio with lawn, Fernau and Hartman arranged them around a winding, paved courtyard that funnels cool breezes and captures varying amounts of sunlight depending on the season. In the house, an east-facing porch extends off a bedroom to capture morning sunshine. Between the workrooms in the studio, a west-facing porch provides a perch for viewing the sunset.

Connect outdoors and indoors in unexpected ways. Red clapboard is repeated inside to recall the exterior while providing an unexpected jolt of color. In the son's bedroom, the bed is mounted on wheels so it can be rolled onto a sleeping porch for viewing the stars. Windows are positioned in each room according to the activity, so the views can be enjoyed whether one is standing or sitting.

Anticipate work-space expansion. In the freestanding pavilion across from the house, an adaptable second room next to the art studio offers more work space for Kitty Mann should she need it in the future. "The whole idea was to make these rooms as flexible as possible," says Fred Mann.

FREE PARKING

Remodeling the garage is a common way of carving out work space at home. Debbie Klein, an artist in Dallas, went one better: she tore down her carport and replaced it with an airy studio elevated over a covered parking area. "It's given me the freedom to spread out and try new things," declares Klein, who used to create her vibrant paintings and collages on the dining room table.

Now she walks across the back-yard patio and climbs a metal-and-wood staircase to reach the sunny aerie, where two large tables and a built-in desk for a computer provide plenty of work room. Visible through a long, east-facing bank of windows are the leaves and branches of red oaks and cedar elms lining an adjacent alley. "It's like a nice tree house," maintains Klein of the 22-by-28-foot space topped by laminated wood beams and exposed ductwork.

The new studio and carport were built as part of a renovation of the house that Klein shares with her husband, Ron, and their two young daughters. Originally designed by the local architect Stark West as a house for himself,

Working
Inside the studio, large metal-sash windows, exposed metal ducts, and laminated wood beams create the feeling of a loft. Back-to-back tables provide a generous work space where Klein creates her collages.

Adding on
"The simple planes of stucco enhance the basic forms of the architecture, allowing the shadows of trees to appear on the surface," says Dan Shipley, architect of the Kleins' addition. "The buildings are really backgrounds for the landscaping."

Growing
The Kleins' Dallas home was originally designed with a high-ceilinged, open living area at the center, flanked by a bedroom in each of the four corners. The couple added a master suite off the house's northeast corner and a studio over a carport at the northwestern edge of the property, next to an alley.

Peeping
In remodeling the 1964 house, the architect Dan Shipley started by installing a new metal roof and a front door filled with forty-five peepholes.

his wife, and their three sons, the one-story dwelling was built in 1964 in the Forest Hills neighborhood east of downtown Dallas. It was arranged with a high-ceilinged, open living area at the center, flanked by a bedroom in each of the four corners. "We've always been drawn to modern," acknowledges Debbie. "I do very modern art inspired by Rauschenberg and Kandinsky, and our furniture is modern."

Seeking to expand and reconfigure the rooms, the Kleins consulted a local furniture store for the name of an architect who could design additions sympathetic to the midcentury modernism of the house. Based on that recommendation, they hired Dan Shipley. He began the project by installing a new metal roof and a front door punctured with nearly four dozen peepholes. "Dan has a great sense of humor," reports Debbie. "From that work we went on to do a plan for the studio, master bedroom, and back-yard patio."

Angling
Dan Shipley maintained the original house's modern aesthetic with planar architectural elements: the patio's outdoor fireplace and copper-topped canopy, stucco walls, and PVC-paneled fencing screening the studio and the carport from the house.

Shipley extended the new spaces off the rear of the house, linking the master suite to one of the back bedrooms. The original carport was demolished to make way for a new one, with the art studio on top of it. This freestanding structure roughly occupies the footprint of the razed garage but is slightly angled away from the house. A concrete-and-steel structure supports the second story to frame a covered parking area next to a motor court off the alley. "By putting the studio above the carport," explains Shipley, "you save site space and help enclose the back yard. The height of the second story also helps screen views of the houses across the alley."

In between the bedroom and studio additions, the architect shaped an outdoor living room with a fireplace. A steel canopy covered in resin-coated plywood shades the space and keeps out the rain. The new carport-studio reflects a similar sensibility in a projecting roof supported by exposed laminated wood beams. It extends far enough to provide cover over the staircase leading up one side to the upper-level studio entrance. "The intent was to make a real distinction between the new architecture and the original," Shipley comments. While the stucco-clad studio and master suite are clearly different from the 1960s brick house, their boxy, unadorned shapes fitted with aluminum-framed windows clearly harmonize with its modern design.

Independent from the house, the studio is fitted with a utility sink, a bathroom with a shower, and a fold-down sofa so that it can be converted into a guest suite or a "granny flat" should the Kleins decide to sell. But for now, Debbie Klein is content to work amid the light and the trees. "I never allowed myself to have such a special place before," she says. "The scariest part of building it was not being sure you could work in the space. But now I'm doing a lot more work than I was a few years ago. It definitely doesn't stifle my creativity."

Relaxing
The new patio is strategically positioned between the 1964 house (right), the new master suite addition (center background and left), and the studio (not shown). Its outdoor space is sheltered from rain and sun by a steel canopy topped by resin-coated plywood panels and a copper roof.

Calming
A low metal fountain and pebbled paving under the overhang of the remodeled house add a note of Zen tranquillity to the back garden, with its patio and outdoor fireplace. The red wall next to the stuccoed chimney matches the underside of the canopy, brightening the space.

Warming
The patio focuses on an outdoor fireplace set within a stuccoed chimney. Furnished with sofas and chairs upholstered in weather-resistant fabrics, it serves as the family's second living room.

Sleeping
The new master bedroom has a fireplace positioned on the interior side of its outdoor counterpart. A cast concrete shelf holds firewood or magazines. Between the chimney and the door to the patio, quarter-sawn oak cabinets house the television and stereo equipment. A glassy bay furnished with chaises provides a place to relax or read.

LESSONS LEARNED

Rebuild when necessary. Rather than trying to shoehorn a workplace into an existing structure that is not a good fit, sometimes a fresh approach makes more sense. Debbie Klein replaced an existing carport with a freestanding structure to gain studio space without compromising the architecture of the original house or the existing landscaping. And the new pavilion still offers a place to park the car.

Don't always worry about blending in. It is acceptable to set a new design apart from an older structure, especially a historic building, rather than to mimic a past style. By designing the new studio-carport in a contemporary style, the Kleins' architect clearly distinguished old from new and house from work space.

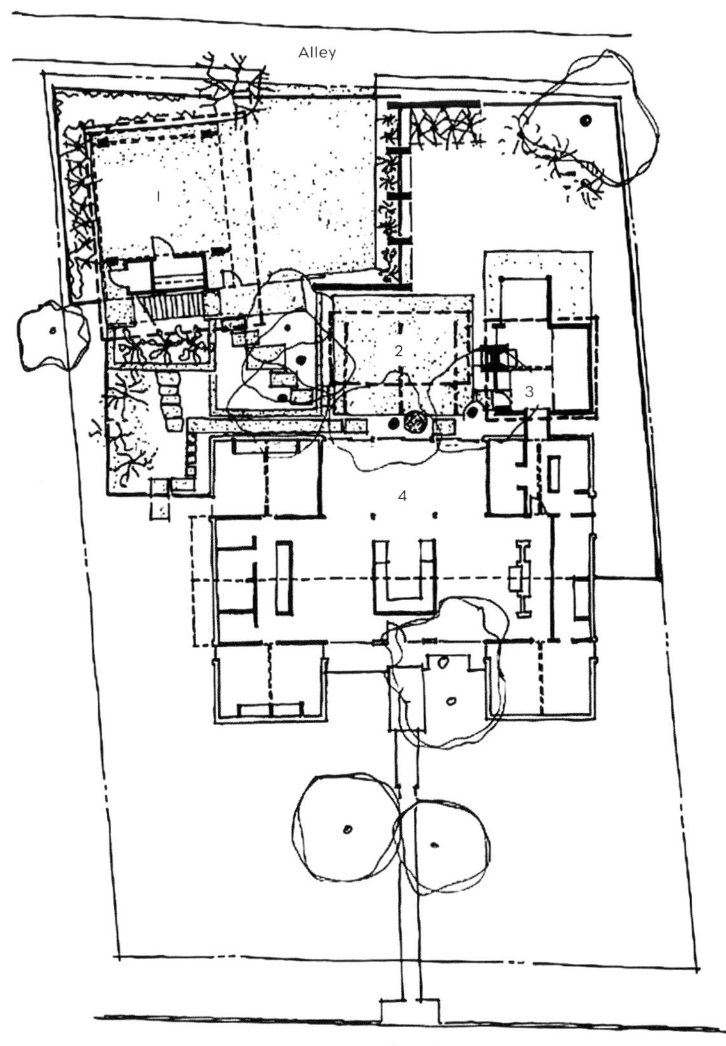

1 Carport/Studio
2 Porch/Pergola
3 Master Suite
4 Existing House

Framing
Shipley marked the threshold to the private wing of the house with a portal in the doorway of the master suite. It is clad in quartersawn oak to match the bedroom's cabinetry.

Looking
In the master bedroom, a tall slot of glass separates the chimney from the corner window bay. It aligns with the steel canopy over the patio and provides a glimpse of that outdoor space.

THINK TANK

David Wild develops his ideas for television commercials and short documentary films in a back-yard retreat he calls the Brain. "It's a think tank," says Wild of the two-story pavilion. "It's an introspective place, almost monastic, where I can get work done." Part factory loft, part playhouse, the 20-by-40-foot box is a short walk from the Seattle house that Wild shares with his wife and sometime collaborator, Lulu Gargiulo, and their young daughter, Michiko. Its architecture of unfinished concrete walls and industrial steel-sash windows is an austere counterpart to the wood-sheathed walls and gabled roofs of the home. "David likes simple, straightforward spaces, and I do too, so it was a match made in heaven," notes Tom Kundig of Olson Sundberg Kundig Allen Architects. "He basically needed a big, open room."

Revealing
The Brain, says its architect, "is meant to express the inherent nature of its materials, which are left unfinished to reveal their intrinsic colors, textures, and aging."

Spotting
Industrial sash windows open up the interior, while a tiny lookout over the door allows the dog to spot visitors.

Wild commissioned Kundig after admiring one of the architect's buildings down the street, a combined house and studio for a photographer that was also constructed in concrete. "I had never worked with an architect before," admits the filmmaker, whose projects have included Saturn car commercials and ten-second shorts for MTV. "Tom was a great filter for what I like. He really understood the importance of proportions."

Topping his wish list were tall ceilings and a symmetrical layout in a structure clearly separate from his house. "I lived in a loft but I never liked seeing the bed while I was working," Wild says. "It made it too easy to take a nap. Having to put

Thinking
The Brain's central space is furnished with Wild's Steinway grand piano and midcentury-modern classics, including Hans Wegner's Ox chair and ottoman, Poul Volther's Corona chair, and Charles Eames's work table. Blackout drapes can be pulled to darken the room for film screenings. "It's like a temple for your thoughts," says Wild of his creative cranium.

on shoes to get to work and leave the house behind is important." His vision for the freestanding studio also came from working years earlier in Michigan, where he converted a cottage, once part of a boys' camp, into his office. "I was told by a friend it was cluttered and dank, like my brain," he recalls.

The name stuck, but Wild made sure that his new Brain was pared down and filled with light. The pavilion sits on the side of a forested ravine with a garage tucked into the lower side. Its main room provides a neutral backdrop for creative work as well as related hobbies such as piano playing, still photography, and reading. After working hours, the space becomes a hangout for family and friends. "Acoustics were important for playing music, so there's an ever slight angling of the walls and ceiling," explains Kundig.

Behind the tall bookcases at one end, a darkroom and a storage space are tucked under an office mezzanine, all framed in hot-rolled steel plates that continue the raw aesthetic. The metal also serves a practical

Reading
An Eames work table provides a place to crack open a book next to the library on the main level. The tall bookshelves, illuminated by industrial light fixtures, extend under the steel floor of the office mezzanine. Through the doors behind them are a darkroom and a storage space. The slotted window extends upward to the second-floor office to bring in daylight.

Seeing all
One of the many humorous touches that keep David Wild's Brain lively are marbles set into the concrete walls—like a camera's all-seeing eye. They fill holes left when the metal construction ties were removed.

purpose, allowing photographs and images to be attached to the walls with magnets. Welded onto the treads of the steel staircase leading up to the balcony are the words, "You'll have lots of time to rest when you're six feet under," a favorite saying of Wild's father. "It reminds me to get to work," relates the filmmaker.

Wild's no-nonsense attitude is reflected not only in the Brain's tough materials, but also in its orientation on the site. The structure could have offered dramatic panoramas of the Olympic Mountains, but Wild chose to frame nearby trees and foliage through sixteen-foot-square windows made for warehouses. "It was a conscious decision not to have a view. I didn't want to be distracted," he observes. "Discipline is an important part of the deal." During film shoots, curtains and theatrical scrims can be pulled over the glass to block the light.

Working
Wild's desk on the mezzanine overlooks the two-story main level. The no-nonsense decor includes stereo speakers and hanging bare light bulbs. A whiteboard for brainstorming is at the ready next to the raw concrete wall, which doubles as a projection screen. The electric pulley and wheels mounted on the ceiling are for raising and lowering the lights.

Playing
Attention to detail was essential to the visual success of such a minimalist space. Among the Brain's special features are electrical conduits left exposed, a fireman's pole for quick exits beside a spy hole for the dog, bare light bulbs, and a motto to quicken anyone's steps up the stairs.

Within the minimalist setting, whimsical elements inject a sense of the owner's personality. A brass fireman's pole, purchased at a local surplus store, extends through a round hole in the mezzanine for quick exits. Bare light bulbs on dangling cords are raised and lowered from pulley wheels mounted on the ceiling. A small window is positioned near the office floor so the couple's dog, Oscar, can spot visitors as they approach the front door. Even the studio's somber gray walls incorporate playful touches. Instead of patching the missing areas of concrete left by the metal ties in the formwork, Wild inserted light-emitting marbles into the holes. Each tiny glass orb acts as a lens—an apt symbol for this photographer and film director.

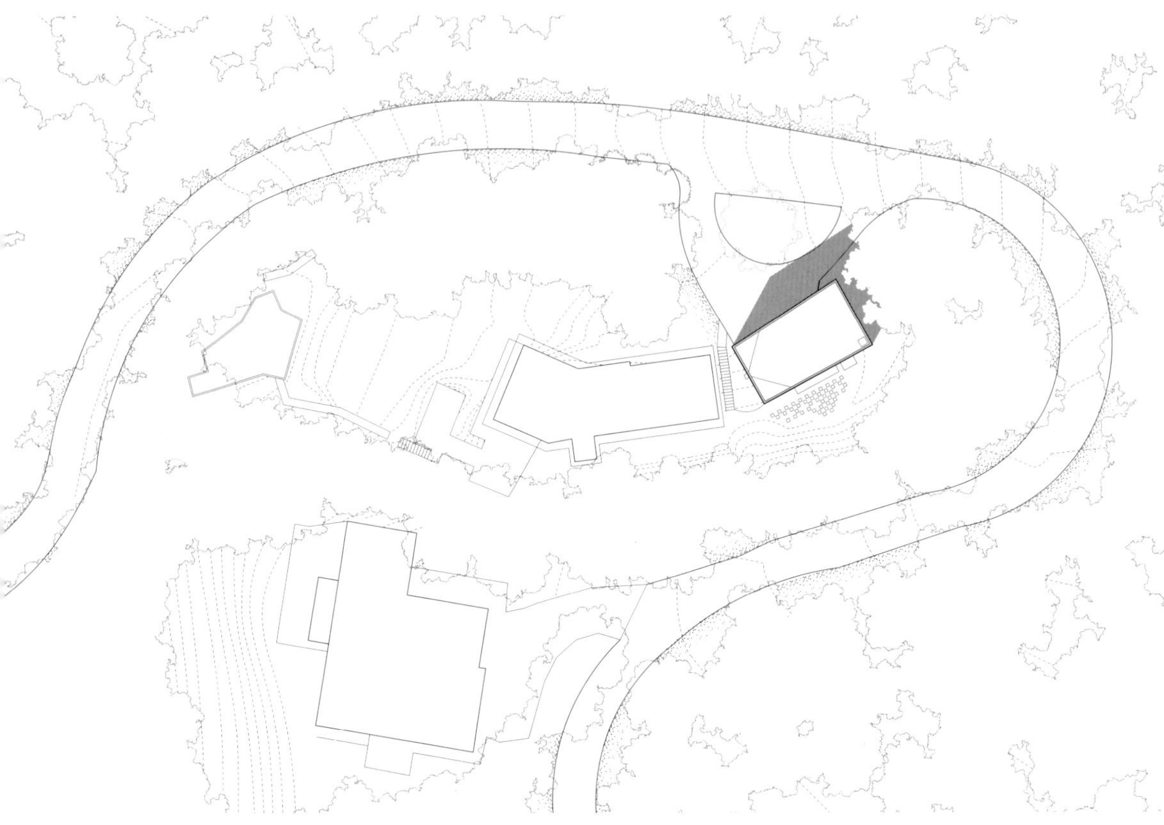

LESSONS LEARNED

Individualize your work space. David Wild gave the Brain quirky elements reflective of his personality. Displayed in his mezzanine office space, in addition to the fireman's pole, are Jacques Tati movie posters and collections of fishing bobbers and circus throwing knives ("I did a short film for MTV on a guy who made them," he discloses). Even a mundane air duct is curved to recall a submarine periscope, adding "a touch of Jules Verne" to this bare-bones space.

Leave room to dream. "I wanted plenty of head room and brain room," states Wild of his tall, airy studio, where distractions are kept to a minimum. Like a blank canvas, the adaptable interior allows the filmmaker to fill in the space with furniture and equipment as needed or to leave it empty for parties. Office work is confined to the second level, so messes are kept out of sight.

Consider loftlike finishes. Concrete and steel-plated walls contribute to the industrial Zen aesthetic in Wild's studio. Unfinished materials including brick, concrete block, and wood could create the same modern loft feeling while saving on construction costs. They can also make a space seem larger because both exterior and interior walls look the same. However, without wallboard or moldings to cover seams and connections, the exposed surfaces require careful detailing and craftsmanship.

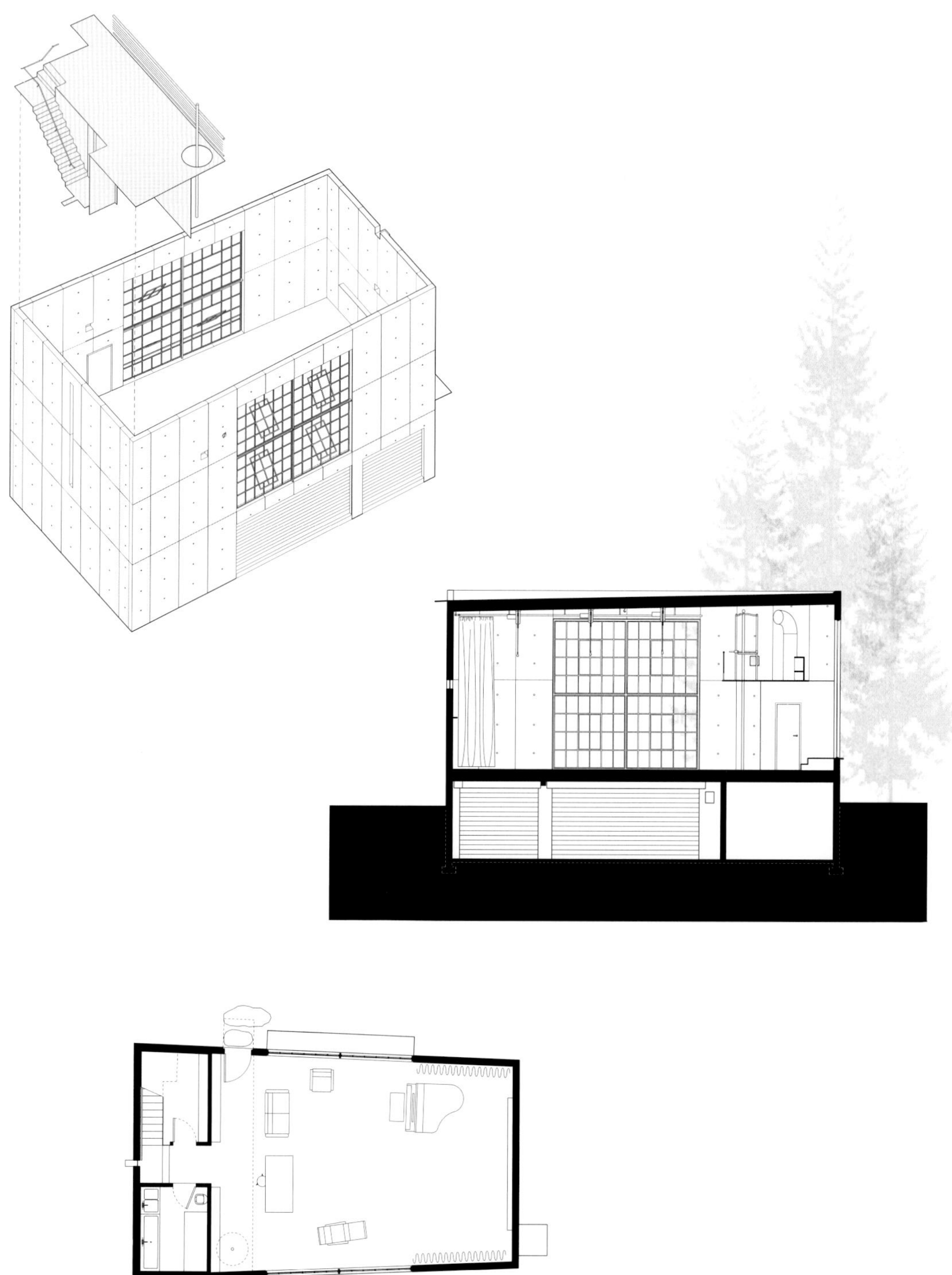

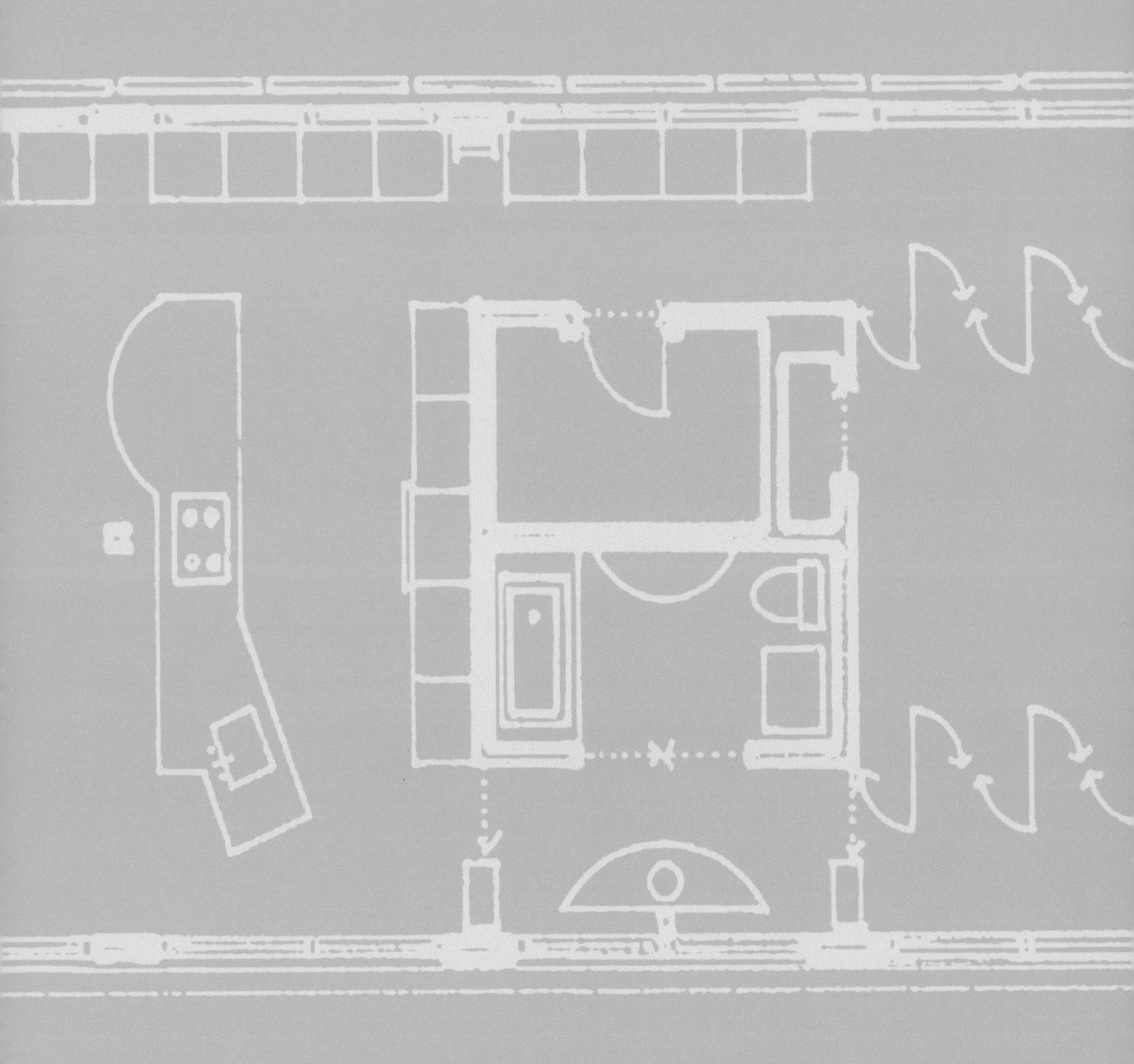

Shades of Green

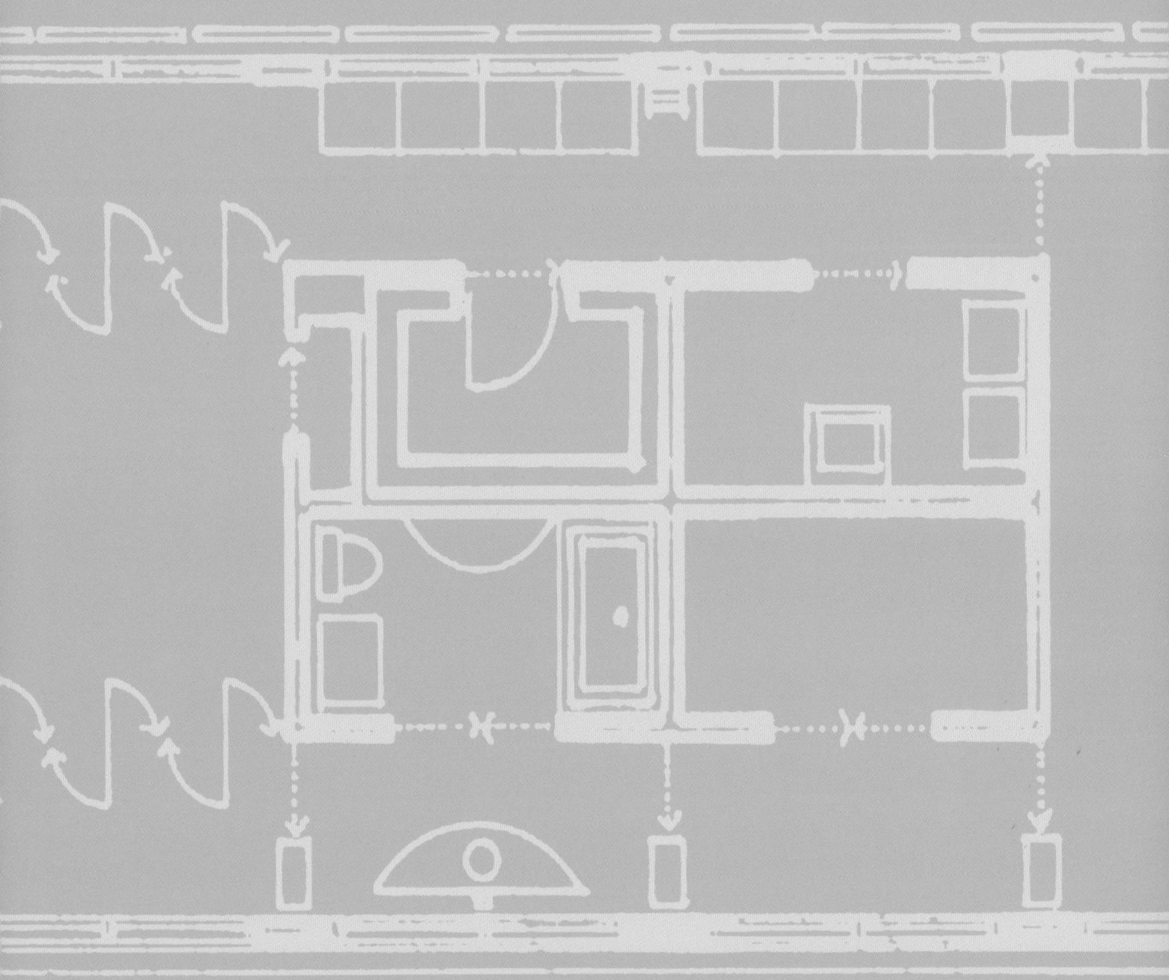

Minding Mother Earth

MA HOUSE

Even before they quit their jobs, the architects Christopher Hays and Allison Ewing made sure that they built a work space at home. The two were designing for William McDonough and Partners, a firm in Charlottesville, Virginia, internationally known for creating environmentally responsible architecture, when they decided to apply what they learned to building a home of their own. Their search for land led to an abandoned house on a corner lot near the Rivanna River in the Woolen Mills district, a working-class neighborhood that had grown up around a textile factory on Charlottesville's eastern side.

After tearing down the small house, Hays and Ewing built a two-part live/work structure that combines their interest in environmentally sensitive building, Japanese architecture, and modern design. "This was an opportunity to build on our interest in sustainability and the connectivity between the landscape and the building," relates Hays. "We began the design of the house with the desire to weave together indoor and outdoor spaces, allowing our two young children to roam easily between the two."

Bridging
Cypress louvers shade the wooden trellis that extends along the back face of the live/work compound. In this bridge area, the Japanese sense of *ma* and *hashi* are almost palpable.

Hiding
From the street, the north-facing side of this green live/work compound in Charlottesville, Virginia, is nearly windowless—keeping a secret as to what awaits behind the facade.

Greeting

The live/work compound is entered up a staircase and through a pivoting door that opens to the courtyard between the residence (left) and the office (right).

Framing
Just off the dining area, a corner of the back porch overlooks the yard's gardens and pond and is used for outdoor meals and entertaining. Timber posts and beams are exposed throughout the house.

The rural-feeling site, next to a riverside park, allowed them the freedom to explore a contemporary design unencumbered by historical context and design review. It also meant raising the building above the flood plain, allowing for an elevated courtyard and a back porch. The architects then pulled the house apart to create two wings centered on the courtyard, which is entered from the street through a pivoting screen. The arrangement recalls southern dog-trot houses, but Ewing explains that it is also based on experiences in Italy, where she and Hays lived while working for the renowned architect Renzo Piano. "We loved the idea that you arrive in the garden first," she says, pointing to the landscape visible from the front entrance. "It was one of the generating concepts of the house."

On the left side of the courtyard is the main wing, containing an airy, double-height living room, a dining area, and a kitchen on the first floor. Play space and bedrooms for their two children, Emily and Christopher, are located on the second level. To the right is the couple's one-room studio and on the floor above it a master bedroom and a bathroom. Bridging the two sides of the house on the upper level is a hallway that doubles as a sitting area.

Connecting
From the back yard, the house opens to the south with an expansive elevated porch connecting the architects' office (left) and their living spaces (right).

"We first thought about the studio as an away building, one built in the yard, but it was more cost effective to do it within the house," notes Ewing. Yet the work space, reflective of the idea of a freestanding building, is independent of the master suite above it—there is no staircase connecting the two—and can be entered only from the courtyard. It was also conceived as a

guest suite or an apartment and incorporates a bathroom with a shower. "We wanted that built-in flexibility," comments Hays. "The idea was to rent it out if we needed the extra income."

Since completing the house, the couple have actively used the remote room for designing residential projects, first for Hays, who set up his own practice in 2003. "I was traveling so much before then that being home was a relief," he admits. "Being around the kids was appealing." His flexible schedule and closeness to the children persuaded Ewing to follow her husband and leave McDonough's firm in 2005—with some trepidation. "Moving from a steady income to being on our own was frightening," she admits. "But we both had projects and it made sense financially."

Divided down the middle with two identical desks and shelving on either side, the light-filled headquarters of the Hays + Ewing Design Studio faces south to a yard landscaped with flowering plants and a pond. Eames chairs are pulled up to a table in front of the tall windows to provide a place for meetings and

Living

Furnished with a contemporary sofa and chairs, the double-height living room flows into the dining area. Stained and waxed fiber-cement panels are arranged on the living-room floor like Japanese tatami mats. The second-floor balcony provides a play space for the children.

Dining
Located at one end of the house, the dining area occupies the space next to the kitchen island, which features open overhead shelving and tall stools.

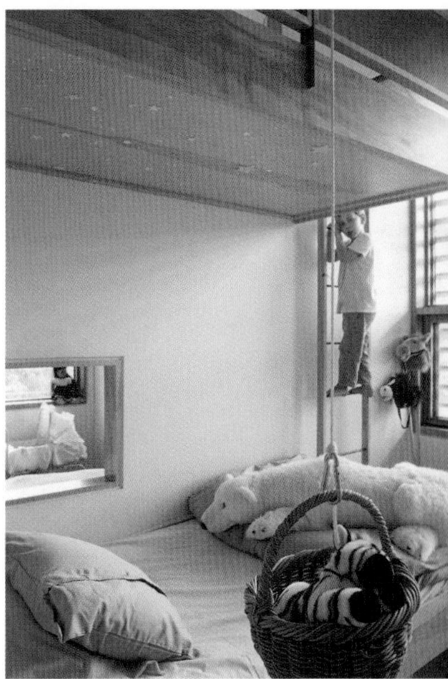

Nesting
The hallway connecting the kids' and parents' bedrooms serves as a lounge and a reading nook.

Playing
The couple's two children, Chris and Emily, share a loft between their second-floor bedrooms.

extra work space. "We'll be working on our drawings and then we'll look out our window and see a heron fishing in the pond," reports Ewing. "There are these wonderful moments in the day when we can take a mental break. The quality of daylight makes a real difference in our sense of well-being."

Sunshine, a generating force in the design, is both embraced for passive solar heat gain in the winter and shielded to reduce it during the summer. From the north-facing street side, the warmly stained, wood-framed house practically closes out daylight with few openings. On the back, it opens to the south with large windows fronting a wide wooden deck. The porch extends the full width of the house and is shaded by a timber trellis. Louvers screen the windows on the upper story and are turned sideways to cover the top of the trellis.

The house's exposed post-and-beam architecture was influenced by the couple's time spent in Japan, she on a grant and he working for the firm Nikken Sekkei in the early 1990s. It also reflects the architects' experience working for Piano, whose precise buildings celebrate the inherent beauty of structural systems. The framework adheres to an eight-by-eight-foot grid, which is expressed throughout the house in Douglas fir columns and beams, as well as heart of pine timbers, some reclaimed from abandoned factories

Separating
Tall, south-facing windows in the office open onto the cypress deck and trellis that extends along the house's back side.

Working
Hays and Ewing work at identical desks in the center of the office. A long table in front of the expansive window walls provides a place for meetings and extra work space. Shelving and pin-up surfaces are built into the walls.

in New York and milled in Virginia. "The grid is close to the size of tatami mats," explains Ewing, referring to the basis of Japanese proportioning systems. "But we organized the spaces in a very rational, Western way." Bathrooms, closets, and stairs are placed on the north side to create a buffer to the street, while rooms for living, working, and waking face south to take in daylight and views.

Their long-held interest in green architecture led Hays and Ewing to select unconventional building materials aimed at saving energy and natural resources. Walls were constructed from structural insulated panels consisting of a polystyrene foam core sandwiched between oriented strand boards made from waste wood chips. This well-insulated assembly creates a heat-efficient shell that reduces noise and air filtration. Higher efficiency heating and cooling equipment added about a 20 percent premium, Ewing notes, but the costs will be recouped in about four years.

Local Virginia cypress was applied to exterior walls, decking, louvers, and the trellis. Low-maintenance fiber-cement panels clad the north facade, and sustainable-yield lumber was used to frame windows and doors. On the floors, panels of fiber-cement sheathing, called Plycem (typically used for subflooring), were installed in a grid and then stained and waxed to look like leather.

Crisply outlined in wooden planes and lines behind an inscrutable facade, the house and studio convey the serene feeling of a modern Japanese tea house removed from the bustle of city life. Hays and Ewing drew not only on architecture seen during their travels, but also on the Japanese concepts of *ma* (the space between two objects or two edges) and *hashi* (elements that bridge two edges). "Our house is broken into two volumes, and the gap

Gathering
Allison Ewing and Christopher Hays sit in their living room with their two children, Chris and Emily.

between them embodies this concept of *ma*," explains Ewing. "It is the space between the public and private centers of our house, between our work and home activities and between our lives with our children and as a couple."

Hays adds that the house reflects the idea of *hashi* as a bridge between the urban setting of Charlottesville and its more pastoral outskirts. "To carry this further," he relates, "the house is split in two parts with a bridge spanning the entry court." These concepts of *ma* and *hashi* might also well symbolize the design projects now shared by the architects and the connections made between Western and Eastern architecture in their light-filled green house.

LESSONS LEARNED

Follow green design principles to be environmentally responsible. From insulated wall panels to high-efficiency air conditioning and from passive solar heating to recycled timbers, the live/work compound created by Hays and Ewing reflects what architects call sustainable design—meant to conserve energy and natural resources. The U.S. Green Building Council has created benchmarks for achieving such ecofriendly structures under its LEED (Leadership in Energy and Environmental Design) rating system. Benefits of a LEED-certified home include lower utility and water bills and the absence of mold, mildew, and other indoor toxins. For more information, go to www.usgbc.org.

Treat outdoor spaces like indoor rooms. The wood-floored courtyard between the office and the house serves as a foyer, a mud room, a play area for the couple's children, a storage area for bikes, and a place to entertain. It connects to the rear yard and the porch off the living area, allowing plenty of room for a crowd to gather during a party.

Draw design inspiration from other cultures. Hays and Ewing once lived in Japan and applied their knowledge of that country's architecture to create a Zenlike sanctuary. They not only dimensioned their wood-framed structure to mirror the proportions of Japanese houses, they also applied Japanese spatial concepts in both separating and linking home and office.

1 Porch
2 Foyer
3 Kitchen
4 Dining Area
5 Living Area
6 Powder Room
7 Office
8 Sitting Area
9 Bathroom
10 Mechanical
11 Master Bedroom
12 Closet
13 Bridge/Sitting Area
14 Balcony/Play Area
15 Laundry
16 Bedroom
17 Play Loft

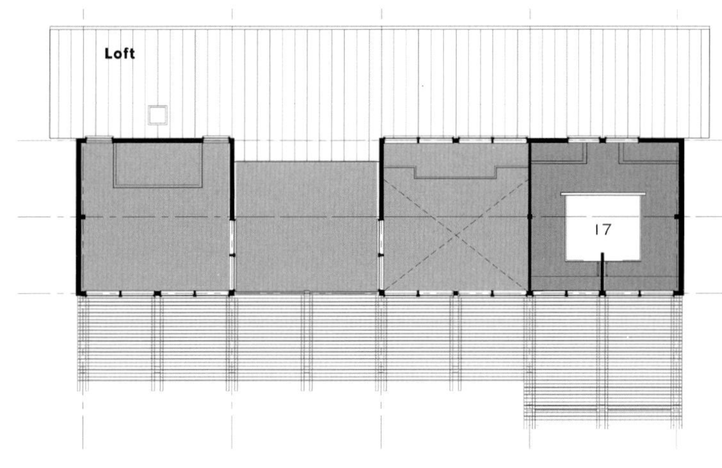

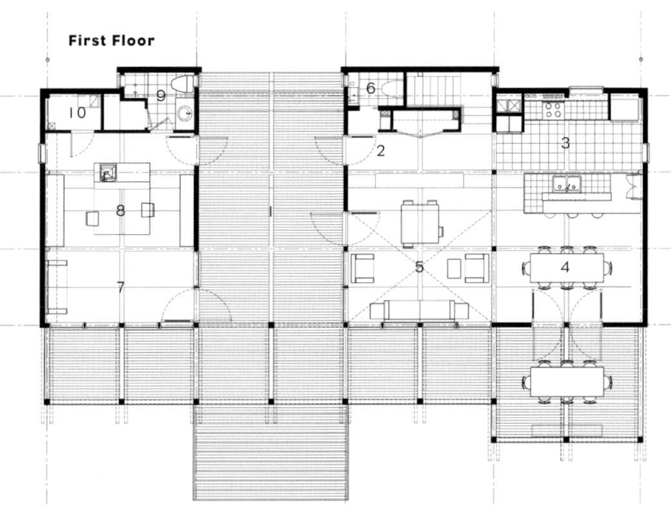

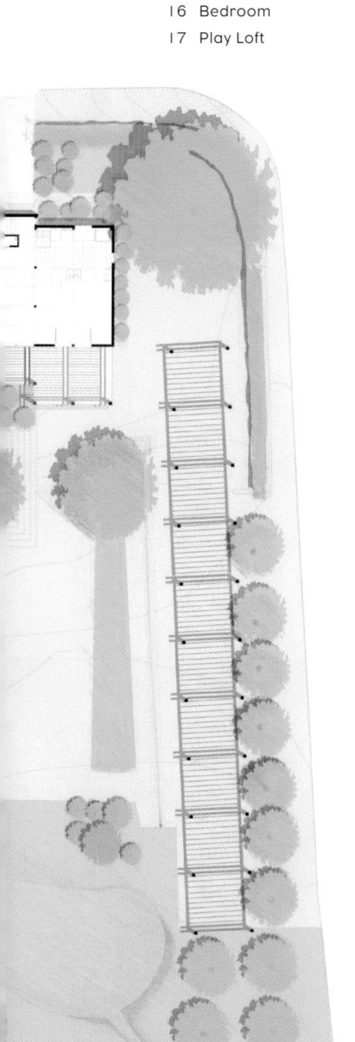

A WHITER SHADE OF PALE

From her pearly white home office, Robin Culbreath forecasts color and design trends for retailers and manufacturers such as Target, Wal-Mart, and 3M. "Because I work around color every day, all day, I wanted my surroundings to be very quiet and calm," states Culbreath. The minimalist, almost monastic house that she shares with her husband, Mitch, a manager at 3M, sits within Jackson Meadow, a new 315-acre development in Marine on St. Croix, one of Minnesota's oldest European settlements.

As are all the buildings in Jackson Meadow, the Culbreaths' home was custom-designed by the award-winning Duluth architect David Salmela, who draws his inspiration from local farm structures and houses, some built by Swedish pioneers. By early 2007 Salmela had designed thirty-four of the sixty-four houses planned for development, all in collaboration with the landscape architect Shane Coen, who lives in the community. The buildings are clustered on only 30 percent of the land; the rest is a nature preserve, protected from development by conservation easements. Although a few utility structures are painted midnight blue, all of the houses are snowy white. The ghostly uniformity is radical, but Salmela insists that he intended the opposite effect. "White is a conservative color that epitomizes rural American architecture, from New England to the Midwest."

Connecting
The bridge connecting office (left) and home (right) is illuminated by a nearly six-foot-square window. It spans a stone patio to create a sheltering canopy over the entrance in the side of the house.

Parking
At the front of the property, two freestanding garages flank the entrance alongside the bridge linking the house and the office. Like the home, they are topped by pitched metal roofs and covered in white-stained clapboard to create the look of farm cottages.

On their first visit to Jackson Meadow, the Culbreaths were immediately drawn to its monochromatic consistency. "It was like a beacon," recalls Robin, who cried at the sight of the alabaster-hued houses. "It had everything I had been looking for from a design standpoint. I knew that this was the place for us." The decision to build a 2,000-square-foot home led her to include an office separate from the main building. "I wanted to work at home but not in the home," she notes. Salmela responded by applying the same simple rules he used for the neighboring houses: a rectangular structure no more than twenty-four feet wide that is covered in white-stained cedar siding and topped by a silvery standing-seam metal roof with a 45-degree pitch. Detached garages, resembling cottages, repeat this architectural vernacular.

The architect deviated only slightly from the formula in shaping Robin's office. Placed over a screened porch, it is separated from the house by a second-level bridge, which frames a gateway to the Culbreaths' property. Vertical battens further distinguish the office from the more conventional clapboard on the home's exterior. Otherwise the buildings and two free-standing garages are unified in their white-painted silhouettes, creating the impression of farm sheds clustered in a meadow.

Working
In her office, Robin Culbreath arranges a dress on a mannequin to demonstrate the latest color trends. A built-in maple desk provides room for several computers and task lighting for freelance employees. Bookcases and files are tucked under the desk to eliminate clutter. A matching table in the center is used for client meetings.

Sculpting

Rather than being enclosed by partitions, the stairway leading down to the basement and up to the second floor was designed as a sculptural element within the open living floor. It is simply separated from the living area by a white screen.

Bridging

House and office are separated by a hallway simply furnished with an Alvar Aalto bench and a rug placed in front of a big window. "I'll sit here talking on the phone and looking at the birds," says Robin Culbreath. "It's a great place to unwind." Rembrandt, the Culbreaths' yellow Labrador, enjoys soaking up the warmth from the sun and the radiant-heated slate floors in the long space.

Robin Culbreath is now one of a dozen Jackson Meadow residents who work at home. They include real estate agents, commercial artists, and business consultants who spend at least part of the work week in their white houses. "My biggest fear was not being taken seriously because I worked at home," admits Culbreath. "Now it's a source of pride. I've had so many people from corporate America walk into this space and say 'I envy you so much'." Their reaction is understandable, given that her second-story work space overlooks preserved field and forest lands through windows more than five feet square. Outside a wood-slatted awning shades the southeast-facing opening, and interior blinds reduce glare on the computer screen. "Mitch calls this the control tower," jokes Robin. "The view is incredible. You don't get that in the typical office cubicle."

Below the windows, a pale maple desk wraps around the room's perimeter and a central table, providing enough space to accommodate freelance employees and client meetings. Bookcases and files are tucked under the

Living
Most of the furniture in the open living-dining area is by the Danish designer Hans Wegner, including his Wishbone chairs and dining table, purchased especially for this house. Floor-to-ceiling windows fill the interior with daylight and warmth during Minnesota's cold winters.

Sleeping
Framed daisies above a floral-patterned Marimekko comforter and pillows brighten the Culbreaths' pale bedroom. "It's easier to change the color scheme with bedding than painting the walls," says Robin Culbreath, who rotates the decor with the seasons.

desk to eliminate clutter. Bentwood stools designed by the Finnish architect Alvar Aalto can be pulled up to the table and work surfaces as needed. A rainbow-striped dress mannequin, used to demonstrate trends to retailers, provides some of the only color.

Next to the office, the long bridge leading to the staircase down to the main living level serves as a decompression chamber. It is simply furnished with a wooden Aalto bench, which faces the view through a huge window. "I stop before leaving this breezeway," discloses Culbreath. "It's a place to disengage mentally and emotionally from work."

The ground floor is one light-filled room. Tall windows, shaded on the exterior by a bracketed wooden canopy, face the preserved meadow and trees. Only a low partition divides the dining and living area from the kitchen and the family room. "It's as open as Mies van der Rohe's Farnsworth House," Salmela points out. "It feels as if you're sitting in a pristine field. There's an overwhelming connection to the outdoors." The two bedrooms on the second floor are similarly oriented to the views through smaller square windows.

Reflecting the home's Scandinavian sensibility, the furnishings in the living spaces and the owners' bedroom are mostly reproductions of midcentury-modern pieces by the Danish designer Hans Wegner. The furniture is kept to a bare minimum to avoid drawing attention away from the clean-lined architecture. Radiant-heated floors are covered in greenish-gray slate, but all the walls are painted white to match the pristine exterior and the neighboring houses. "If you have to have a purple door," cautions Culbreath, "Jackson Meadow isn't the place for you."

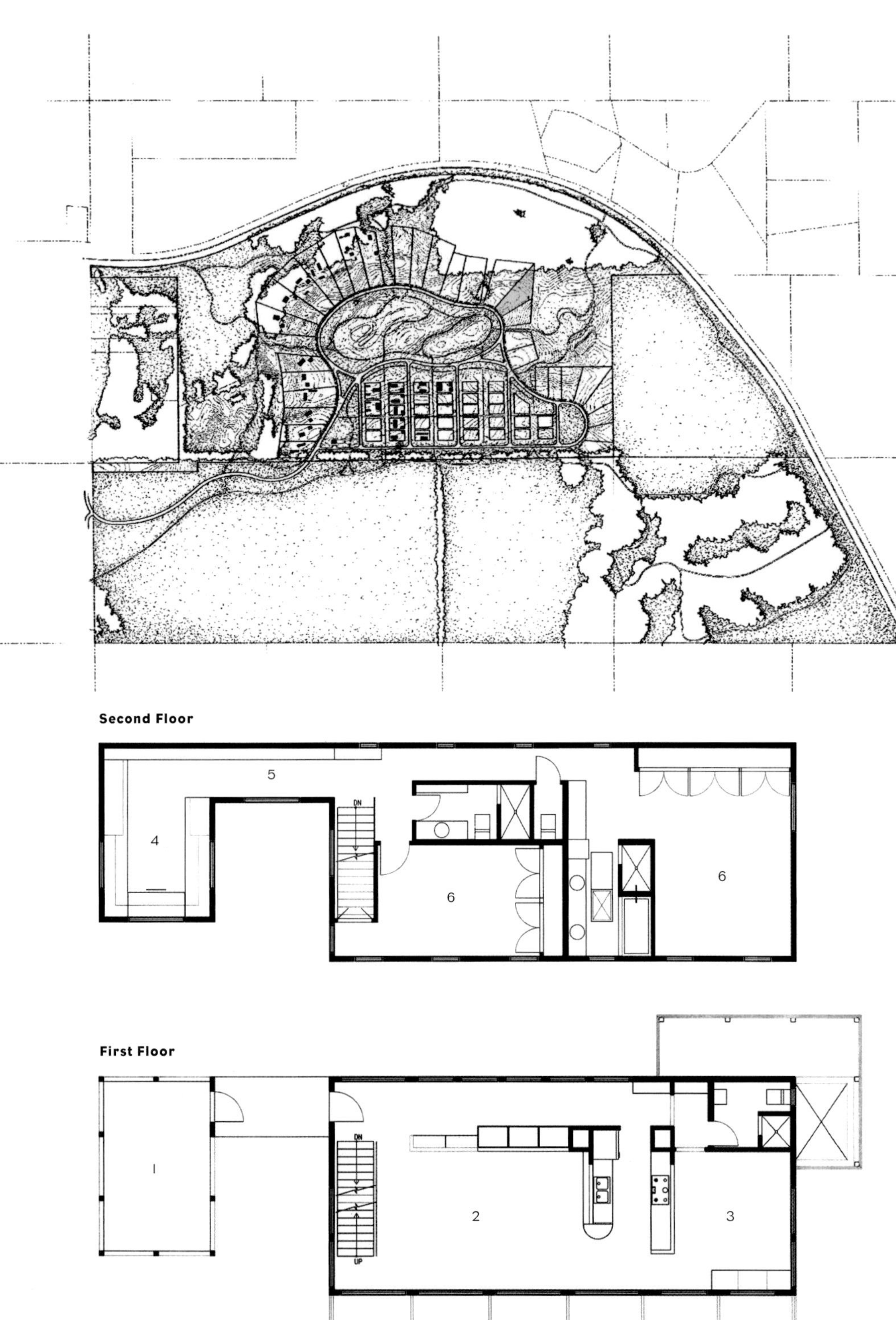
Second Floor
5
DN
4
6
6
First Floor
DN
1
2
3
UP

Grouping
Salmela designed the Culbreaths' all-white garages, towerlike studio, and house to resemble a grouping of farm sheds. Large glass panes in the office (center), perched above a screened porch, and the ground-floor living spaces (lower right) are shaded by wooden awnings supported by brackets. To provide privacy, windows in the upper-story bedrooms are smaller.

1 Porch
2 Living/Dining Area
3 Kitchen
4 Office
5 Bridge
6 Bedroom

LESSONS LEARNED

Don't forget the land in your conservation plans. Clustered developments like Jackson Meadow preserve open space for all residents and visitors to enjoy inside and out. Townhouses and multifamily dwellings also make economical use of the increasingly scarce land available for building.

Elevate your work space to increase separation. Robin Culbreath's office is housed in a pavilion pulled away from the house's main block and positioned on the second level over a screened porch. This location provides distance from the ground-floor living spaces, helping eliminate distractions while providing inspirational views. "It's conducive to creative thinking," she declares.

Use a hallway to decompress. After her work day, Culbreath pauses in the bridge connecting her office and home before entering her domestic space. "It's a place to disengage from work," she maintains. Instead of cluttering up the hallway with storage cabinets and furniture, she installed a single wooden bench for contemplating the bucolic views.

Embrace whiteness for calm. A forecaster of color and design trends, Culbreath is constantly surrounded by a rainbow of hues. To create a sense of serenity, she painted her office and living spaces in the same pure white as the home's exterior. "I mostly use color as an accent in the bed linens," she comments. "That allows me to decorate seasonally with darker bedding in the winter and yellow and pinks in the summer."

OPEN 24/7

Basements—dark and damp subterranean spaces cut off from the rest of the house—are often the last resort for those working at home. Not so in the rectilinear brick dwelling designed by the Croatian-born architect Zoka Zola in a neighborhood northwest of Chicago's Loop. Her office, sunk four feet below the ground, is bright, high ceilinged, and accessible from the front door. Oversized double-hung windows fill the two-story recessed studio with daylight and framed views of street activity.

In this narrow corner house, Zola has overturned conventional ideas about open-plan living. "I was looking to construct a space that was open in a different way than we assume 'open' to be," she explains. "Not by putting in large glass surfaces or knocking down walls, but by creating the feeling that you can exit from the house or change your environment." Instead of designing an unencumbered, horizontal expanse like a loft, the architect stretched the space vertically to create a series of interlocking rooms of different heights linked by an open staircase.

Fitting in
Zoka Zola clad her stripped-down live/work dwelling in red brick to harmonize with the Chicago neighborhood's historic townhouses. "The difference is, our house is more open and connected to the street," she notes. Oversized double-hung windows on the north facade dwarf the door yet fill the basement office and the upper-story living room with sunshine. The garage extends under the library and the bathroom, leaving room for a tall, enclosed terrace off the living room.

Working
Zola's studio is bright and lofty despite being sunk four feet below the ground. The long platform at right, which hides storage, connects the garage and the entrance to the stairs and the studio. It extends to the rear of the house, where the architect plans to enlarge her office space in the future. The work tables, topped by sustainable strawboard, were assembled for the architect by Home Depot.

Simplifying
Rising up through the two-story space is an open staircase leading to the living and bedroom levels. Metal railings curve around the landings. Both stairs and floors are covered in the same white oak applied to the window frames. "If I had introduced more textures and colors, it would have been too cluttered, given all the changes in levels," explains the architect.

Living
A Womb chair by Eero Saarinen occupies one end of the seldom-used living room. A door in the glass wall opens onto an outdoor terrace overlooking the street. Because the home is only eighteen feet wide, daylight penetrates deep into the interior to reduce reliance on artificial sources.

"I designed it knowing that I would spend a lot of time here," acknowledges Zola, who built the house soon after moving from London to Chicago with her husband, Peter Pfanner, a product designer for Motorola. From the start, the architect planned residential spaces private enough for her family (she is now the mother of a young son) as well as a studio big enough for several employees. "It is a small lot, and it made the most sense to put the office on the ground," she says. But that would have meant sacrificing living space or building a three-story house, which according to the local building code would have required two staircases instead of one. So Zola positioned the workroom partially below grade to create what is officially considered a basement, given that more than half of its square footage is underground.

In reality the "basement" is a twenty-two-foot-high sunny space, warmed by radiant heating in the floor. "It anchors the whole house," notes Zola. "If it was on street level, we would feel exposed." From the front door, a platform extends along the edge of the sunken studio to the rear of the house. This bridge provides access to stairs descending to the workroom and to the main staircase winding up through the house. From a landing with a powder room above the studio, stairs lead to an intermediate level, used as a library and a storage area, that is just shy of seven feet tall. This low-ceilinged level essentially acts as a buffer between the sunken studio and the second-floor living space. From there a few more steps lead to the kitchen and the dining area, which sit over the two-story studio. More stairs go to three bedrooms and two bathrooms on the top floor.

Outdoor rooms such as the covered terrace off the living room make the 3,000-square-foot house feel bigger than it really is. "We have business meetings there in warm weather," reports Zola. "My husband brings people home nearly every evening and we entertain them there." A balcony off the kitchen also provides a place for a meeting or a meal.

To create continuity, Zola painted all rooms white and used white oak, a material common to Chicago houses, for floors, cabinets, stair treads, and window frames. "Different materials and colors would have cluttered up the space," she insists. Both paint and wood sealers applied throughout the rooms are environmentally friendly—part of a larger conservation strategy for the structure.

Because the home is only eighteen feet wide, sunshine from big windows on either side of the studio penetrates deep into the interior to provide natural light and heat. Cooling cross-ventilation, shading from tall cottonwood trees

Gathering
A sunny eat-in kitchen is off the open staircase that winds up through the house. Nearby Zoka Zola enjoys the views through the kitchen's generous corner windows. A balcony off the space provides a place for outdoor meals.

on the property, and a heat-reflective white roof reduce the need for summertime air conditioning. Among its other environmentally green features are low-energy appliances and bathroom vent fans on timers. A high-efficiency commercial boiler heats water for bathing and dishwashing as well as for the radiant heating that extends within the floors as well as to the bathtub and shower. The home's urban location and integral architecture office also contribute to its environmental benefits. "There is life in the house twenty-four hours a day," notes Zola, who is a certified LEED (energy leadership) designer. "We are only two and a half miles from downtown and keep a Prius in the garage."

A 1,500-square-foot addition will eventually be built at the rear to provide more work space. Like the main structure, it too will envelop unadorned, uncompromised space. "The site requires a tough cookie," says the architect of her efforts to both embrace and transform Chicago traditions.

Meeting
The terrace off the living room, with its generous fireplace, is used for meetings. "The knowledge that there is some other place to go is built into the space," Zola points out. "You are always aware that there is a world outside the house." The architect carefully chose the house's wall color so it would not be too stark. "I tried ten different shades of white before I got the right one."

Looking out
On the top floor, views of Chicago's skyline stretch out through the window walls. By pushing the narrow building to the corner of the lot, Zola was able to allow room for an L-shaped side garden that winds around the back and serves as a shortcut through the block.

Bathing
The house's openness extends to the top-floor master bathroom, where a window offers an expansive side view. Radiant floor heating, fed by water from a high-efficiency commercial boiler, extends under the tub as part of a larger energy-conservation strategy.

East-West Section

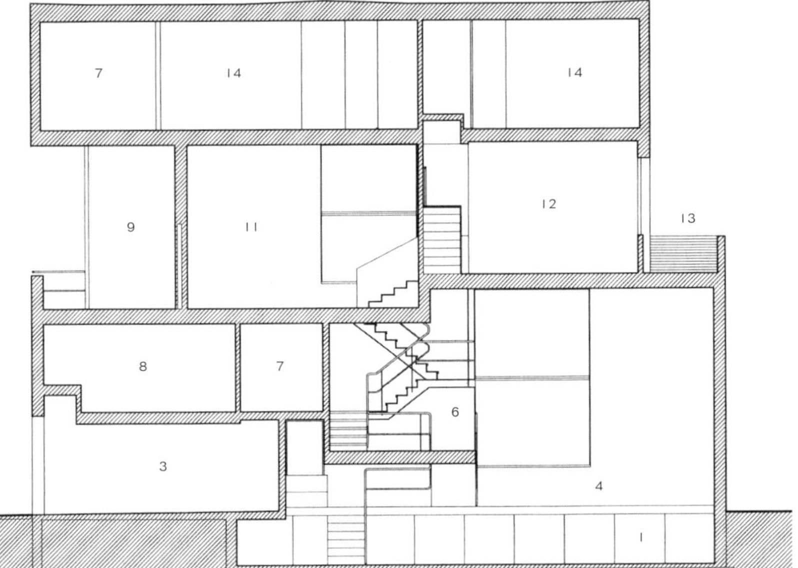

North-South Section

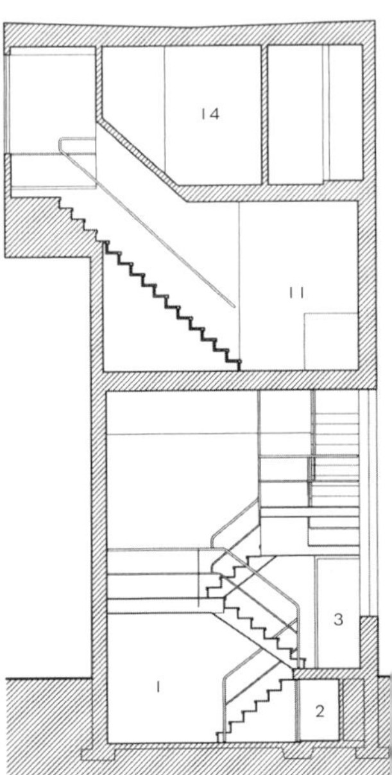

LESSONS LEARNED

Think up, not out. One way of adding more space on tight urban lots is to go vertical. Zoka Zola took advantage of high ceilings to insert half levels for a powder room, a library, and storage spaces. Even removing part of a floor can open up a basement or a lower level room to light and air.

Reduce utility bills through design. Zola maximized daylight and ventilation by creating a narrow footprint with large side windows. Cool breezes through white-painted rooms, shading from trees, and a heat-reflective roof lessen the need for air conditioning during the summer.

Take your business outdoors. Use porches and balconies as places for working and meeting as well as for off-hours entertaining and relaxing. Zola transformed her living room terrace into a welcoming spot for clients and colleagues by building in a bench and a fireplace.

Relaxing
The architect Zoka Zola and her husband, Peter Pfanner, a product designer, enjoy their terraces for work and play.

Second Floor

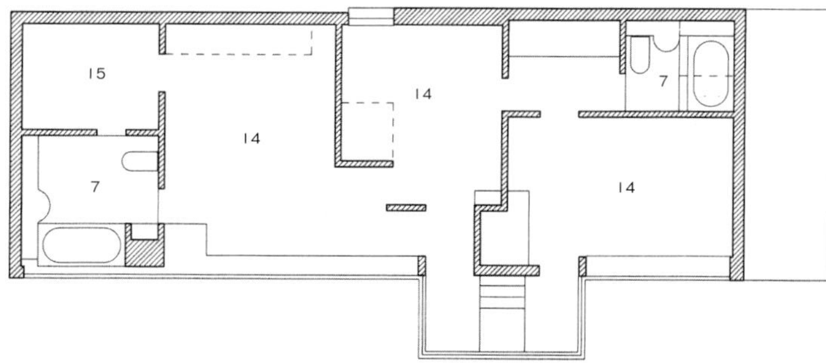

First Floor

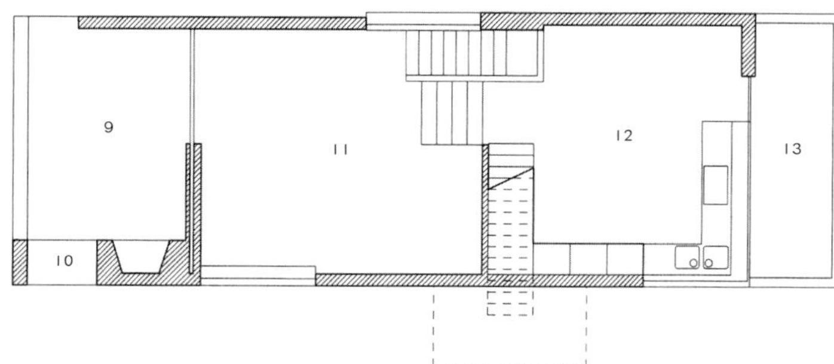

1 Studio
2 Storage
3 Garage
4 Entrance Platform
5 Open to Below
6 Entrance Hall
7 Bathroom
8 Library
9 Sunroom
10 Bench
11 Living Room
12 Kitchen/Dining Area
13 Balcony
14 Bedroom
15 Closet

Entrance Level

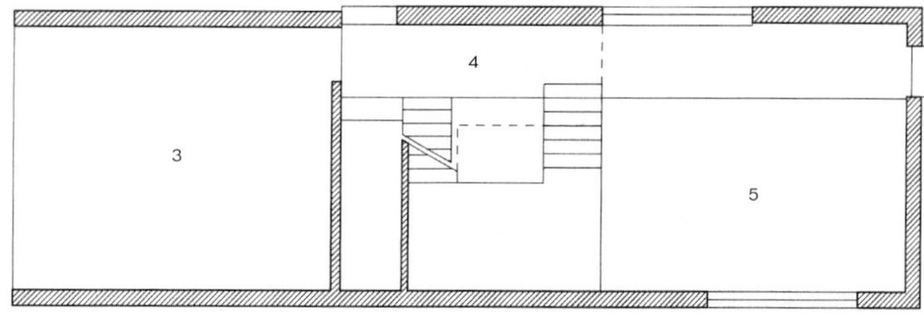

Basement Level

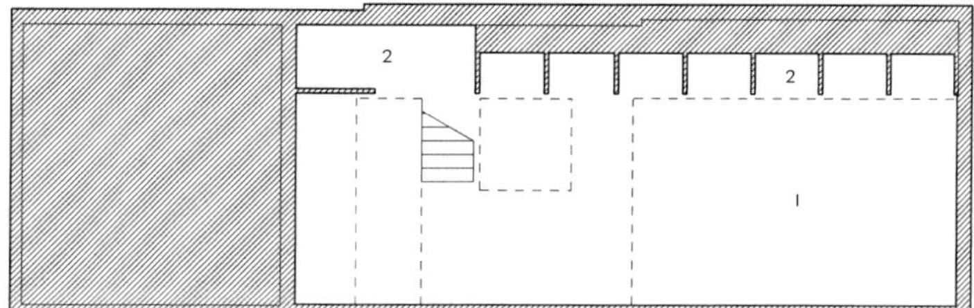

INSIDE OUT, OUTSIDE IN

When he is not working in Los Angeles, the bicoastal architect Scott Hughes can usually be found in Hobe Sound, Florida, a tony community on a barrier island north of Palm Beach. In the vacation house he shares with his wife, Lisa, a documentary filmmaker, Hughes maintains an office in which he designs his Florida projects. No need for California dreamin' in the Sunshine State: the couple's low-slung, L-shaped residence, wrapped around a swimming pool, would look right at home in L.A.

In designing the house, Hughes took inspiration from the California modernism of Richard Neutra, particularly the Austrian émigré's 1946 Palm Springs house for Edgar Kaufmann, the Pittsburgh department-store magnate who had earlier commissioned Frank Lloyd Wright to design his country estate, Fallingwater. "I admire Neutra's ability to handle light and to create openness," reflects Hughes. "His skill was to bring the outside in and the inside out."

Shading
Inspired by Richard Neutra's modern houses, Scott Hughes wrapped his low-slung, L-shaped house and elevated guest "motel" (left) around a swimming pool. The living spaces face the water through floor-to-ceiling sliding-glass doors. The pool deck is shaded by a generous overhang. Grass planted on the roof helps insulate the house while providing a verdant view from the second-story office.

Like the Kaufmann house in Palm Springs, this Florida retreat is planar and largely transparent, using overhanging roofs to provide shade from the ever-present sunshine. The sides facing the neighboring properties and the street are sheathed in gray-green stucco, while the frontage along the sixty-four-foot-long pool is enclosed by huge sliding glass doors that open onto a terrace at water's edge. Fronting this movable boundary are a kitchen, dining room, living area, and master bedroom, all strung along the length of the pool. To enhance a feeling of spaciousness, the interior is divided by partitions that stop short of the ceiling. An open hallway is placed next to the perimeter glass to link the rooms while providing a clear view through the house and making the interiors feel airy and expansive.

Perpendicular to the living wing is what the couple calls the "Motel 6," a two-story block housing the garage and, on the upper story, guest suites for visiting family and friends, plus a lounge. "The idea was to give visitors a sense of privacy and independence," explains Scott Hughes. The three suites and the lounge are connected by an outdoor corridor that terminates in a staircase leading down to the pool.

Access to the second-floor rooms is provided inside the main house by stairs located between the dining room and the kitchen, which serves as the hub of the house. "The kitchen has become the center of the house, where everyone comes together," reports Lisa Hughes. "We rarely use the living room." An eating nook at the end of the kitchen focuses on a flat-screen television. Just outside the room, a terrace under the upper story of the "motel" provides a sheltered spot for outdoor dining.

Living
In the main living area, partitions stop short of the ceiling to enhance a light, airy feeling. The poolside wall serves as a long hallway linking the kitchen to the dining area, living room, and master bedroom. The dark print on the wall is Jasper Johns's *Figure 6* from his 1968 black numeral series. Brad Dunning custom designed the ultrasuede green sofa under the staircase, which leads to the office and divides the public rooms from the private master suite at the end.

Fitting in
In contrast to the glass-lined pool side, the street facades are sheathed in gray-green stucco. Shutters protect the windows of the upper-story guest bedrooms from harsh sunlight. The house is entered through a large, pivoting steel door flanked by a low onyx bench.

Painting

In the dining area is a 1971 abstract by Thomas Downing, and between the sofas is Gene Davis's *Pale Pulse* from 1964. Le Corbusier's LC7 chairs are arranged around a Carlo Scarpa-designed dining table, while a Warren Platner table sits between Linea club chairs in the living area. The stairs lead to the bedrooms.

To leave space for the pool courtyard, the architect had to push the main house and guest wing to the boundaries of the half-acre property. That left little room to add an office where he could meet clients and design his residential and institutional projects. "Because we had built out to the max, there was no more footprint available," explains Lisa Hughes. "So we went up."

The office sits in its own pavilion atop the master suite, next to the flat, poured-in-place concrete roof over the living spaces. Scott Hughes shaped the roof so that it could be fitted with a waterproof membrane to hold soil and grass. "In order to be more ecologically friendly, we planted some grass to create insulation and make it a bit more interesting to look at from the second floor," he notes. This green roof provides a pleasant view from upper-story rooms in the "motel" while insulating the house to save energy costs, absorbing pollutants, and blocking out noise.

The office, 17 by 34 feet, is reached from a staircase positioned between the living room's television nook and the master suite to separate the public and private parts of the house. "Originally it was supposed to be a shared office for the two of us," says Lisa of the second-story room. "But Scott sees it strictly as his domain." Still, between the desks in the master bedroom and the kitchen, plus the meeting space in the "motel" lounge, there is plenty of work space in the house for both wife and husband.

As on the floor below, the office overlooks the pool and ficus trees in the yard through south-facing windows. "The glass is sloped to give it the look of an airport control tower," notes Scott, who commands the room from

Sleeping
Each guest room in the "Motel 6" features a different twist on 1950s and 1960s decor. The artist Mark Bennett's blueprints of homes featured on the hit television shows *Lost in Space* and *Perry Mason* hang above twin beds by George Nelson. In the master bedroom, the PK 24 woven cane chaise from 1965 by the Danish designer Poul Kjaerholm is paired with a Duxiana bed that has a custom-upholstered headboard. A tall, narrow window overlooks a corner of the back garden.

a built-in, 15-foot-long desk. The angled glass, he explains, also allowed the roof overhang to be shorter while still providing shade from the afternoon sun. The ceiling slopes upward to the glass to direct the eye toward the view and reduce the height of the north side facing the neighbors. In the lower part of the office near the entrance is a space for meetings, arranged with midcentury-modern Charles Eames office chairs pulled up to a conference table.

To help them furnish the house with the appropriate modern flair, the Hugheses tapped the Los Angeles interior designer Brad Dunning, who blended midcentury classics with contemporary and custom pieces. "Lisa and I needed a sounding board, and we felt that Brad's eye was similar to our own," comments Scott. "The furniture is intended to look as light and clean as the lines of the house itself." White walls and ivory terrazzo on the floors and stairs, flecked with mother-of-pearl and marble chips, reinforce the casual, tropical feeling throughout the rooms.

Since completing the home and office, the architect has used them as a calling card to secure commissions and persuade his clients that modern architecture can be livable, especially in Florida. "It is beneficial for people to come here in order to visualize the detail and massing of what I do," asserts Hughes. "My residential clients often say, 'Let's do it like Scott's house'."

Working
Set apart from the residential spaces above the master bedroom, Scott Hughes's Florida office commands the tropical scene like an airport control tower. The glass angles outward to meet the overhang of the grassy roof, providing plenty of natural light as well as shade when needed.

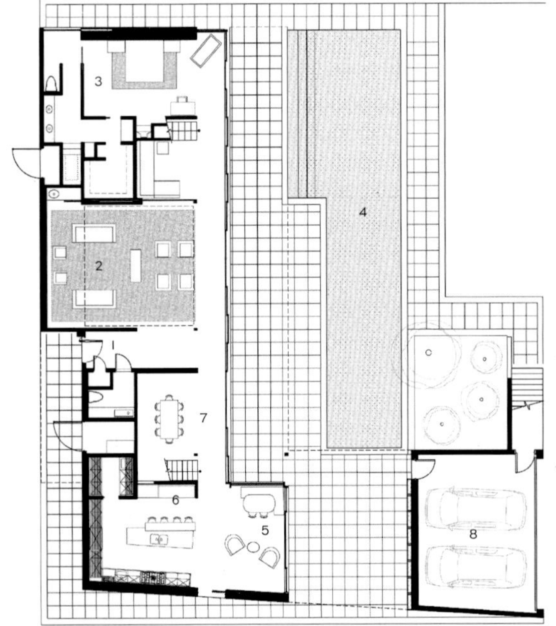

First Floor

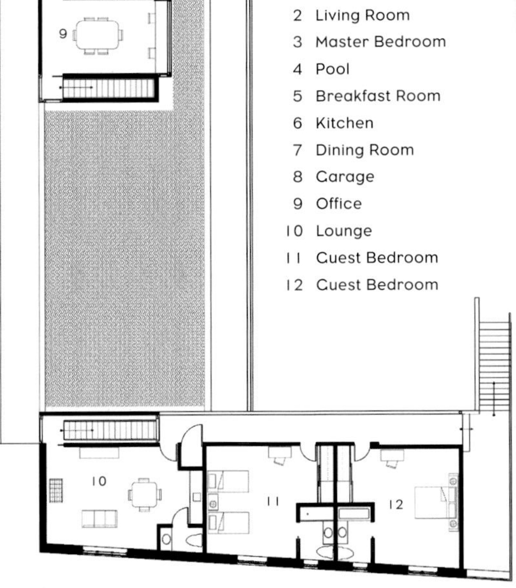

Second Floor

LESSONS LEARNED

Green roofs don't grow themselves. Before planting a roof with low-maintenance grass, sedum, or wildflowers, make sure that the structure is protected from moisture and can support the garden's weight. Check out www.greenroofs.com for resources and information.

Incorporate the hallway into the rooms. Instead of enclosing the corridor that extends along the side of the house next to the pool, Scott Hughes treated this open passageway as part of the living and dining rooms to save space and make the interiors seem larger. Partitions that do not reach the ceiling also increase the feeling of spaciousness.

Use a staircase to sequester private from public spaces. The stairs leading up to Hughes's office divide the master bedroom from the living spaces, providing both physical and acoustical separation yet allowing all the rooms to remain within the house's main block.

Build in a desk next to a window. Space in this one-room office was saved by extending a Corian countertop under the windows at the front. The 15-foot-long work surface tapers from 30 to 24 inches deep to fit into a structural recess. A sloped window supplies abundant daylight to illuminate the work surface, reducing the need for artificial lighting.

LITTLE HOUSE ON THE PRAIRIE

From the approach down a long driveway, the sod-topped house almost disappears into the surrounding grasses. "It fits into the landscape perfectly," relates its owner, Jon O'Neal, a screenwriter who is also a physician. "You see the grass roof first, and then the house appears. It's amazing to sit inside and watch turkeys fly over the cornfield or thunderstorms roll in."

Dubbed the "Kansas Longhouse," this one-story shed outside Lawrence, Kansas, is the modern-day equivalent of the little house on the prairie. Located on an eight-acre parcel, it was designed to withstand the region's tornados, hot summers, and snowy winters—and save energy in the process. With a team from his office, the architect Dan Rockhill built the house as a speculative venture and then sold it to O'Neal in 2004. "It was an opportunity to pursue our interests in regional buildings without the constraints of a client," acknowledges Rockhill.

Disappearing
From the rear, this Kansas longhouse is entered through a door tucked into the side of the covered breezeway between the limestone-clad living quarters (left) and the metal-paneled garage (right). The porch provides a sheltered spot for outdoor dining. Grass planted on the roof visually blends into the surrounding prairie so that, from a distance, the house almost disappears.

Inspiration for the 150-by-24-foot structure came from Native American longhouses, homestead dwellings, and farm sheds typical of the area. "Like those buildings, it's a long, thin form that takes advantage of the southern exposure to bring in light and to heat the interior," explains the architect. "On the north side, high windows exhaust the air flow. It's the way chicken coops were built. All we did was borrow from the guys who came before us."

Well, hardly. Rockhill put a contemporary spin on the old henhouse by sheathing the wood-framed building in painted steel and bolting slabs of local limestone onto the metal. Steel louvers shade the nearly all-glass south wall, and custom metal brackets support the overhanging roof, now covered in insulating sod. "We were enamored of the idea of slicing out the prairie grass, moving it to the side while we built, and putting it back on top," comments the architect, who constructs his designs with a team from his firm. "The problem is, prairie grass is really deep and needs at least eight to twelve inches of substrate." Instead fescue was planted over a green roof system; volunteer prairie grasses—and weeds—have subsequently taken root.

The environmentally friendly design appealed to O'Neal, who was returning to Kansas from film school in Los Angeles. "My goal was to have a writing retreat in the country were I could create regionally based films," he admits.

Conserving
Large windows on the south side of the 150-by-24-foot home bring in daylight during the winter when the sun is lower. In the summer, projecting steel louvers shade the glass from higher rays.

Working
Jon O'Neal writes his film scripts at a U-shaped desk in one of two adaptable rooms at the house's center. Like the rest of the structure, the view is oriented to the prairie outside the tall south-facing windows.

"This house is inspiring for doing that." His scripts so far include *Casino Rez*, a film noir about unsolved murders on an Indian reservation, written at a large, U-shaped desk in the center of the house. Rockhill designed the space as one of two adaptable rooms enclosed by pivoting doors that could be used as extra bedrooms, guest quarters, an exercise area, or offices. "When we designed the house, we didn't know who would end up buying it, so we built in as much flexibility as possible," he explains.

After moving in, O'Neal removed the doors so the room would connect to its surroundings, especially to views of the prairie outside the window. "It opens up the house from the central core. I can turn my head and look out at the layering of green grass, gray farmland, and green trees—planes of color that look like something Milton Avery would have painted," muses the screenwriter, who serves part time at a local hospital. "To work in a space that's inspiring helps build your own creativity."

Relaxing
A chaise pulled up to the south-facing window wall provides a place to contemplate the prairie. Birch-veneered wall paneling and pine window frames maintain a light, airy feeling throughout the interior.

Anchoring the ends of the longhouse are the main living space and the bedroom. From a breezeway between the garage and the house, the front door opens directly into the open living-dining-kitchen area, which is fitted

with a projector and a pull-down screen used for nighttime screenings. Past the office and adjacent bathrooms is the master bedroom, where O'Neal wakes with the sun pouring in through floor-to-ceiling windows.

All the enclosed rooms—bathrooms, closets, flex spaces—are located in the center of the house, allowing for long, open hallways along the perimeter. The spaces include a necessity in this Wizard-of-Oz country, a tornado shelter, off the bedroom. The setback rooms allow sunshine to shoot straight across the narrow interior during winter months, heating the rooms and reducing utility bills. "In January, I have to wear shorts it's so warm," reports O'Neal, who also appreciates the radiant heating in the concrete floors.

In the summer, when the sun is higher, light is blocked by steel louvers projecting over the south-facing windows; breezes cool the narrow interior. Air entering from these windows flows through the interior to exit through clerestory windows on the more solid, northern side of the house. This long facade is shielded by the slope of a hill that protects it from gusty winds and is further insulated by Ikea cabinets lining the length of its interior wall. The storage is particularly welcome, notes O'Neal, because the house has no basement.

The ceiling is an inversion of the gabled sod roof, slanting upward from the interior to the perimeter. It conceals a generous attic space below the roof for heating and electrical equipment. Accented by concealed cove lighting, the angled ceiling also serves to accentuate the south-facing window wall and direct the view outward to the prairie and its changing weather. Observes O'Neal, "It's the only house I've ever lived in that is more beautiful when it's raining or snowing."

Dining
In the kitchen and dining area, the glass-fronted kitchen cabinets and island, birch-veneered plywood paneling, and pine window frames maintain a light, airy feeling. The hallway along the southern perimeter is left open to maximize daylight.

Sleeping and washing up
A conventional sash window brings morning light into the master bedroom. Just outside, the Rockhill-designed sink and mirror are mounted in front of the window to offer uninterrupted prairie views. Partitions that stop short of the ceiling allow sunlight from the south-facing windows to filter deep into the interior.

Viewing
The end of the open living area is a home theater with comfortable lounge chairs in front of a pull-down screen.

Grazing
Inspired by Native American longhouses and settler homesteads, the architect Dan Rockhill designed this work/live space to take advantage of sunlight and breezes. Under its overhanging grass roof, metal louvers on the south wall naturally shade the windows.

Sheltering
Because there is no basement, a bedroom closet is enclosed in concrete block walls to double as a tornado shelter.

LESSONS LEARNED

Site to save energy. The architect Dan Rockhill increased the energy efficiency of this longhouse through solar orientation. Tall, south-facing windows capture direct light during the winter, when the sun is low; in the summer, when the sun is higher, they are shaded by metal awnings. Breezes flow through the narrow interior to exit through windows on the north side, which is nestled into a sloping hillside to buffer the winds.

Consider design-build. "Few people in Lawrence like modern architecture," admits Rockhill, "so I do what I call 'design-build extreme.'" In contrast to typical custom-home construction, where the architect and contractor are hired separately, a design-build firm offers both architectural services and construction supervision. Rockhill takes this one step further in both designing and building his projects, without the help of outside subcontractors, to ensure that his unconventional details are executed with the utmost quality.

Center work space in the house. Jon O'Neal turned one of his home's middle flex spaces into an office that is both private yet connected to the rest of the house. "A lot of people don't think about being inspired by their workplace, but it's important because you spend so much time there," O'Neal declares. Although centrally located, the office is flanked by a guest room, a bathroom, and a closet that visually and acoustically separate the work space from the bedroom and living space occupying opposite ends of the longhouse.

1 Carage
2 Living Area
3 Kitchen
4 Mechanical
5 Office
6 Shelter
7 Laundry
8 Master Bedroom
9 Bathroom
10 Master Bathroom
11 Closet

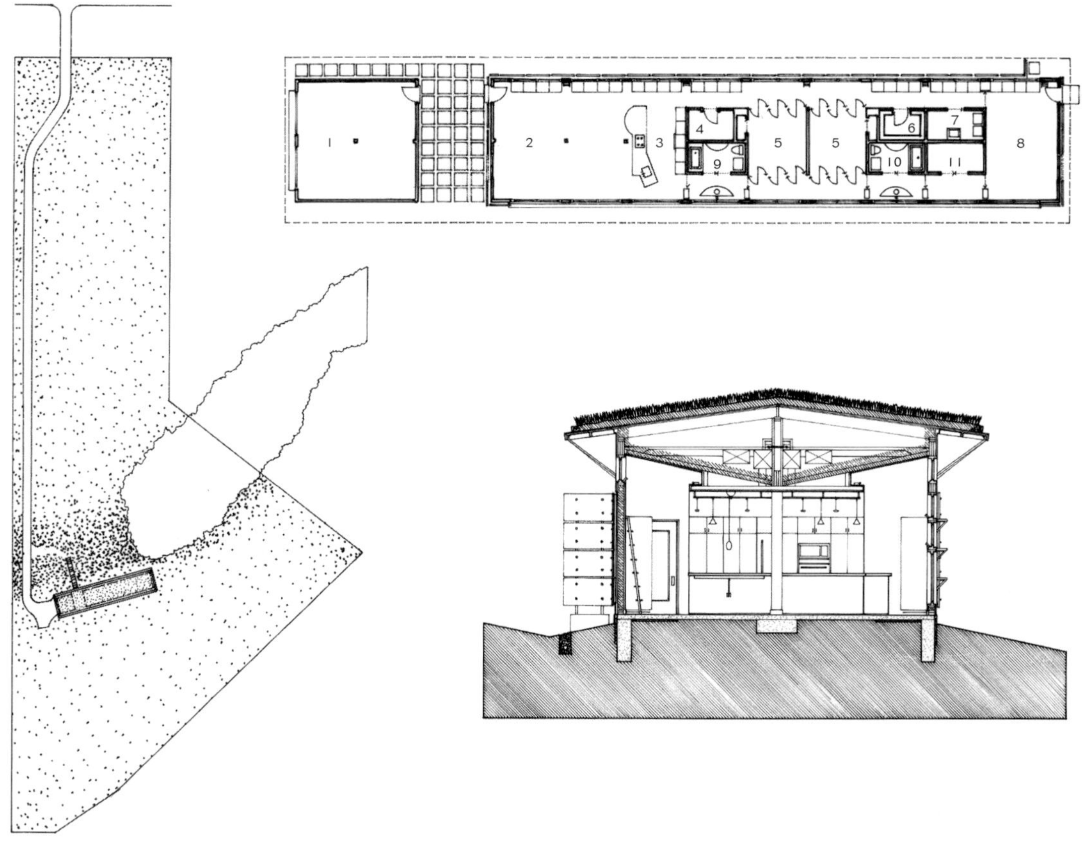

YANKEE INGENUITY

The Boston architect Elizabeth Gibb jump-started her own practice by designing a house for her family with a ground-floor work area for herself. "I knew that I didn't want to pay rent for office space," says Gibb. Instead she added 545 square feet below the home's living quarters that can pay rent to her. The long, narrow space next to the garage offers not only a sunny, multipurpose room but also a kitchen, a bathroom, and a separate entrance. "In the future, it could become a rental apartment, an au-pair unit, or an in-law suite for our parents," observes the architect.

Gibb's entrepreneurial approach to her own real estate began with researching city tax records to find an affordable property in Cambridge near Harvard University, where her husband, Markus Meister, is a neurobiology professor. "We wanted to buy a property that allowed us to renovate and add square footage without the need for a zoning variance," she explains. "After an initial search for properties that were owned for thirty-plus years, had

Interpreting
Elizabeth Gibb, the architect and owner, designed a modernist interpretation of the triple-deckers common to her Cambridge, Massachusetts, neighborhood.

Prefabricating
The architect's father, James Gibb, fabricated the staircase's aluminum and stainless-steel components and then shipped them in pieces from his home workshop in Florida for assembly on site.

Living
Instead of positioning the living room at the front, Gibb moved it to the sunnier rear of the house, next to the dining area and the kitchen. Above this two-story room is a balcony with tall bookcases that serves as a library and a play area for the couple's children.

Dining
As viewed from the kitchen, the living-dining space opens onto a deck for outdoor entertaining and relaxing. Clerestory windows positioned at the top of the southeast-facing wall supply sunlight during the winter.

Cooking
Because of its openness to the livng area, the kitchen is designed with the same attention to detail as the rest of the space. To allow space to flow around it, the white cabinet wall does not touch the ceiling.

a paid-off mortgage, and were in need of work, we sent out 250 letters asking selected owners if they would be interested in selling their house. We had only one reply, from the owner of the house that we eventually bought."

The two-story clapboard house purchased by Gibb and Meister was located within a neighborhood of triple-deckers, duplexes, apartment buildings, and single-family homes, built mostly in the early 1900s. Because local zoning permitted such multifamily dwellings, Gibb was allowed to incorporate a separate apartment into her home. But renovation of the existing residence was out of the question. "The foundation had sunk about a foot on the west side," relates Gibb. "I did extensive research with geotechnical engineers to try to figure out why. That's when we discovered that this area had been used for mining clay to make bricks. The clay pit under the house had been filled with construction debris and not property compacted." After the sinking dwelling was razed, a structure of concrete caissons, grade beams, and retaining walls was erected to ensure the new home's stability.

Mindful of the neighborhood architecture, Gibb designed a taut, modernist interpretation of the surrounding triple-deckers. "I wanted it to look like it was built in 2004. But the mass and scale fit in with every other house on the street," she notes. "I made some references to their porches and bays but reinterpreted them in a contemporary way." Instead of sheathing the exterior in conventional clapboard or shingles, the architect chose durable, low-maintenance exotic hardwoods (all from sustainable forests) and left them unpainted. Tongue-and-groove siding of Australian jarrah, a species

Designing
Gibb's office incorporates a kitchenette past the bookshelves so that it could be converted into a rental apartment. The narrow space—just 11½ feet wide—is illuminated by windows along one side to make it appear larger. "Spaces can feel bigger if they have proper light and views to the outdoors," Gibb points out. "A glass wall can make it feel more open," she adds.

of eucalyptus, covers the first two levels, and wood-composite paneling called Parklex clads the topmost story and soffits under the overhanging eaves. German-made windows are framed in mahogany, and structural columns and outdoor decks are made of ipe, a Brazilian ironwood.

Gibb fleshed out the design in a bedroom-turned-office in her previous residence, a three-level townhouse, which inspired a similar vertical separation of functions in the new home. Instead of positioning the living room to front the street, she moved it to the sunnier, south-facing rear of the house next to the kitchen and the deck. Above this two-story room is a balcony with tall bookcases that also serves as a library and a play area; paired front bedrooms accommodate the couple's teenage daughter, Michela, and son, Florian. On the third floor are master and guest bedrooms and an office at the back for Meister with its own terrace. The levels are connected by a staircase that projects from the side of the house.

The building mediates a slope so the basement apartment extends above ground at the rear. It is in this raised area where Gibb has her office, which she reaches from a staircase inside the house near the front door. "I can work at any time and not waste time going back and forth to an office," she comments. The stairs lead down to a mechanical room with a door that can be locked should the architect decide to rent the unit. "I don't want to feel like I'm at home when I'm working. There is nothing here to remind you of the living space," Gibb points out. Well, almost nothing. A sofa, chairs, and a table are arranged in front of sliding doors to the garden, where the architect and her employees eat lunch in warmer weather. "When we are working on architectural projects, the furniture is converted to work use or moved out of the room," she says. "Then when a client comes for a presentation, we use the table for meetings. The sofa converts into a bed in case we have a guest who wants privacy from the rest of the house. It's also just for relaxing too."

To save money, Gibb bought some of the building materials wholesale and others from companies abroad, allowing for an advantageous exchange rate. She supervised construction and did some of the work herself, including finishing the custom mahogany trim around windows and doors. Her husband helped out, as did her father, James Gibb, an automotive tool and die maker who fabricated the aluminum and stainless-steel components of the staircase connecting the main living floor to the bedroom levels. "Because he lives in Florida, we had to design it like a kit of parts," recalls the architect, who received the metal pieces by FedEx and then had them assembled just before the house was completed in 2004.

Since then, the contemporary residence has helped win her clients, including a couple seeking a renovation of their midcentury-modern dwelling just around the corner. "Building my own house and office has allowed me to show people what I can do," declares Gibb.

Working
Although it is tucked into the sloping ground at back, the basement office extends sufficiently above ground to allow a separate entrance for Gibb's two employees. Sliding glass doors open onto the garden, where the architect and her staff eat lunch in warmer weather. Similar projecting bays on each side of the building are glazed with translucent glass planks for privacy.

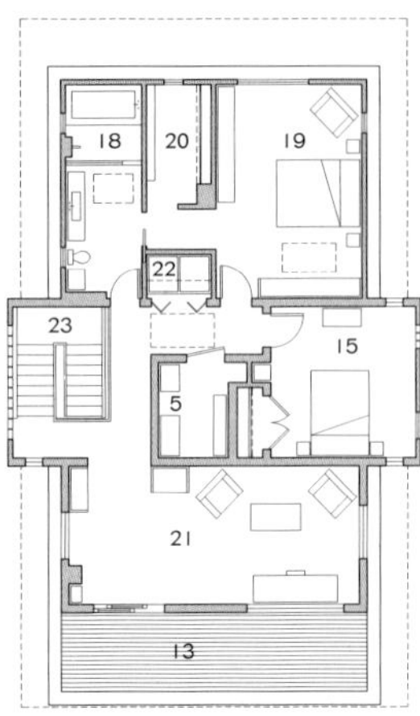

Third Floor

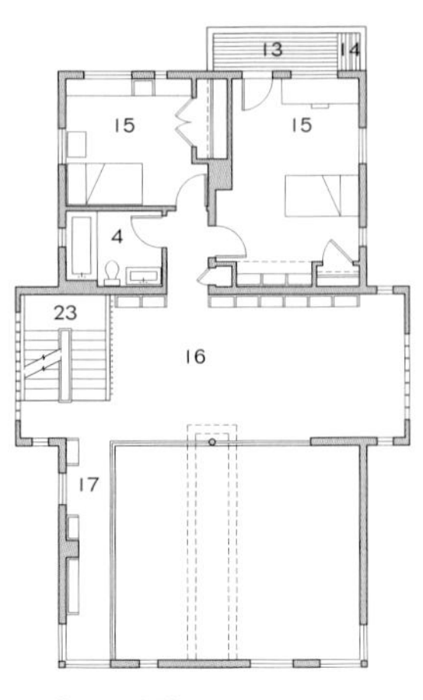

Second Floor

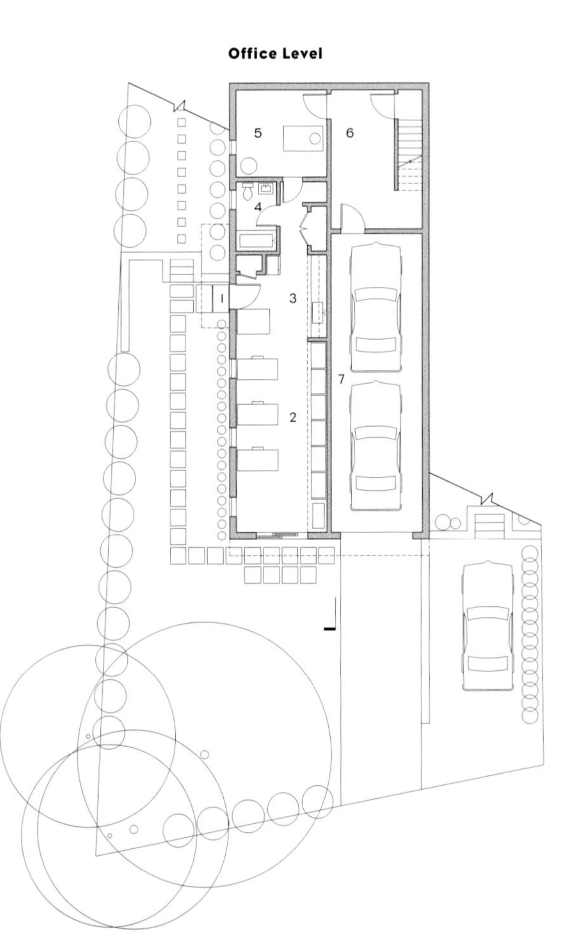

Office Level

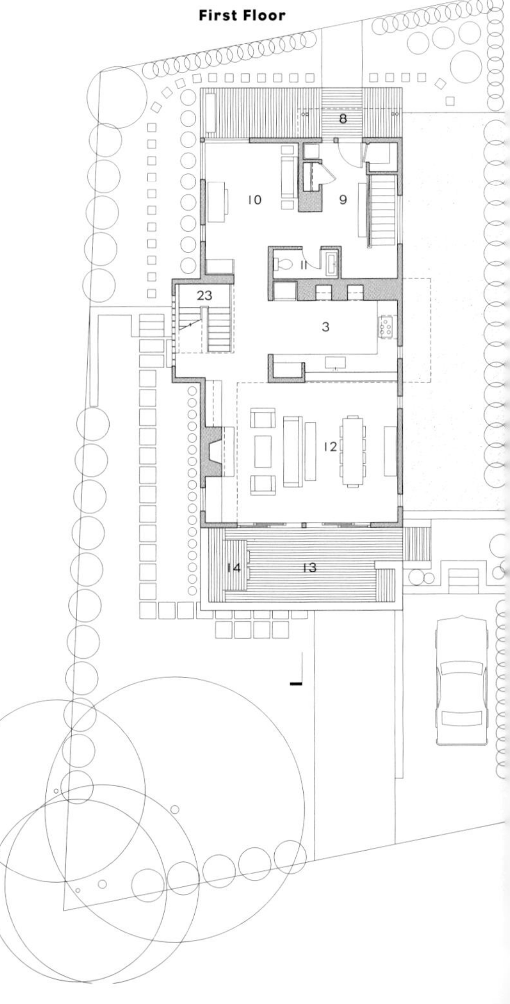

First Floor

1 Office Entry
2 Work Space
3 Kitchen
4 Bathroom
5 Mechanical Room
6 Storage
7 Garage
8 Main Entry
9 Vestibule
10 Music Room
11 Powder Room
12 Living/Dining Area
13 Deck
14 Built-in Bench
15 Bedroom
16 Play Space
17 Library Wall
18 Master Bathroom
19 Master Bedroom
20 Master Closet
21 Study
22 Laundry
23 Custom Stair

LESSONS LEARNED

Make local zoning work to your benefit. Although the existing multifamily zoning was in her favor, finding the right configuration for Elizabeth Gibb's home and office was challenging, given restrictions on setbacks from property lines. "The setback dimensions are determined by a formula that takes into consideration the height, width, and length of a building. If any one of those dimensions changed, they all did," she points out. The architect came up with a winning solution. "We didn't need a single variance," she exclaims.

Orient rooms to the sun. Gibb reduced energy costs by positioning the offices and main living spaces to face south and gain heat during the winter through generous windows; only the bathrooms and service spaces are located in the northern corners. All the bedrooms face east to receive morning light. During summer months, spaces are shaded by tall Norway maple trees in the back yard and, on the top floor, the overhanging roof. The only sources of heating inside the house are hot water-filled tubes embedded in the floors to radiate warmth.

Choose low-maintenance building materials. Exotic woods from sustainable or replenished forests, including jarrah and ipe, supply richness to the minimalist, boxy exterior without forsaking New England's timber vernacular. Extremely durable and rot resistant, these dense woods absorb less water than softer woods and are less likely to bow or twist; they also do not require painting.

Looking
Elizabeth Gibb and her husband, Markus Meister, a neurobiology professor at Harvard University, enjoy treetop views from the third-floor terrace adjoining his study at the rear of the house. Lead-coated copper edges reinforce the crisp lines of the overhanging roof.

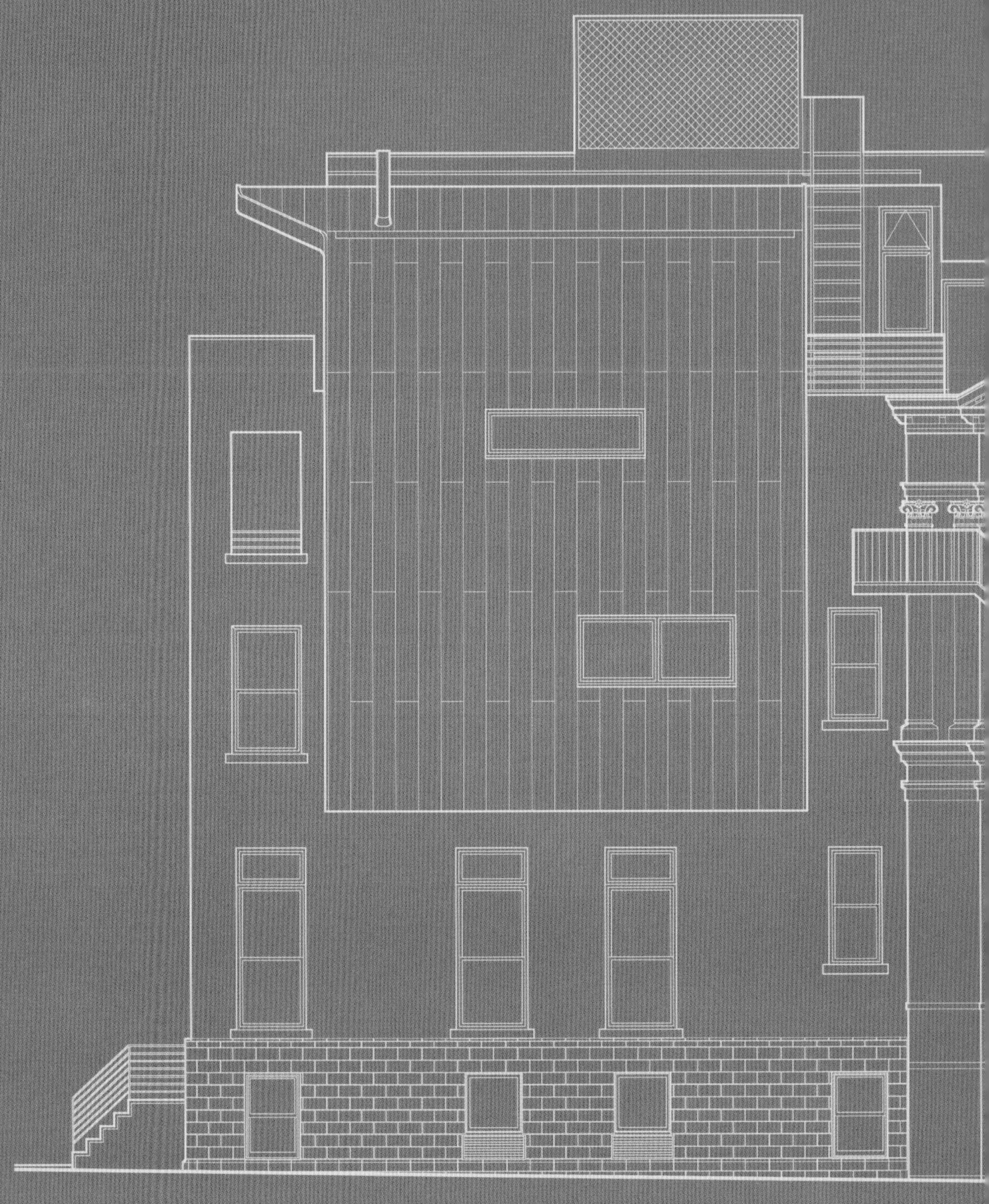

Built to La

Born-Again Buildings

worked in the same place," declares the artist David for nearly two decades combined home and studio in a Lower Manhattan loft. Success in the art world led Salle to think about buying his own building, a place where painting and privacy could coexist in larger, more separate spaces. When presented with the opportunity to purchase a former Masonic lodge and its neighboring townhouse in Brooklyn, he seized it. "My assistant found them while bicycling through the neighborhood and realized that they were sitting empty," recalls the Oklahoma-born painter, who has also dabbled in photography, set design, and film directing. "They had been uninhabited for a long time. Not much was here except pigeons."

Juxtaposing
David Salle paints and lives in two conjoined historic buildings in Brooklyn: one an antebellum townhouse refinished in stucco and fitted with new windows plus a zinc-clad addition and the other an 1890s Masonic lodge. A cast-iron dog guards the studio entry and the stairs to the living quarters.

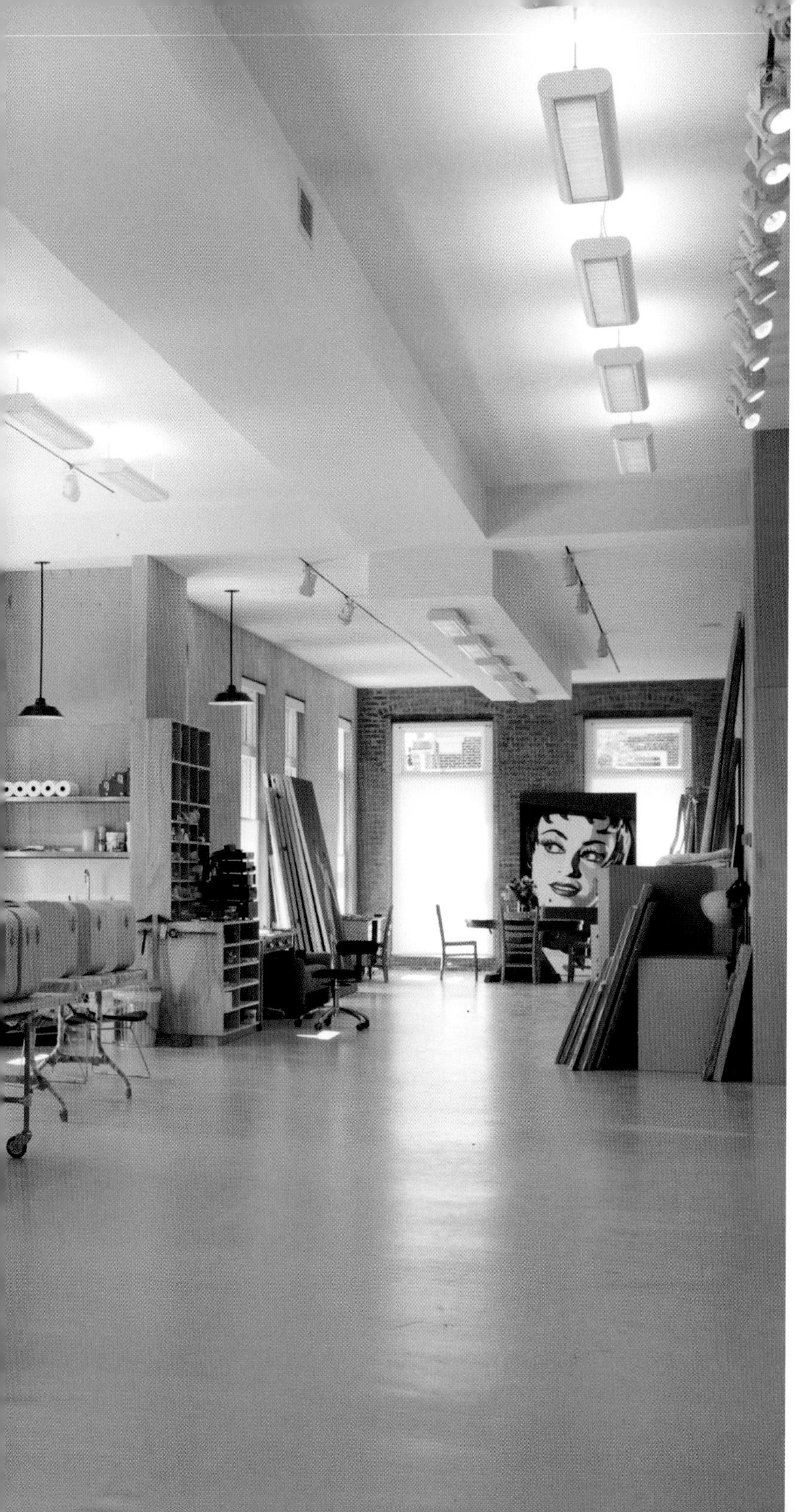

Painting
Salle's 15-by-40-foot painting studio on the townhouse's ground floor features exposed brick walls, east-facing windows, and a built-in kitchenette. The larger part of his studio, located in the renovated lodge, measures 65 by 25 feet and takes up that building's ground floor.

24 GIANT SIZE PKGS.
New!
Brillo
soap pads
SHINES ALUMINUM FAST
24 GIANT SIZE PKGS.

Dining and cooking
Tom Brokish, a carpenter in Portland, Maine, built the dining room cabinets and a sideboard of limed oak as well as a table topped in salvaged chestnut that complement Salle's sculptural 1940s chairs. Limestone countertops in the kitchen are paired with limed oak cabinets and stainless-steel appliances, including a professional-quality Wolf range for the chef.

Living
Salle furnished the twelve-foot-tall living room with midcentury-modern pieces such as a Florence Knoll sofa and a Hans Bellman tripod table. Christian Hubert designed the fireplace surround with bricks laid vertically.

Sightseeing
On the townhouse's top level, the study is finished with bamboo flooring and heated by a wood-burning stove. The window and the adjacent terrace overlook city views as well as bamboo growing up from the bedroom corner terrace on the floor below.

Bathing
Tucked under the curved roof of the zinc-clad addition is the master bath. Its deep soaking tub, teak vanity, and cedar walls and ceiling convey a Japanese feeling. The glass-framed room opens onto its own private terrace, carved out of the lodge building.

To renovate the structures, Salle turned to the man who had designed his Tribeca loft in 1984, Christian Hubert. The Manhattan-based architect quickly realized that the conjoined nineteenth-century buildings, even in their decrepitude, presented several advantages for a painting studio and a home. They were located on a corner with exposures on three sides and provided street access and a basement for an office, a guest room, and a garage. "The ground floors of both buildings were already connected, so we knew that level would be the studio," he notes. "But the upper floors were nasty with very little light. The brickwork on the townhouse was in bad structural condition, enough so that we had the upper stories demolished right away."

Reshaping the townhouse into living quarters led the architect to replace its missing portions with new stucco-clad walls and double-hung windows similar to the originals. He then broke with tradition to design a modern, metal-clad addition on the side nearest the lodge. Its seamed, zinc-paneled wall curves over and above the townhouse to form the roof while leaving room for big windows and front and back terraces on the top floor. A portion of the lodge next to the townhouse was also carved out to provide another terrace and more daylight for the addition.

"The mix of contemporary and historic architecture is my analog to David's sensibility of mixing different elements in his paintings," Hubert explains. Inside the juxtaposed buildings, the rooms feel seamlessly connected and surprisingly high and open. The studio runs the entire length of the ground

Contemplating
The pebbled bamboo garden off the master bedroom provides a contemplative touch of Zen in this decidedly urban building.

floor, offering more airy, unobstructed space than the artist's previous column-filled loft. On the level above, a smaller workroom for drawing is tucked off the main living-dining area. Behind the dining space, the kitchen, with a built-in banquette, occupies the addition with a window overlooking the street. The master bedroom suite and its terrace take up the third level; and on the townhouse's top story are a sitting room and a study, each with its own deck. "I can stay here for days at a time," admits Salle of his spacious, 10,000-square-foot surroundings. "Sometimes, I have to force myself to leave."

During the two years of construction, Hubert collaborated with his associate architect, David Fratianne, as well as with Salle, who chose every material and finish. "David was very involved after the basic spatial ideas were worked out, and the house is very much his self-portrait," says Hubert. "Having designed his Manhattan loft, I knew from the beginning of this project that there was not going to be uniformity of color and texture."

Within the live/work compound, subtly variegated backdrops—exposed wooden trusses and old brick arches; walls covered in felt, teak, and wallpaper; and floors of rift-cut oak, walnut, and bamboo—highlight the midcentury-modern furnishings collected by the artist since the 1980s. Salle's artistic eye is particularly apparent in the choice of paint colors, which range from chocolate brown to sky blue. "We came up with them through trial and error," the artist acknowledges. "There was a lot of repainting before we decided on the right one."

Sleeping
At its southern end, the master bedroom opens onto a small glass-enclosed bamboo garden, one of several outdoor areas in this live/work hive; a larger sitting terrace is off the room's opposite end. Walnut floors, a platform bed, a lounge chair by Jens Risom, and a Tulip side table by Eero Saarinen extend the midcentury-modern look found elsewhere in the house.

Fourth Floor

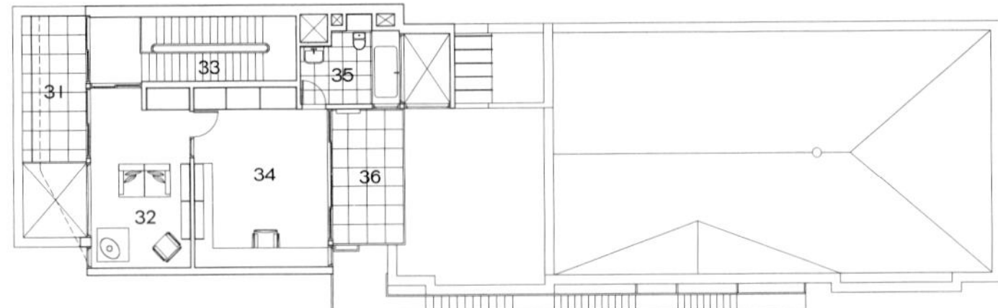

Third Floor

Second Floor

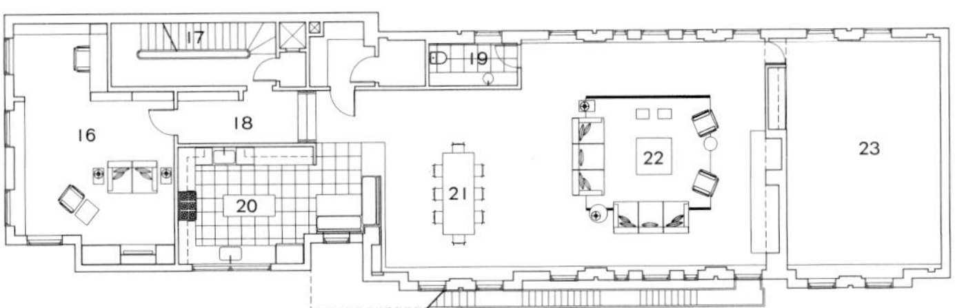

First Floor

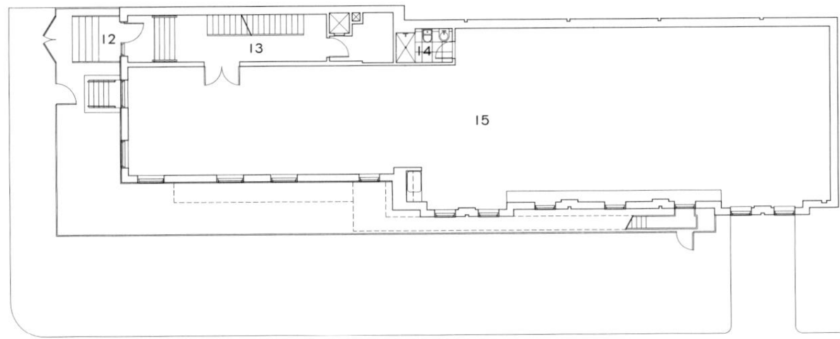

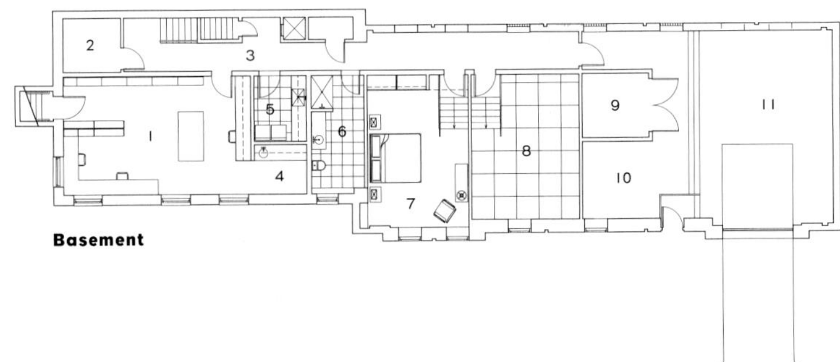

Basement

Making art
Salle contemplates the progress of his art in his Brooklyn studio. Built-in shelving and tools mounted on the wall save space for his oversized canvases, which often juxtapose contrasting elements.

LESSONS LEARNED

Mix styles and materials to enrich the space. David Salle is known for imagery that appears to be randomly juxtaposed. His studio and home reflect the same layering of disparate elements. On the exterior, historic and contemporary architecture in masonry, metal, and glass create a lively montage of materials and styles. Each room inside conveys a slightly different modern character, from the Japanese-style master bathroom and the Arts and Crafts-inspired library to the 1940s-style limed-oak cabinetry in the dining room and the kitchen.

Relieve urban stress with outdoor space. By reconfiguring the existing buildings, the architect was able to redistribute the floor area without increasing the overall square footage—a local zoning requirement. "It was a matter of pulling in the building and pushing it out in different places," notes Christian Hubert. "I took chunks out of the building to create outdoor rooms." Hidden from the street, the plant-framed terraces, including a bamboo garden next to the master bath, supply contemplative oases rarely found in city dwellings.

1 Office
2 Storage
3 Hall
4 Kitchenette
5 Laundry
6 Bathroom
7 Guest Room
8 Gym
9 Storage
10 Shop
11 Garage
12 Entry
13 Hall
14 WC
15 Studio
16 Den
17 Stair
18 Hall
19 Bathroom
20 Kitchen
21 Dining Room
22 Living Room
23 Studio
24 Terrace
25 Closet
26 Master Bedroom
27 Stair
28 Bathroom
29 WC
30 Terrace
31 Terrace
32 Den
33 Stair
34 Study
35 Bathroom
36 Terrace

INDUSTRIAL HACIENDA

Industrial buildings are well suited for live/work spaces. Their large, open bays and tall ceilings can be partitioned off in numerous ways, and their tough floors and walls are indestructible to daily wear and tear. The graphic designer Jill Giles of San Antonio, Texas, has long taken advantage of their versatility, first living in a warehouse and then renovating a 1920s-era laboratory complex in a more marginal area of the city.

With the help of the architect Ted Flato of the nationally recognized San Antonio firm Lake/Flato Architects, Giles turned one building of her industrial hacienda into a living loft and the other—a larger, more warehouselike structure—into studio space. "It had a nice set of bones," says Flato of the original architecture. "We just had to make the most of the great proportions and spaces between them."

Reusing
In what once was the Petty Geophysical Laboratories, a metal staircase now leads to a mezzanine holding files and storage. Wood trusses, exposed ductwork, and concrete floors reflect the complex's industrial past.

Enclosing
A pool creates an oasis in the courtyard between the work building (left) and the living quarters, with its sawtooth roof (right).

Daylighting
An air-conditioning equipment plant in San Antonio inspired Ted Flato in his design of a sawtooth roof fitted with glass panes over the laboratory testing building. Supported by steel trusses and columns, the roof adds height to the living loft and fills its open space with northern light. Each section corresponds to a bay of the old lab.

Rising
A metal pipe supports the work building's office mezzanine. Such low-budget details maintain the industrial spirit of the original buildings.

The bigger work building at the property's southern end focuses on a tall, multipurpose room topped by wooden trusses. When Giles is not using it for her own design projects, she rents it out for photo and film shoots. "The space has been set up with a full boxing ring to shoot a TV spot for Corona beer," recalls Giles. "I've used it to refinish a hundred antique mirrors for a local restaurant. It's a great all-around space for studio work."

On the other side of the building is a rental live/work unit, designed by Flato with a sleeping loft inserted over a kitchenette and a bathroom. Giles now leases the apartment, which has its own private garden, to an art dealer who uses it as gallery space. The building also houses a bedroom suite for visiting guests and a garage with easy access to the street.

To the east of the studio, along a major street, the structure originally used for lab testing was converted into Giles's living quarters. "There was more finish in that building," explains Flato. "It had a stamped tin ceiling, skylights, and a lower ceiling space where offices might have been." Seeking to preserve the character of the building, the architect and the homeowner

Living
Steel columns and trusses frame the living room's sawtooth roof and clerestories. Sliding doors set into the wall's wood paneling open into the master bedroom. Furnishings include an Arne Jacobsen Swan chair and other modern classics.

Dining
From the bedroom, the former blasting chamber is visible at the living room's far end. This steel-lined room for seismic experiments, where the renovation fire originated, now serves as the dining area. Jill Giles designed the low, two-sided bookcase.

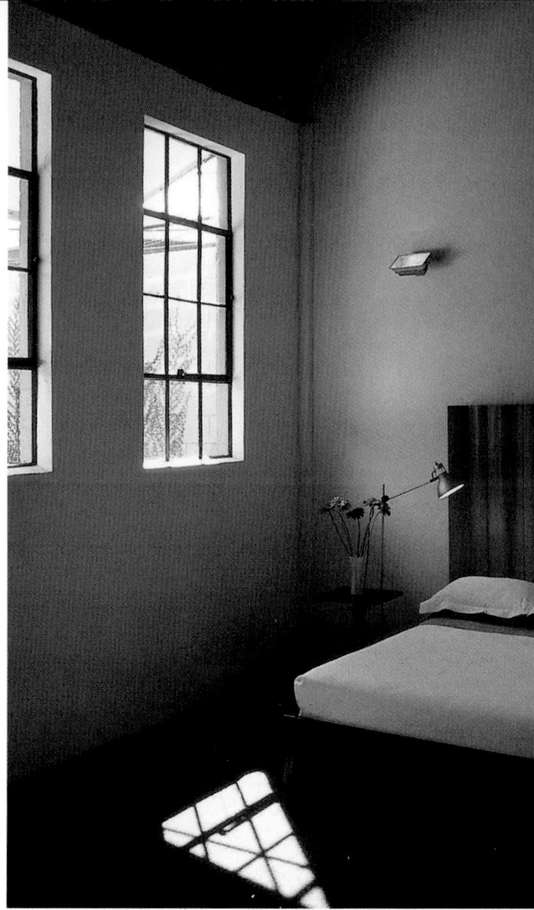

agreed to turn what had been a blasting chamber for seismic experiments into a dining room. Cork was removed from the walls to expose steel plates lining the space; they were left in place and repaired.

But just before the renovation was scheduled to be completed, disaster struck. A spark from a welder's torch, smoldering behind one of the metal wall panels, erupted into a huge blaze that burned the home, leaving only the exterior masonry walls, concrete floor, and remnants of the interior steel columns and plated walls. Fortunately the flames did not spread to the remodeled studio building, which survived largely intact: "It had just a little smoke damage," notes Giles.

Rebuilding the charred living quarters fired up the design. "The building had beautiful old skylights that you could never reproduce," Giles observes. "But it also had a low ceiling height that bothered me." Inspired by an air-conditioning equipment plant in San Antonio, Flato designed a factory-style, sawtooth roof of clear glass panes and plywood angles that adds height to

Bathing
The living area's concrete floor continues into the minimalist master bathroom, with its deep soaking tub and metal chair by Harry Bertoia.

Sleeping
In the guest room occupying one corner of Giles's studio building, a wavy plywood screen by Charles Eames serves as a headboard. Metal sash windows and brick walls retain the lab's original industrial character.

the loft and floods the open space with northern light. "When you stand at the southern end of the space and look north, the glass in the roof appears to fold together. From one direction it looks like you have a glass ceiling and the roof seems to disappear," explains Flato. "The space turned out far more exciting than it was before."

Inside the urban block shared by the live/work buildings, Flato transformed what had been an alleyway and a parking lot into an outdoor room that takes advantage of the southwestern climate and provides a gracious entrance into the complex. "A lot of times you walk right into a loft, which doesn't have the sequence of spaces that a house has," he remarks. "The outside spaces here did that for us. They already had hallways and rooms built in."

From the alley at the western edge of the property, a steel gate opens into a narrow passageway that leads into the large courtyard with a raised concrete lap pool and potted plants. In one corner of the space, a small, freestanding structure, once used to house heating and cooling equipment, was gutted to create a one-room pavilion with a fireplace for outdoor dining. "It's my secret paradise," discloses Giles.

Coming in
From the street, a door opens onto a passageway leading to the courtyard between the living and work buildings. Stone paving repeats the patterns of the brick walls.

Going out
Metal and glass doors open from the living quarters onto the courtyard in front of the work building, where the raised concrete pool beckons.

Camouflaging
"From the outside, it has a hard, nobody-lives-here quality," notes Jill Giles about her L-shaped complex of historic red brick buildings. "Inside, everything opens up and is very airy." The sawtooth roof designates the living area.

LESSONS LEARNED

Preserve architectural character. Instead of disguising the rooms of the laboratory compound with wallboard and other new finishes, Jill Giles kept their original features intact. She left brick, roof trusses, and even the steel-plated walls of a former blasting chamber exposed to create visual interest through evidence of the buildings' history.

Don't forget the roof. Reconfiguring the top of a building can add space and light. Giles seized the opportunity of a fire to insert angular skylights that create a sense of spaciousness by extending the ceiling and illuminating the interior. The sawtooth roof mimics factory architecture in keeping with the industrial character of the original laboratory buildings.

Minimizing
The simple canopy shading the front door exemplifies the minimalism of the architect's insertions into the old structure. "The brick facade was restored to maintain its historical feel," says Ted Flato.

1 Living Loft Entry
2 Study
3 Master Bedroom
4 Master Bathroom
5 Living Area
6 Dining Area
7 Kitchen
8 Studio
9 Rental Apartment
10 Pool Courtyard

CIBOLO FILMS

HOUSE ORGAN

Playing a violin or even a grand piano is easily accomplished in most areas of the house. But when your instrument is a pipe organ, the living room, study, or extra bedroom is usually too intimate for its immense size and sounds. The organists Sonja Kahler and Matt Larson, who play in churches around Washington, D.C., solved the problem by extending a soaring music room from the back of their remodeled rambler.

The centerpiece of the fine-tuned addition is an eleven-foot-high mechanical action organ that was custom built in Cornish, New Hampshire, by a friend of the musicians from their days at Northwestern University's music school. The main internal works and some of the pipes came from a century-old Connecticut church organ. "I really appreciate what complex machines they are," declares Larson, who dismisses the idea of a smaller electric organ. "It is a thrill to be able to make so much sound." Adds Kahler, "You can play a whole symphony by yourself."

Before building their dedicated music room, the couple had shoehorned the ten-rank organ into the enclosed porch of their former home. "It was a bit like stuffing a grand piano into a large, walk-in closet—workable but hardly optimal," recalls Kahler. "We always knew we'd build a room for it." Their desire for a space big enough for the instrument, plus a harpsichord and a grand piano, prompted a search for a house on a large lot that could accommodate a sizable addition. That led the husband-and-wife musicians to buy a 1957 rambler in Kenwood Park, a suburban Washington, D.C., neighborhood that is home to politicians and diplomats. As Larson describes the midcentury-modern home: "It was the perfect blank canvas because we didn't have to rip out anyone else's remodeling."

Performing
This harpsichord is one of the three instruments that take center stage in the family's new music room, separated by a simple glass door from their living area. The appropriately cathedral-like ceiling was designed with acoustical needs in mind.

Adding on
The couple purchased a rambler that would accommodate their new music room. "It was like the set of *The Dick Van Dyke Show,*" says Matt Larson. The addition rises discreetly in the rear on the house's right side.

Playing
"This is the first place where we've ever had all our instruments together in the same room," notes Larson about the couple's organ, harpsichord, and grand piano. Ground-level and clerestory windows supply northern light at strategic places to indirectly light the instruments. Glass doors slide open to unite the room with the adjacent living area—creating one grand space.

To find an architect to design the addition, Kahler consulted her big file of clippings from shelter magazines. "I'm an addict," she admits. She noticed that she had saved many pictures of projects designed by the local architect Mark McInturff. "His work is contemporary yet so elegant." So Kahler sent a picture of the organ to McInturff with a note explaining the need for a music room.

"Someone coming to you to design a room around a pipe organ is pretty special," observes the architect, who responded positively to Kahler's request. "The challenge was how to place this big, delicate, and precious instrument in such a way as to allow someone to practice in the room and not blow away everyone else in the house." McInturff, who also works at home (see pages 132–41), took his inspiration from a chapel designed by the French architect Le Corbusier for the Convent of La Tourette, built near Lyon, France, in the 1950s. Like that building, the music room is attached to the house at the rear but distinguished as a separate chamber by its sculptural shape.

The addition is as finely tuned and crafted inside as the instruments it holds. The organ is given a place of honor in its own center bay, outlined by narrow windows and copper sheathing on the exterior. "The idea was to bring light in around the organ but not put sunlight onto it," McInturff explains. A crawl space under the floor provides enough room for the electric blower that supplies pressurized air to the wood and metal organ pipes. Placed on either side of the organ with plenty of room to spare are the harpsichord and the grand piano.

Welcoming
In the house's entry, space soars to new skylights and a ceiling that hints at the elevated spaces beyond that hold the owners' unique music room.

Acoustics also played an important role in the design. "Organists often say that the most important stop on the organ is the room," notes Kahler. "A dry, dead room can really muffle an instrument." In shaping the walls and the ceiling, McInturff worked with the Baltimore-based acoustician Neil Thompson Shade to prevent reverberation and reduce sound transmission from the inside of the room to the outside. "The purpose of the angled surfaces is to break up the flutter echo that occurs between parallel surfaces and to scatter the sound throughout the room in many directions so you feel like you are enveloped by the music," explains Shade. Double-thick gypsum board on the walls and two layers of plywood under the bamboo floor help reflect low-frequency bass notes ordinarily absorbed by conventional residential construction.

As part of his design, McInturff remodeled the living room with a slate fireplace and expanded the kitchen into an existing carport to incorporate a breakfast nook and an office area. He divided the addition from the living area with sliding glass doors so that when they are opened, the two spaces feel like one big room. "Music is so critical to our lives," admits Kahler. "We wanted to be able to combine our music and living spaces at any desired point."

Kahler and Larson use the 550-square-foot music room not only for practicing the organ, harpsichord, and piano. It additionally serves as a place for parties, concerts, and ballroom dance lessons. "We also use it for practice sessions with other musician friends, nursery-rhyme singing with our two children, and Christmas carol singing with extended family," comments Kahler. "We've even had a guest or two sleep in there on an air mattress for a night or so when we've had a houseful of company. We will surely think of other uses for the room as time goes on."

Warming
A slate fireplace with an integrated mantel scribes a horizontal line in the lofty, angled living room. Through the use of glass doors, the musical instruments are never far from view.

Cooking
In the remodeled kitchen, the owners can keep an eye on their instruments. A dining nook provides a view of the angular music room addition through a glass wall.

LESSONS LEARNED

Sometimes you just have to move. Finding a comfortable place to work may not always be possible in the typical home. Practicing their music on a cramped porch led the organists Sonja Kahler and Matt Larson to sell their house and buy a rambler with enough land to build a spacious room to hold several of their instruments.

Special professions require special solutions. Expertise outside the design professions may be needed to meet unconventional live/work needs. Creating a room for the couple's pipe organ required the skills of an acoustician to fine-tune the angles of the space and ensure live sound. Other spaces featured in this book, including a restaurant, required advice from lawyers and other experts.

Push work spaces to their full potential. Positioning an office or a studio next to the most frequently used room in the house allows the space to be used after work hours for more than one purpose. Kahler and Larson attached their addition to the living space so they can use the music room as spillover space for entertaining or an extra guest room. During their concerts, visitors can sit in the living room and still enjoy the music.

Separating
The slanted, laminated-glass ceiling over the music room helps reflect sound and provides acoustical separation from the adjacent living room. "It's remarkably live," says Larson, "with only about a second of reverberation."

Sculpting
Dark gray fiber-cement panels on the addition are outlined in a rhythmic pattern with copper bands "like musical notations," according to the architect, Mark McInturff.

ALMOST A LOFT

The real estate developer Matthew Hood lives and works on the other side of the tracks—literally—in a former lumber warehouse. Hood's loft was originally the sales office and model home for his eight-unit conversion on the outskirts of Royal Oak, Michigan, next to an active railroad line. "I didn't build what would sell quickest but rather the type of place where I would like to live," Hood relates of his 22,515-square-foot development called the Parent Avenue Lofts. "I found myself hanging out in the model all the time, so I decided to make it my home."

The loft has also become the developer's own office. He works from a mezzanine overlooking the two-story living room at the back of the building, where south-facing windows flood the entire space with daylight. His glass-topped desk is placed under a skylight, with a convertible sofa nearby to accommodate casual meetings and overnight guests. "Working at home saves a lot of time, and it's much more efficient than commuting to an office," Hood says, adding, "You don't have to get dressed in the morning and roll out to the highway. I try not to schedule a lot of morning meetings."

Living
The two-story living room is illuminated by sixteen-foot-tall windows along the back wall. Patios, reached from a glass door, provide outdoor space for each unit.

Rezoning
The developer Matthew Hood took advantage of rezoning to remodel a 1960s warehouse into eight townhouse-lofts in a light industrial area north of Detroit. On the front facade, box bays covered in wood veneer punctuate the cement-block exterior. They project from the second-floor bedrooms over the garages.

Living and working
Open from front to back, the townhouse is organized so that the kitchen and the dining area occupy the space under the second-floor office. Metal balcony railings and concrete floors maintain the original warehouse's industrial character.

Descending
Along one side of the living space, a staircase leads down from the office and the bedroom on the upper level. Exposed steel trusses, original to the building, and new industrial lighting further the warehouse sensibility. Matthew Hood furnished the loft with contemporary furnishings, including a rug that matches the paint color of the kitchen and office walls.

One of several loft buildings in Royal Oak, a leafy community north of Detroit, the remodeled structure is located in a light industrial area next to a neighborhood of single-family homes. The warehouse district was rezoned in 2001 to allow a mix of uses, including multifamily housing. Hood took advantage of the change by purchasing a 1960s cinder-block structure he envisioned as the perfect setting for the type of contemporary lofts that he admired in Denver and Portland, Oregon. "It had an interesting shape—trapezoidal, not square," he notes. "It was tall enough so we could put in a second floor without having to change the original roof height."

But the building had no windows, only a few roll-up doors. That led Michael Poris of McIntosh Poris Associates, an architecture firm based in nearby Birmingham, Michigan, to puncture the back wall with sixteen-foot-high windows and to create an entirely new front facade using the original materials, concrete block and steel. Box bays covered in wood veneer extend from the second-floor bedrooms over garage doors to add visual punch. "We didn't want to change the character of the warehouse and sanitize it," explains Poris, whose experience includes converting a Detroit vacuum cleaner factory into lofts. "At the same time, we wanted it to be a little more interesting than a blank, block building and give individuality to the units." His solution was to create a hybrid of a townhouse and a loft. Each of the units, most of them fifteen feet wide, has its own garage and entrance from the street, while its interior, centered on a core of kitchen and bathrooms, is kept open and flexible.

The floor plan is fairly unusual: the bedroom fronts the street while the two-story living room faces a terrace at the back, on the side of the property flanked by single-family homes. To preserve the warehouse character inside, the architect left the original steel roof trusses and concrete floors exposed in the living area. Balustrades made of steel grating and thick wood planks on the stairs reinforce the industrial look. Poris explains that he designed the mezzanine above the twenty-two-foot-high back room as a work area but points out that other spaces in the unit could also serve the purpose. "Someone could make the bedroom into work space, and an artist could make the living room into a studio," he comments, adding with a laugh, "It's almost a real loft except it has bathrooms."

"It was always part of my plan for people to turn the space into what they wanted," explains Hood, who admits that working at home can be isolating. His antidote is to frequent the shops, coffee bars, and restaurants of downtown Royal Oak, all within walking distance of the converted warehouse. "It's a small-town atmosphere that is attractive to young people," he observes, noting that several of his twenty- and thirty-something neighbors also have home businesses in their lofts.

Cooking
The kitchen's compressed ceiling is released in the two-story living area at the unit's rear. It occupies the center of each townhouse under the wooden joists supporting the second-floor work space.

Dining

Located adjacent to the kitchen, the dining area is also tucked under the exposed wooden ceiling joists. Visible down the red hallway is a two-story slot of space next to the front door, designed to funnel daylight from the second-floor windows to illuminate the entrance foyer.

Gleaming

Furnished with stainless-steel appliances, the kitchen includes an island with stools for casual dining. The partition separating the space from the adjacent corridor supports the second-floor work balcony. It is edged in metal to match the upper-level railing.

Second Floor

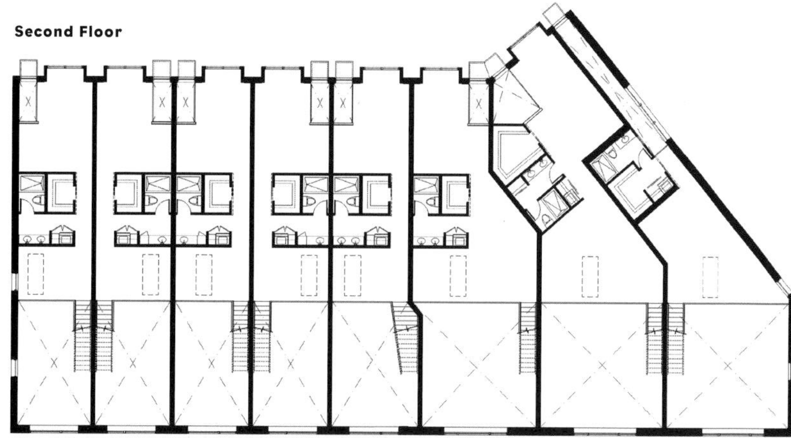

First Floor

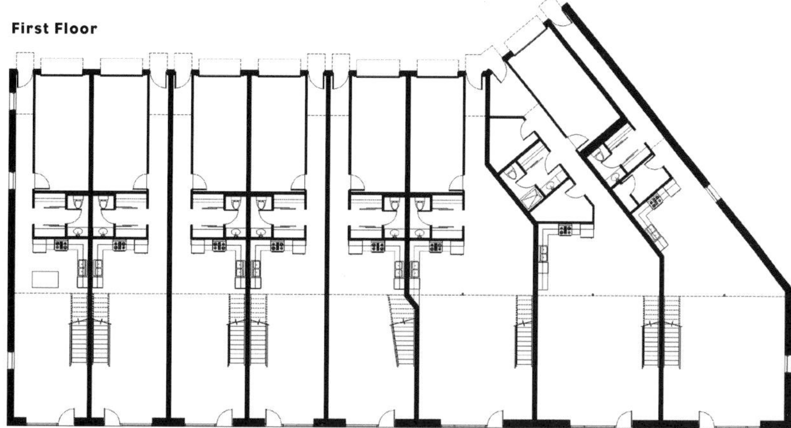

Concealing
The second level is designed so that each of the two major spaces can be used as either a bedroom or a work area. A red box between the bedroom and the office in this unit—recalling the color of the carpet downstairs—encloses the bathroom and a closet. To allow for exposed ductwork and a feeling of spaciousness throughout the loft, the partitions around these spaces were kept free of the ceiling.

Sleeping
The floor of the front space, used here as a bedroom, is cut out in one corner to create a two-story entrance foyer on the level below. It can be seen through the metal-mesh balustrade framing the opening.

Bathing
In the hidden bathroom, paired sinks are mounted on a wooden vanity with drawers and shelves for storage. This space is one of the few enclosed rooms in the loft.

LESSONS LEARNED

Develop it yourself to get the space you want. Matthew Hood was inspired by the high ceilings and trapezoidal shape of a warehouse to configure space flexible enough for any number of live/work variations, including his own office. He combined the narrow, vertical arrangement of a townhouse with the open, industrial character of a loft to create unusual contemporary residences that appeal to young home buyers.

Arrange living and working spaces around a central core. Placing the kitchen, bathrooms, and utility rooms at the center of a loft or an open-plan house allows the spaces at the front and back to remain flexible. It is easier to switch the perimeter spaces for living and working than to move the rooms that require plumbing. And because kitchens and bathrooms do not need tall ceilings, they can be tucked under a second-level mezzanine, allowing front and back spaces to extend higher.

WEDDED TO WORK

David Egan not only works and lives in an old stone parish house—he also uses it to generate income. The 1879 Cothic Revival building once belonged to Christ Episcopal Church in Baltimore's historic Mount Vernon neighborhood, a place for Sunday school and social events. Today its ground-floor rooms and garden are rented by Egan for weddings, receptions, holiday parties, and celebrations. "I'm honoring the building's sacred purpose with what I do," he suggests. "I feel a spiritual connection to the space."

A commercial photographer for most of his career, Egan bought the parish house in 2002 in order to start his events-staging business. One of the advantages of Chase Court, as he calls the building, is that it is hidden from the street behind the church and adjacent townhouses. A walled garden between the parish house and the church forms a private space for outdoor events. Here stone steps lead to a raised wooden platform under a wisteria-draped canopy for weddings and other ceremonies.

Wedding
On one side of the courtyard, a raised wooden platform under a wisteria-draped canopy allows the wedding party to be seen by guests seated in the space.

Enclosing
The courtyard in front of the old stone parish house forms a private space for outdoor events. The 1879 Cothic Revival landmark was originally owned by the neighboring Christ Episcopal Church (left) in Baltimore's historic Mount Vernon neighborhood.

RESERVED

Toasting
Illuminated by antique pendant light fixtures, the ballroom accommodates various table arrangements and festive decors.

Catering
Behind the ballroom, the catering kitchen is illuminated by an arched Cothic window. Tables can be rearranged for preparing and assembling meals for varying numbers of guests.

Primping
A bride prepares for her wedding in the second-floor suite next to the office. A draped and skirted counter under the original windows is arranged with mirrors and stools for last-minute touch-ups.

By the time Egan arrived, much of the property had been renovated by a previous owner, an architect who ran his practice from an upstairs space. "He did all the heavy lifting," Egan acknowledges. "But there was more work to be done. When I got here, all the floors were painted green, so I stripped them down to the oak." He updated the electrical system and repainted and remodeled parts of his living quarters.

Just through the front door is a reception room called the "library," although it has no books, and down the hall is a spacious high-ceilinged ballroom with a baronial fireplace, now converted to gas. In both rooms, pointed-arch windows with diamond-shaped leaded glass and dark-painted woodwork lend a Gothic atmosphere. At the rear of the larger space, a painted and gilded partition, bearing images of saints, screens the entrance to the catering kitchen at the rear.

Up a broad wooden staircase is a second-floor suite with a powder room and stools pulled up to a long makeup counter. Here brides and their attendants can change or prepare to walk down the aisle. Adjacent to this room is an office where Egan books events and meets with prospective clients. In addition to his Web site, Egan has created a DVD so "people can see how other brides and grooms have decorated the rooms and how the spaces flow."

Home is just next door to the office, a big open room under a soaring vaulted ceiling that once served as a chapel. "I've always wanted to live in a loft," discloses Egan. "This goes beyond my expectations." At the center is a freestanding kitchen enclosed by light birch cabinets and red-tiled countertops that were put in by the previous owner. Arched windows with stained-glass rosettes flank the sides of the space, above built-in shelving and benches. Furniture is casually arranged next to the banquettes and in the center of the room.

At one end of the room, a large wood-paneled wall conceals a staircase to a loft. Used as a guest room and a storage area, this upper level offers a clear view of the enormous living area and wooden trusses in the ceiling. Below it, behind the wall and the staircase, are the main bedroom and the bathroom.

Egan leaves the furniture rental, catering, and photography to his customers, but he is always on hand to help with the events that take place on the floor below his home. At the end of the day, he is often found sweeping up the rice and rose petals thrown by wedding guests. "I want to make sure everyone walks out happy," he asserts, "So far, so good. I've never had anyone left at the altar."

Living
David Egan's living space occupies a former chapel topped by large wooden trusses. At the left, a tall wood-paneled wall conceals a staircase up to a guest room and a storage area. The doorway to the right leads to the bedroom and the bathroom.

Cooking
The freestanding kitchen at the center of the living space is designed like a big piece of furniture. Built by a previous owner, it incorporates the refrigerator and other appliances and an island for dining. The upper birch cabinets use glass on both sides to avoid blank surfaces.

LESSONS LEARNED

Rent out the ground floor. Like an old-fashioned shopkeeper, David Egan lives above his "store," whose meeting rooms are rented for weddings and parties. No furniture is required, yet his business has to be approached as a full-time job, says Egan. "It takes a lot of energy and set-up time. A large part of the work is letting people know that the space exists. I do a whole lot of tours and booking online."

Create spatial variety. Although Egan lives in a chapel with high vaulted ceilings, his bedroom is designed for coziness. The kitchen is also a compact island within his tall-ceilinged living area, independently lighted by halogen bulbs strung across a cable.

Join a support group of like-minded business owners. Every month Egan meets with other local owners of historic properties in Baltimore who rent out their spaces. "The group is tremendously helpful in sharing information about contracts, rates, and promotion," he notes. "We'll have lunch in each other's spaces. That allows us to try out different caterers that we can recommend to our clients."

Gazing
The loft offers an unobstructed view of the original beams and arched windows, the living and dining areas, and the freestanding kitchen.

Arriving
Metal gates at the street open onto a brick path leading to the old parish house. Another entrance is off the courtyard used for ceremonies, allowing wedding parties to reach Chase Court without running into each other.

Ground Level

1 Foyer
2 Ballroom
3 Entrance to Catering Kitchen
4 Fireplace
5 Library
6 Garden
7 Pond
8 Bridge
9 Walkway
10 Pergola
11 Wall
12 Iron Fence

WINDOWS ON THE WORLD

Madeleine Keesing creates quiet abstractions by painstakingly applying tiny strokes of oil paint in consecutive rows. Layer upon layer of the droplets is applied until the canvas is saturated with a discernible texture. The results are subtle, yet radiant, as different colors emerge from beneath the surface.

Until recently Keesing had little room to create her labor-intensive canvases. She painted in a second-floor bedroom at the back of her 1923 brick home in Washington, D.C. The cramped quarters were less than ideal for a serious painter, but she nevertheless continued to pursue her vision and win admiration from art dealers and museum curators.

Critical acclaim for her work at gallery shows in New York City, Baltimore, and Washington during the late 1990s led Keesing to seek a more commodious environment: "I finally decided that I needed a beautiful studio." On the recommendation of a photographer friend, the artist hired the husband-and-wife team of Robert Cole and Sophie Prévost of ColePrévost, a D.C. architecture firm known for edgy design, to remodel and expand her old house with more space for both painting and living. "I told them that I'm obsessed with windows, doors, and light," she discloses.

Glowing
Clad in stucco, big sheets of clear glass, and translucent fiberglass, the angular studio addition is a complete departure from the traditional architecture of Madeline Keesing's original house. A tall door next to the window on the side wall opens to a tiered, wooden deck set with Adirondack chairs.

Fitting in
From the front, the 1920s home in a leafy neighborhood of Northwest Washington, D.C., bears no evidence of the artist's contemporary painting studio at the rear. She used to work in a small second-floor bedroom in the old house.

Layering
Keesing's abstract paintings layer rows of paint droplets to saturate each canvas with color and texture.

Painting
A view from the upper level reveals the tall windows and fiberglass panels—patterned like Japanese shoji screens—that enclose the painting studio. Near the west-facing window, Keesing paints at the movable easel in front of the stool. The easel can be raised or lowered on cables into a slot in the floor. The adaptable stand accommodates canvases of different sizes and allows the artist to dab the top surfaces of her paintings in comfort. Her work table faces the wooden side deck. The studio is large enough to house a printing press, a work sink and storage cabinets, and a small powder room in the corner.

Magnetizing
Paneled in hot-rolled steel—allowing Keesing's artwork to be hung with magnets—the side wall facing the studio conceals the stairway up to the second-floor office. Behind the wall are a storage space and a powder room, shown with its door open. To take spills, the floor is simply covered in gray-painted plywood that could later be covered with more finished boards. "Several shades of light gray were used in the studio, as it needs to remain neutral for the paintings," notes Sophie Prévost, one of the designers. Adjoining the studio is the dining room, visible through one of the "Deep Throat" archways linking the old house and the new studio.

All of those elements are abundantly evident in the luminous two-story studio now affixed to the back of the house. "Fortunately this is exactly where Madeleine wanted her studio, smack dab in her garden, so she could paint with an excellent source of natural light," says Cole, noting that the constraints of setting back the new construction from adjacent properties made it almost impossible to build elsewhere on the lot.

Clad in lavender and red-painted stucco, the angular addition is enclosed on two sides by huge sheets of glass. The big windows bring in daylight and views of the lushly planted garden, designed by the local landscape architect Rhonda Dahlkemper. A tall door next to the window on the side wall leads to a tiered, wooden deck furnished with Adirondack chairs and cheerful pots of flowers.

Striking in its bold outlines, the contemporary architecture marks a departure from the traditional brick home, with its big front porch, gabled roofs, and dark wood-trimmed rooms. "Madeleine's life is making her art," explains Cole. "This was in direct conflict with the spatially segregated nature of the existing house. So we deliberately opened up the stuffiness as much as possible." The visual bravado of the studio, however, is hidden from the street, and its presence is apparent only well inside the house. "I love that you can come into the house and not know about the studio," adds Keesing. "It's a surprise."

Cooking
Stainless-steel appliances, black limestone countertops, and open shelving continue the studio's contemporary look into the renovated kitchen. Old linoleum was peeled up to reveal an oak floor.

Reaching the open, light-filled space requires walking from the front hallway, across the living room and through the dining room. A new archway framed in oak separates the dining space from the studio; by staining the oak to match the existing dark wood trim, the designers related their contemporary look to the home's traditional style. "We took special care in framing the passages from old to new," comments Cole, who points to what he calls the "Deep Throat"—the wide wooden door jamb in the dining room that is repeated in the other spaces opening into the studio to accentuate the transition from house to work space.

Extending along one side of the studio is a staircase leading up to a newly configured master suite. Paneled in hot-rolled steel, the side facing the work space allows Keesing to hang her prints with magnets. Underneath the stairs, a small orange-painted nook is used for storage. "I call it the Harry Potter room," the artist jokes, relating how her young grandson likes to play in it.

Now Keesing paints in front of the studio's rear window on a custom-designed, movable easel. "Traditionally a painting is a reflected window on the world," says Cole. "The juxtaposition of the easel in front of the picture window reinforces this interpretation. Madeleine wanted to look at her work in progress as though it were hanging in a large space." Above the easel, a row of halogen lights on steel rods extends from the ceiling to light the work space.

Working and sleeping
Under a translucent fiberglass skylight on the second-floor balcony, the long built-in desk, where Keesing works at her computer, overlooks the studio. A custom cabinet separates the office from the adjacent bedroom, while allowing daylight to filter through both spaces. Slots between the drawers eliminate the need for hardware.

Creating art was not the project's only motivating factor. Keesing's husband, Donald, an economist with the World Bank, suffered from a debilitating neurological disease, and part of ColePrévost's charge was to design a new master bedroom and adjacent bathroom with a wheel chair-accessible shower. "He loved sitting in here, feeling the water come down," recalls the artist of her husband's final days. Most of the remodeling took place during the difficult period of his illness, but Keesing relates that the project kept her going. "It refocused my energy. I wanted to look ahead."

The new master suite partially opens to a wide balcony that serves as an office. This space is also used as a guest room with a daybed for Keesing's visiting grandson and a place to do yoga. A long built-in desk along the balcony edge overlooks the two-story studio, the artist's easel, and the garden outside the studio windows. Overhead more translucent fiberglass panels form a luminous ceiling that matches the studio wall and filters daylight down to the work space. Behind the desk, a thick storage cabinet, with drawers on one side and bookshelves on the other, screens the office from the bedroom without completing separating the two spaces. "I don't need to get away from my work," Keesing remarks of the interconnected suite. "I like to get up at night and look at my paintings."

After completing her studio and master suite, Keesing decided to upgrade her kitchen: "As a single woman I thought it would be important to cook for friends." Naturally the kitchen opens to the studio; an old table and chairs are pulled into a nook of the work space to create a breakfast area. Standing in her studio in front of a yellow-daubed canvas on her movable easel, Keesing insists, "This is really where I live."

Bathing
In addition to the large, open shower with a "rain" head recessed into the ceiling, the limestone-paneled master bathroom incorporates a deep rectangular tub for tension-soothing soaks. A notched corner, edged in stainless steel, allows overflowing water to drain through the shower floor. A wall-hung toilet reflects the contemporary design found throughout the addition.

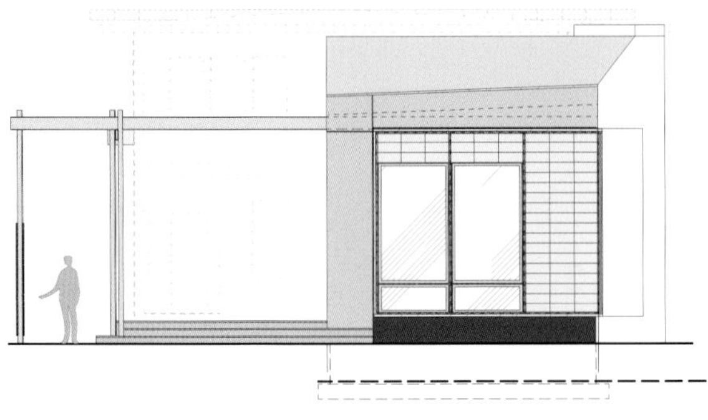

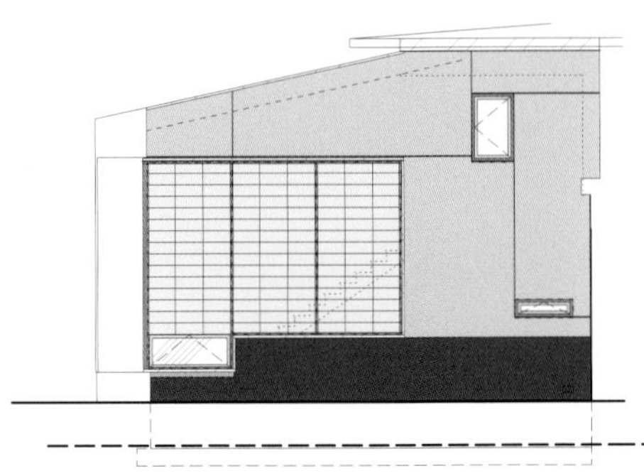

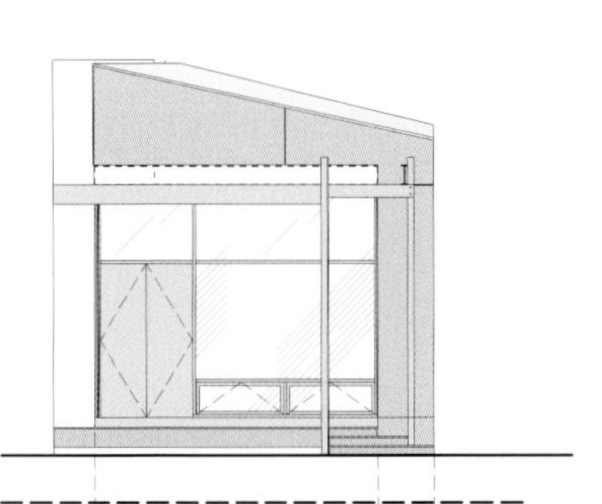

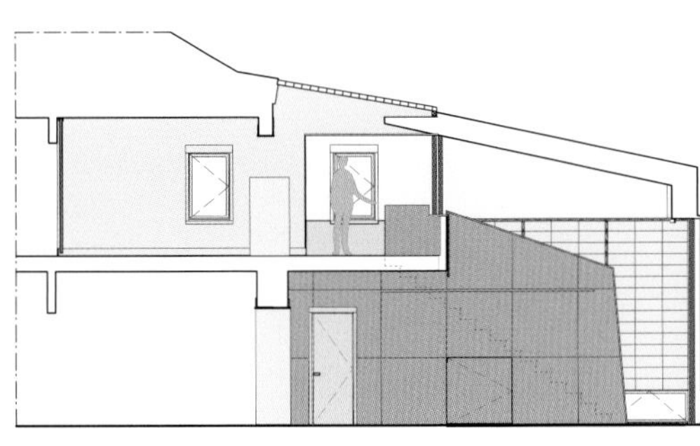

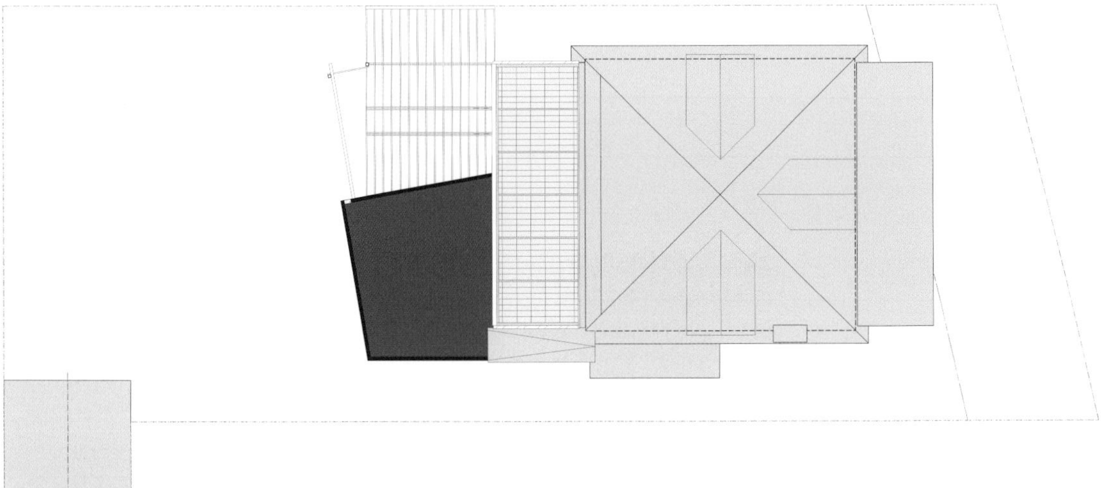

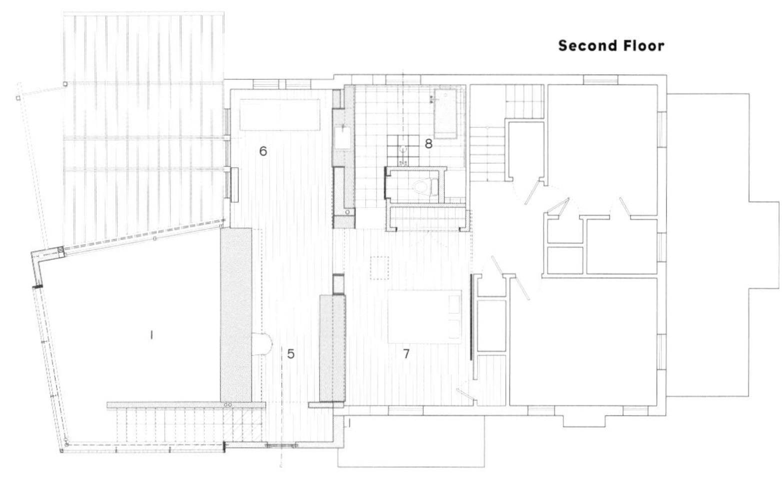

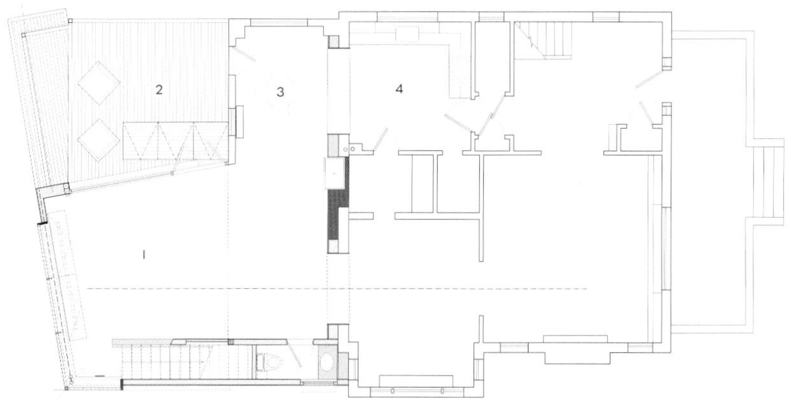

Addition

1 Painting Studio
2 Deck
3 Breakfast Area
4 Kitchen
5 Office
6 Yoga Area
7 Master Bedroom
8 Master Bathroom

LESSONS LEARNED

Be mindful of light sources, especially in design studios. Panels of translucent fiberglass, gridded like Japanese shoji screens, frame the studio's rear, west-facing window to shield the afternoon sun. The room was painted gray, explains the designer, because "white would be too bright for this space, which gets so much light."

Custom design work-saving features. Framed in steel, Madeleine Keesing's movable easel is hoisted and lowered on cables operated by a winch. "It looks like a Giacometti sculpture," notes the artist. The mechanism allows her to lower her large canvases into a five-foot-deep slot in the floor, making it easier for her to reach the top surfaces without having to stand on a ladder.

HOME—AND OFFICE—ON THE RANGE

Frequent trips to supervise the construction of a venture capitalist's Montana ranch led Richard Fernau to consider a family getaway in Big Sky country. "When the job started winding down, I kept wondering why we didn't have a place here so I could keep coming back," recalls the architect. But instead of building a trophy house amid the state's wide-open landscape, Fernau opted to remodel a commercial building in the center of Clyde Park, Montana—population 296—right next door to the local supermarket. "The idea was to invest in the town instead of bleeding the resources of the land," he explains. "Ecologically it makes sense because the infrastructure is already in place. You don't have to drill for water or extend the road, and they even plow the sidewalks in the winter."

The two-story town house serves not only as a personal vacation retreat but also as a field office for local building projects designed and managed by Fernau's firm, Fernau and Hartman of Berkeley, California. Its open, airy

Colorizing
On the front facade, the original clapboard was replaced with black asphalt shingles—a humble material reflective of the unpretentiousness of Clyde Park, Montana. The brightly painted windows, door, and canopy strike a contrast with the supermarket next door.

Anticipating
Before the building was renovated, Fernau's wife, Sarah Cunniff, and sons Eli and Owen posed in front.

SHIELDS

interior is a far cry from the low, dark spaces that the architect found after purchasing the property in 2004. "The front facade was a wreck, the cinder block on the sides had eroded, and the building had three false ceilings," acknowledges Fernau. Still intact was a room-sized concrete vault, a leftover from the days when the building was the town's only bank. Before that the early 1900s structure was home to a gambling den, a barber shop, and a bordello. It was referred to in one deed of sale as the "Bucket of Blood."

The newly minted urban cowboy adopted a similar frontier spirit in reshaping the building into a dual-purpose modern dwelling. First on his agenda was reinforcing the roof and portions of the side walls to ensure protection against Montana's severe winds and weather. Then the inside of the shoe box was scraped clean to allow sunshine to filter into the center from both front and back. Within this two-story-high shell, an office mezzanine was inserted at the front, overlooking Main Street, and a sleeping loft was created at the back over the kitchen and the bathroom. To make room for this rear mezzanine, the roof was raised and the back facade extended with new windows to supply daylight and a view of the Crazy Mountains. Each upper level, framed in composite beams and pine floors, is reached by its

Playing

A second-floor balcony at the front of the narrow building projects over the door and part of the living space, providing a work area overlooking the street. Reached from a staircase extending along a side wall, it is framed in wood composite beams and joists. A punching bag and floor mat testify to the pine-floored space's double life as a rec room.

own staircase extending up the sides of the open interior. Stair treads are made from wooden planks recycled from the building's original ceilings. The bank vault now serves as a pantry off the kitchen.

As in early settlers' homes, the main level is left open as one big communal room focused on a wood-burning stove. Furniture, some of it designed by Fernau, is moved around the space to form seating and meeting areas or pushed to the side to allow for recreational activities during Montana's frigid winters. "The flexible interior is an alternative to the small, closed rooms of our city house," comments Fernau. "We like to change it all around." On family vacations, the architect and his wife, Sarah Cunniff, an attorney, can retreat to the mezzanines to work, while sons Eli and Owen hop on their skateboards, shoot a few hoops, or practice fencing, karate, or boxing on the main level. "There is no movie theater close by, so we're thinking of installing a big screen and a projector," adds the architect.

Living
From the main living space at the rear of the building, a dedicated staircase leads to the bedroom level. The slatted enclosure in the corner provides storage and a private bedroom. Under this "duck blind," the original bank vault serves as a pantry off the kitchen. A wood-burning stove heats the interior, furnished with a mix of modern and custom-made pieces.

Upstairs on the rear mezzanine, mattresses are pulled from a stack to provide as many beds as needed. A small chamber to one side, enclosed in wooden slats and camouflage fabric (nicknamed the "duck blind") supplies storage or a second bedroom for the kids. Parked in the back yard is an Airstream trailer that provides extra space for visiting employees and guests. This portable addition comes in handy during firm retreats when Fernau and his business partner, Laura Hartman, host their employees at the Montana getaway.

From the street, the live/work building presents a crisp, graphic image that stands out from the adjacent white-painted commercial structures. To reflect the town's unpretentiousness, bland pale brown clapboard was replaced with black asphalt shingles—a humble material typically applied to roofs. New windows, a door, and a canopy, in contrast, are painted bright yellow, green, and red, respectively, to brighten the dark facade and clearly indicate the architect's creative claim on this property.

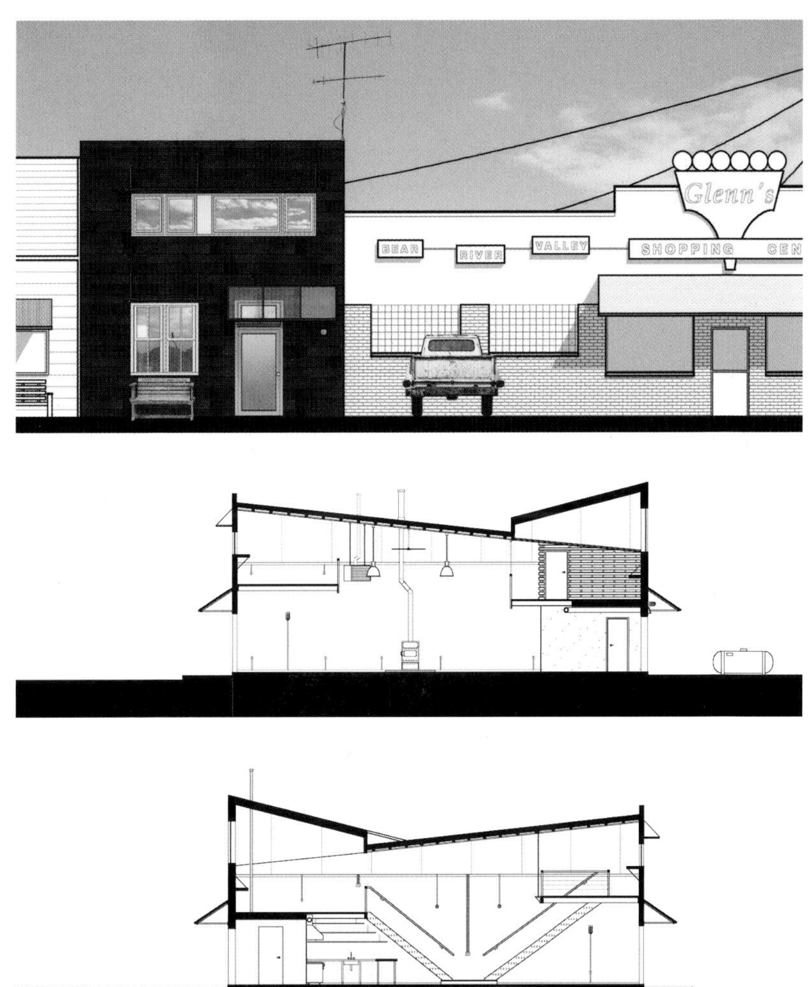

Rolling along
Before the renovation was complete, the unfurnished interior welcomed all manner of indoor games. The separate staircases leading to the upper-level bedroom at the back and the office mezzanine at the front are made of wooden planks recycled from the original ceilings. On the rear sleeping loft, a row of windows captures daylight and mountain views.

LESSONS LEARNED

Use a second home as a live/work outpost. The need for a field office in Montana led Richard Fernau to create an unconventional retreat that allows him to manage architectural projects in the region and also vacation with family and friends. The tiny hamlet encourages easy access to neighbors and services. "Townspeople keep an eye on the place when we're not there," he relates.

Frontier style does not have to mean log cabin. Without resorting to stereotypical Wild West imagery, Fernau combined economical materials in inventive ways: black asphalt shingles on the front of the building, wood strips lined in camouflage fabric to enclose a tiny bedroom on the second floor, planks from the original false ceilings recycled in the mezzanine staircases.

Illustration Credits

Thad Allender, 28, 29, 142, 144–45, 146 top, 147, 149, 150 top, 234, 236 (both), 238, 239 top and bottom left, 240 (both)

Kevin Bauman, 19, 283–88

Philip Beaurline, 198–206

Timothy Bell, 33, 299, 303, 304 (both), 305 right

Tom Bonner, 76–83

Aaron Britton, Place Architects, 2, 3, 34, 58, 60–63, 65

Janet Century, 4, 5, 88–97

Ayla Christman, 124–27, 129

Langdon Clay, 22

Lydia Cutter, 32, 298, 300–302, 305 left

David Egan, 36, 37, 290–97

Elizabeth Felicella, 252–59, 261

Robert Ferguson, Place Architects, 59, 64

Richard Fernau, Fernau & Hartman Architects, 308, 312, 314

Doug R. Fogelson, Zoka Zola Architects, 216, 222, 223 top right

John Reed Forsman, 208–13, 215, back cover (both)

Just visiting
At the back of Richard Fernau's Montana office-cum-vacation getaway, an Airstream trailer provides guest quarters for visiting colleagues and friends. This portable addition comes in handy when Fernau and his business partner, Laura Hartman, host their employees for annual retreats.

Peter Gorman, 233

Roland Halbe, 1 (both), 217–21, 223 top left and bottom right, 225

Julia Heine, McInturff Architects, 30, 31, 272–74, 276–81

Paul Hester, 262–68, 269 right, 270, 271

Historic American Buildings Survey (Library of Congress), 23

John Horner, 245

Matthew Hranek, 226–31

Timothy Hursley, 68–74

Lake/Flato, 269 left

J. K. Lawrence, 309, 311

Stephen Lee, Elizabeth A. Gibb Architect, 242–44, 247

Juli Leonard, *Raleigh News and Observer*, 12–17

John Edward Linden, 106–14, 152–57, 170–77

Maxwell MacKenzie, 50–57

Mariagabriela Manrique, Elizabeth A. Gibb Aarchitect, 246, 249

Mark McInturff, McInturff Architects, 132–39

Juergen Nogai, 41, 43 (both), 46 (both), 47 top right

Juergen Nogai and Julius Shulman, front cover, 40, 42, 44, 45, 47 top right, 48, 49

Eric Oxendorf, 6, 7, 160–67, 169

Polifilo Architects, 122, 123

Michael Poris, 18, 282

Marco Prozzo, 188, 190 (both), 191, 192, 193 top right and bottom right

Dan Rockhill, Rockhill and Associates, 8–9, 143, 146 bottom, 148, 150 top (both), 235, 237, 239 bottom right

Julius Shulman and Juergen Nogai, front cover, 40, 42, 44, 45, 47 top right, 48, 49

Charles Davis Smith, Shipley Architects, 180–86

Matt Spaulding, 128

Tim Street-Porter, Esto, 24, 25

Stanley Tretick, *Look* (Library of Congress), 20

Albert Večerka, Esto, 116–20

Regis Vogt, 26, 27, 98–103, 105

David Wild, 189, 193 top left and bottom left

Jim Wilson, *New York Times*, 310

Architectural drawings and floor plans were provided by the project architects.

Featured Designers

Patrick Avice du Buisson
Polifilo
1807½ Twenty-first Avenue South
Nashville, TN 37212
Tel: 615-385-0463
polifilo@comcast.net

Tim Carl
Hammel, Green and Abrahamson
701 Washington Avenue North
Minneapolis, MN 55401
Tel: 612-758-4000
www.hga.com

Robert Cole and Sophie Prévost
ColePrévost Inc.
1635 Connecticut Avenue, NW
Washington, DC 20009
Tel: 202-234-1090
www.coleprevost.net

Ralph Cunningham
Cunningham and Quill Architects
1054 Thirty-first Street, NW
Washington, DC 20007
Tel: 202-337-0090
www.cunninghamquill.com

Merrill Elam
Mack Scogin Merrill Elam Architects
111 John Wesley Dobbs Avenue, NE
Atlanta, GA 30303
Tel: 404-525-6869
www.msmearch.com

Richard Fernau and Laura Hartman
Fernau and Hartman Architects
2512 Ninth Street
Berkeley, CA 94710
Tel: 510-848-4480
www.fernauhartman.com

Ted Flato
Lake/Flato Architects
311 Third Street
San Antonio, TX 78205
Tel: 210-227-3335
www.lakeflato.com

Elizabeth Gibb
Elizabeth A. Gibb Architect
12 Newell Street
Cambridge, MA 02140
Tel: 617-864-5762
www.elizabethgibbarchitect.com

Christopher Hays and Allison Ewing
Hays + Ewing Design Studio
1900 Chesapeake Street
Charlottesville, VA 22902
Tel: 434-979-3222
www.hays-studio.com

Christian Hubert
Christian Hubert Architect
48 Gold Street
New York, NY 10038
Tel: 212-349-2752
www.christianhubert.com

Scott Hughes
Scott Hughes Architects
141 Gomez Road
Hobe Sound, FL 33455
Tel: 772-546-7011
1322 Pacific Avenue
Venice, CA 90291
Tel: 310-399-5757
www.sharc.com

Glen Irani
Glen Irani Studio
410 Sherman Canal
Venice, CA 90291
Tel: 310-305-8840
www.glenirani.com

Heather Johnston
with Kevin Spence
Place Architects
119 West Denny Way
Seattle, WA 98119
Tel: 206-281-8225
www.placearchitects.com

Stephen Kanner
Kanner Architects
1558 Tenth Street
Santa Monica, CA 90401
Tel: 310-451-5400
www.kannerarch.com

Tom Kundig
Olson Sundberg Kundig Allen Architects
159 South Jackson Street
Seattle, WA 98104
Tel: 206-624-5670
www.oskaarchitects.com

Mark McInturff
McInturff Architects
4220 Leeward Place
Bethesda, MD 20816
Tel: 310-229-3705
www.mcinturffarchitects.com

Zoltan Pali and Judit Meda Fekete
Studio Pali Fekete Architects
8609 East Washington Boulevard
Culver City, CA 90232
Tel: 310-558-0902
www.spfa.com

Michael Poris
McIntosh Poris Associates
36801 Woodward Avenue
Birmingham, MI 48009
Tel: 248-258-9346
www.mcintoshporis.com

Dan Rockhill
Rockhill and Associates
1546 East 350 Road
Lecompton, KS 66050
Tel: 785-393-0747
www.rockhillandassociates.com

David Salmela
Salmela Architect
630 West Fourth Street
Duluth, MN 55806
Tel: 218-724-7517
www.salmelaarchitect.com

Jonathan Sandvick
and Julie Dornbeck
Sandvick Architects
1265 West Sixth Street
Cleveland, OH 44113
Tel: 216-621-8055
www.sandvickarchitects.com

Adele Naude Santos
Santos Prescott and Associates
27 Village Street
Somerville, MA 02143
Tel: 617-666-6668
33 Zoe Street
San Francisco, CA 94107
Tel: 415-908-3767
www.santosprescott.com

Roger Sherman
Roger Sherman Architecture + Urban Design
713 Ashland Avenue
Santa Monica, CA 90405
Tel: 310-450-7553
www.rsaud.com

Dan Shipley
Shipley Architects
5538 Dyer Street
Dallas, TX 75206
Tel: 214-823-2080
www.shipleyarchitects.com

Sarah Susanka
Susanka Studios
Raleigh, NC
www.notsobig.com

Mike Watkins
Duany Plater-Zyberk and Company
320 Firehouse Lane
Gaithersburg, MD 20878
Tel: 301-948-6223
www.dpz.com

Zoka Zola
Zoka Zola Architecture + Urban Design
1737 West Ohio Street
Chicago, IL 60622
Tel: 312-491-9431
www.zokazola.com

Index

Commissioning Editor: Eric Himmel

Produced by Archetype Press, Inc.
Project Director: Diane Maddex
Designer: Robert L. Wiser

Library of Congress Cataloging-in-Publication Data
Dietsch, Deborah K.
Live/work: working at home, living at work / by Deborah K. Dietsch ; foreword by Sarah Susanka.
p. cm.
ISBN 978-0-8109-9400-3
1. Home offices. 2. Office layout. 3. Interior architecture. I. Title.
NA2856.D54 2008
729—dc22

2007042355

Published in 2008 by Abrams, an imprint of Harry N. Abrams, Inc.

Printed and bound in Singapore

10 9 8 7 6 5 4 3 2 1

115 West 18th Street
New York, NY 10011
www.hnabooks.com

Display illustrations

Page 1: Home and studio of Zoka Zola, Peter Pfanner, and their son, Chicago (see pages 216–25).

Pages 2–3: Heather Johnston and Rob Ferguson's home, Seattle (see pages 58–67).

Pages 4–5: Tower Press Building, Cleveland, and Krisztina Lazar in her apartment (see pages 88–97).

Pages 6–7: Adele Santos in her office and courtyard, Somerville, Massachusetts (see pages 160–69).

Pages 8–9: Jon O'Neal's home, Lawrence, Kansas (see pages 234–41).

Pages 10–11: Elevation of Robert and Molly Krause's home restaurant, East Lawrence, Kansas (see pages 142–51).

Pages 38–39: First floor plan of Clen Irani and Edith Beaucage's home, Venice, California (see pages 40–49).

Pages 86–87: Elevation of Tower Press Building, Cleveland (see pages 88–97).

Pages 130–31: Site plan of Robert and Molly Krause's home restaurant, East Lawrence, Kansas (see pages 142–51).

Pages 196–97: Floor plan of Jon O'Neal's home, Lawrence, Kansas (see pages 234–41).

Pages 250–51: Elevation of David Salle's home, Brooklyn, New York (see pages 252–61).